Hoath and

The Last
of the
Forest

'Histories Make Men Wise.'
Francis Bacon, Essays Civil and Moral

Published by K. H. McIntosh
design/print Thanet Printing Works Ltd.,
81 High Street, Ramsgate, Kent, 1984.

Holy Cross Church, Hoath.

Rene Hummerstone

HOATH AND HERNE
by
Robert Paine, F.R.I.B.A., A.R.C.A.

Hoath and Herne – the 'Jutish Double-Act' strolled on to the stage of history 1500 years ago: Hoath on its windy upland, staring far-eyed across Thanet to the sea beyond; Herne in its hollow, snug and warm, back turned towards the east from whence both came. Bede suggests Jutland but archaeology favours the Rhineland from where the settlers brought skill in farming and the art of jewelry.

Now no place in England (save some crackpot planner's nightmare) is where it is without a reason. We know why Fordwich and Sturry are where they are because of the river, but what shall we say about Hoath and Herne? Their names are the give-away. Hoath was 'the boggy heath' and Herne 'a nook or corner of the valley'.

Clearly before Hoath there were earlier settlements nearer the shore of the Wantsum: Highstead, the most important, was overrun by the Romans and later abandoned, but before that there was one perhaps on the waters edge close to the salt pans. Hoath in fact looks like the last in a series of moves which carried settlement up to the edge of the Blean where there was ample pasturage for swine under the oaks which provided timber for house and boat building and fuel for omnivorous open fires, everything in short that the new settlers needed plus good land for the clearing. It was just off the old track inland from the Wantsum which the Romans made into their road from Canterbury to the Saxon Shore fort at Reculver but close enough to use and benefit from it. Such use and benefit were very real since the road ran to where the estuary could be forded and where it turned westwards to the tribal capital.

Herne may have had a similar beginning as the first landfall of those who, edging further along the coast, ventured inland as far as the forest along the western flank of the high ground above the level of what would then have been a marsh or even a sea inlet extending towards Bullockstone. Whether there was already a track through the woods we do not know but no doubt one was soon beaten out also to lead to Sturry and beyond.

But if Hoath and Herne had similar origins chance caused them to develop very differently. The great change in the relative level of land and sea which made the Wantsum recede from Sturry in time left Hoath well inland whereas Herne retained its lifeline to the strand which is now Herne Bay. This was to become an important outlet for trade of considerable importance to the hinterland and to Canterbury well into the 19th century, a trade controlled and directed from Herne to which considerable prosperity accrued as is well testified by its magnificent church, immense compared with that at Hoath. Herne took top billing and Hoath was relegated to a supporting role.

Their first inhabitants built for themselves simple barn-like homesteads side by side facing the track which brought them there. From these they farmed the land won by clearing the primaeval forest living with their animals under one roof and practising their other skills as carpenters, ironsmiths, thatchers and daubers from which later on came separate trades. They came as pagans but were soon converted to Christianity which provided them with their only

3

other building, a simple wooden church not very different from a house. Everything was done slowly and laboriously mostly with timber. They had no water power, and windmills did not appear for another 700 years. Oxen drew the ploughs which were of a kind which later gave rise to the enclosed field system, water was taken from the communal well and corn was ground in a hand quern.

Herne today is entirely changed but we can get a glimpse of the family face when we look at the narrow houses, many no doubt occupying the same space where once a peasant had his hut with a side way through to the land beyond and a fire break from his neighbour. Garden fences across which neighbours chat today then were wattle barriers which helped to keep out the wolves and bears of the wild wood.

Time ground slowly by: the Normans came; free peasants became feudal tenants of their manors but the way of life was much the same; houses collapsed and were rebuilt with the old timbers; Edward II granted weekly markets to both villages and an annual fair to Herne; the old churches were demolished and those we see today were built; it was no longer necessary as it had been for generations to trudge to Reculver for burials.

But change was in the air. Arable farming began to make way for sheep. Wool was the success story of the Middle Ages and the manors began a process of enclosure which deprived the peasants of their tenancies. With no land to farm they were left destitute and began to drift away to join the great rabble of vagrants and beggars which was to provoke dread among the townsfolk as the old song 'Hark, Hark the Dogs do Bark' reminds us. There would have been yet more had the Black Death not reduced them so cruelly.

At this time, after a thousand years since settlement began, a process of decay set in from which Hoath never truly recovered; certainly its nature was changed quite radically. In both villages homesteads collapsed and were not rebuilt: their gaunt skeletons stood against the skyline and the mouldering thatch smothered the hearths. Like some Irish village after the 'Troubles' they stood abandoned and desolate.

Yet as it is today, while many were out of work others prospered. The manors grew fat and farms of a new sort appeared with yeoman-type houses set in fields which someone more enterprising had managed to acquire by artful manipulation of the copyholds, possibly with money earned by the sea trade.

And trade now tended to vie with agriculture introducing new types of building, certainly in Herne, to serve its convenience – inns, alehouses, dwellings for merchants and shipmen standing side by side with the desolation of the past. Little of all this survives but Smugglers Cottage is sufficient to give the flavour of the new life, different by far from the old hovels, more sophisticated, carefully built with specially formed wrought timbers, with overhanging upper floors and attic rooms all telling the tale of their origins in the town houses of Canterbury and London.

In this newly settled state both villages seem to have pottered right through the brave new Tudor times, the upheavals of the Civil War and the Great Rebellion. A small amount of church bashing followed the dissolution of the monasteries and records indicate a healthy independence among the laity who dodged their churchgoing and refused to pay for the upkeep of the mother church at Reculver. The clergy, freed from the ancient Catholic imperatives, for a while behaved oddly. In 1569 the Vicar 'sent his wife away in travail and gave himself to filthy lykar' and in 1683 Theophilus Beck 'neglected the church, converted the pulpit cloth, got drunk in an ale-house and struck one Allen'.

The sea trade grew, hoys plied regularly from the Bay to London with hops now as additional cargo from Canterbury which, as Defoe was to remark, was surrounded on all sides by the new plantations. Dutch vessels came in for shellfish and brought goods from the Low Countries. The old enemy remained a threat and in 1702 the government was petitioned for guns to deal with French pirates. There had been a kind of 'early-warning' system since the 14th century when one of a national chain of beacons was erected on Mill Hill. Up to fifty outbound shipments a year were recorded from Herne alone which for customs purposes was associated with Whitstable and Faversham.

Yet while this went on there was little change in the appearance of the village. The old ways of building seem to have persisted. Elsewhere oak and elm for construction had become scarce to the point where it was feared there might not be enough for the navy, but here on the heavy, wet, unworkable clay of the Blean enough remained to meet local needs. The new-fangled brick building with its Dutch style sash windows, its tiled roofs and its floors of imported softwood did not begin to appear much before 1700 although all the materials had been trundling through from the coast for nearly a hundred years.

It is not therefore some sudden urge to rebuild in a new style which accounts for the quite extraordinary number of neat small 'georgian' houses 'listed' today in Hoath and Herne. Such houses were for new people even if they were on long-since abandoned plots. They were built in a new way presumably because new men and newcomers from places more up-to-date wanted them so.

During the 18th and early 19th centuries there was an influx of people and it is tempting to think of this as the beginning of that process of migration from Canterbury by the well-to-do who found Herne at least more healthy, as indeed had been its reputation from quite early times. It is tempting too to see it as the start of what made modern Herne Bay a salubrious retreat from the smoke of London. Perhaps it was something of both but it was more besides. Over the years of which there is no detailed record village society had differentiated considerably. Trades established themselves independently from the old way of being a secondary occupation; the availability of more and varied goods encouraged the setting up of shops, perhaps only on a 'front-room' basis or as a stall in front of the house; medicine required a doctor for people and a vet for creatures great and small; a lawyer would certainly be required if only to draw up wills, and the land-surveyor had plenty to do.

Once established the new way of building took a firm hold at first in the simplest form, which as in previous times grew directly from basic needs and the mode of construction.

This is best seen in Hoath. Its numerous small cottages were usually free-standing, squarish in plan, with bold hipped roofs and casement windows rather than sash as if there were some reluctance entirely to throw off the older form. With a neat door-case and well moulded framed door they remain models of 'commodity, firmness and delight'. Settlers in America took the idea with them and it survives in New England to this day.

5

The Herne version had a more town-like character, imposed upon it by the close packed plots, at first very simple and trim with sashes many-paned to suit the size of glass available and neat doors like those at Hoath. But here, the door being now set ajar to change swung wide open. Foreign materials, slate from Wales, sawn painted weather boarding from the Baltic, varied the townscape and brought contrast to the street scene. How much was owed to the newly procurable white-lead paint is a story in itself. Fashion crept in, builders' pattern books appeared, pretty quirks were added and the way was paved for the age of the villa, the semi and the bungalow.

Throughout the 18th century the villages enjoyed a quiet prosperity but with the coming of the railways in Victorian times the sea trade declined and Herne Bay became a resort. Thomas Telford, the great engineer, built the first pier, bands played, horse buses and then char-a-bancs made convivial excursions to Herne, and the scene was set for what had been so long the mistress to become the servant. Sewers were laid, water was piped in, the gasometer appeared, streets were made and a sprawl of villas flowed like lava unchecked to the very edge of the village. Only the construction of Thanet Way to relieve unemployment in the hungry Thirties prevented it from being quite engulfed. Herne was in danger of being vandalised.

Fortunately the passing of the Town and Country Planning Act, the listing of historically important buildings and the establishment of conservation areas averted the main threat; but there is still much to be done by persuasion and example to restore Herne to its proper status as a village in its own right and one of the finest in Kent.

Perhaps this could be celebrated by the ceremonial destruction of that most dreadful of all Victorian horrors, the Workhouse, planted upon the village by the Poor Law Guardians in 1837. In the 14th century people were caused to leave their homes: in what should have been a better age they were brought back but to a misery of degradation and despair. They deserve some memorial, for it was people who won the land from the forest and made Hoath and Herne more than quaint names.

POPULATION OF HOATH 1801-1961

1801	271	1841	394	1881	355	1921	317
1811	296	1851	359	1891	359	1931	357
1821	348	1861	348	1901	282	1951	327
1831	360	1871	346	1921	324	1961	323

POPULATION OF HERNE 1801-1961

1801	1232	1841	1469	1881	4410	1921	1964
1811	1442	1851	3094	1891	5482	1931	2135
1821	1675	1861	3147	1901	1716	1951	2896
1831	1876	1871	3988	1911	1900	1961	4576

NOTES: 1871 Herne District 2097.
1881 Herne District 2816.
(Herne parish included in Herne Bay in 1881).
Amalgamation of Herne and Herne Bay took place in 1841.

OLD STONE AGE FINDS IN THE STOUR VALLEY

by

Derek A. Roe, M.A., PhD., D. Litt. Oxon.

Most areas of south-east England can boast at least a few traces of Palaeolithic man – usually stray finds of his easily recognisable flint handaxes, picked up at a local gravel pit or on the surface of arable land. A few regions, however, have information of a much more substantial kind to offer to the prehistorian, and the Stour Valley near Canterbury is one of them. Well over a thousand flint implements have been recovered, from gravel deposits belonging to several different stages of the Pleistocene, the geological epoch which contains the Old Stone Age; the finds have genuine importance for the interpretation of the British Palaeolithic sequence and are also of considerable interest to archaeologists working in France and other parts of western Europe. For large parts of the Pleistocene, Britain was physically joined to continental Europe by a land-bridge extending over what is now the southern North Sea and the eastern end of the English Channel: North Kent was clearly close to the main routes by which people moved, and is easily the most prolific county of England for finds of earlier Palaeolithic artefacts. Within Kent, there is an area of outstanding importance for Lower Palaeolithic finds in the Northfleet-Dartford region, including the famous Swanscombe sites, and this is complemented by the discoveries made in the Stour Valley.

The main local sources of implements were the gravel pits of Sturry and Fordwich. Many artefacts have also come from the gravels which cap the cliffs between Herne Bay and Reculver, and others have been found during commercial digging or building operations of all kinds in Canterbury itself. The best finds were made by Dr. A. G. Ince of Sturry and Dr. Armstrong Bowes of Herne Bay, during the first 30 years or so of the present century, though implements have continued to be found in smaller numbers right up to the present day[1], the decline in their frequency being directly related to the ending of gravel-digging by hand. It is also worth noting that Reculver was known as a source of Lower Palaeolithic flint implements as early as 1860, at a time when the debate on the antiquity of man versus the Biblical account of the Creation was in full flood. John Evans, later Sir John Evans, in the first edition of his famous book *The Ancient Stone Implements, Weapons and Ornaments of Great Britain*[2], described various finds in the Stour Valley, mostly by Mr. John Brent at locations between Chislet and Chilham, and forecast that more discoveries would be made.

This is no place to attempt a long technical account of the Stour Valley palaeoliths: the present writer has discussed them at some length in their context in a recent book[3]. It will be sufficient to observe here that Middle Acheulian handaxes are abundantly represented, especially at Sturry, and that a few typical Middle Palaeolithic handaxes of Mousterian type have been found. In the writer's view, the collections of crude heavy handaxes from Fordwich represent one of the most important Early Acheulian collections in Britain, even if their geological context has not been well defined or described; if this is correct, they would be not less than 350,000 years old and probably very much older. Chronometric dating of the earlier stages of the British Palaeolithic is notoriously difficult. It is only fair to record that arguments for a younger age for the Fordwich industry have recently been put forward[4]; there

7

is no space here for the writer to explain why he finds them unconvincing and stands by his own reading of the situation. Artefacts made by the well-known 'Levalloisian' flaking technique are also quite common in the Canterbury area and are of late Lower Palaeolithic or Middle Palaeolithic age. An interesting industry dominated by use of this technique was discovered a little way to the west of Bapchild.

It is sad that the Stour Valley gravels have produced little in the way of faunal, environmental or clear geochronological evidence to accompany the admirable implements they have yielded, but we should not despair that important new discoveries may yet be made and examined with all the modern aids now available to the archaeologist and his colleagues in Quaternary Research. The arguments over Fordwich, for example, are unlikely to be settled without productive new exposures on that particular gravel terrace of the Stour.

Much of the best material from the area is now in the collections of the British Museum, but various implements can be seen in the local Museum collection at Canterbury.

References
(1)   e.g. three ovate handaxes found during building operations at Rough Common, Canterbury, in 1978: (See *Arch. Cant.* 1978. Vol.XCIV pp.158-165).
(2)   Published by Longmans in 1872.
(3)   *The Lower and Middle Palaeolithic Periods in Britain,* published by Routledge & Kegan Paul in 1981.
(4)   e.g. by A. M. Ashmore in her paper The Typology and Age of the Fordwich Handaxes in *Arch. Cant.* 1980. Vol. XCVI pp. 83-107.

A ROMAN SITE AT HOATH

In the summer of 1971 two buried features disturbed by ploughing were investigated in Mile's Field, Shelvingford Farm, Hoath (NGR. TR 216649), very close to the parish boundary with Chislet.

The first was provisionally identified as a small furnace room of stones bedded in clay, and comprised a roughly square inner chamber about 4 feet each way, clasped on two sides by a corridor about 2 feet wide, one limb of which extended beyond the limits of the chamber, and evidently represented a firing tunnel. The orientation was NW-SE (approximately 157° Magnetic) with the open end of the tunnel to the NW. There was some evidence of a flue at the SE corner of the structure. Little dating evidence was available due to the few finds and lack of stratification. After examination, all but the lowest two courses of stone were removed at the request of the farmer, Mr. S. Harbour.

The associated structure was a linear chalk feature, parallel to the longer axis of the building, and about 32 feet east of it. It extended about 72 feet, with a return arm towards the south end of the building, about 9 feet long; its width averaged about 28 inches. This had been planed down by cultivation, and was covered by only 10 inches of topsoil. West of the chalk feature were several pits containing animal bones (cow and sheep), but positive association was precluded by the removal of stratification.

The two main structures seem by their alignment to have been associated, but the lack of undisturbed soil over the site made any conclusions unclear. The few pottery fragments in the filling of the building made a Roman origin probable.

See: Kent Archaeological Review, No. 28 (Summer 1972) pp.249-50.

THE ROMAN ROAD FROM STURRY TO RECULVER

by

Cyril Wardale, F.S.A.

It is now nearly eighty years since Codrington (a) wrote:

'A Roman Road from Canterbury towards the northeast appears to have crossed the Stour at Fordwich. A parish boundary follows the present road from the river at Fordwich through Sturry and for two miles on through Westbere. At about three-quarters of a mile from Sturry the road to Reculver branched off represented by the present road through Upstreet which a parish boundary follows for two miles near Hoath....'

Although Codrington made his point with directness and authority its value is diminished by the lack of supporting evidence, without which his statement can only be seen as an opinion no matter how convincingly put; and it is an inescapable fact that the ensuing years have failed to produce indisputable evidence in support of his statement. Even so, the idea of a road from Canterbury to Reculver is still attractive and worth looking at in detail if only to marshal such evidence as there is.

The northern termination of the road is Regulbium (b) a Roman fort situated in a prime position at the northern end of the Wantsum Channel where this enters the Thames Estuary. The Wantsum was navigable in Roman times, providing good anchorage and a safer route into the Thames than the still hazardous rounding of the North Foreland. The fort, which was undoubtedly sited to guard both the channel and the estuary, has been badly eroded by the sea, the southern half only surviving. This loss has occurred since 1685, as a map of Reculver of that date (c) shows it entire, with the sea close to the north wall. If the rate of erosion of the coastline has been reasonably consistent then the sea at the end of the third century was about 500 metres to the north of the fort. Here, presumably, was the harbour and the town, but this is not certain as the Wantsum would have provided a more sheltered site. Nonetheless, the internal arrangements of the fort indicate the main entrance was in the north.

In the latter years of its life Reculver was one of the series of forts known as the Forts of the Saxon Shore. This was a coastal defence system devised specifically to deal with the acute problem of Saxon and Frankish pirates who infested the sea routes between Britain and Gaul. The forts protected the harbours of the Classis Britannica, which had been reformed, and also served as barracks for the military, whose task it was, inter alia, to handle any land incursions the pirates might make. Ten forts of the system are known for certain: from Brancaster on the north Norfolk coast, to Portchester in Portsmouth Harbour. All are massive, stone-walled structures, and the majority date from the organisation of the defence system in the late third century; even so, many occupy sites with known connections with the original Classis Britannica.

However, Reculver and Brancaster stand out from the others not only in date, but in form, for both are in the earlier, true military fort tradition with regular plan and rounded corners, and stone walls lacking both tile courses and bastions. Brian Philp's excavations at Reculver (d) uncovered an important inscription which, although open to some minor differences of interpretation, refers to the building of the principia of the fort in the early third century.

9

D. E. Johnston (e) has suggested this may refer to the refurbishing of the fort when the original Classis Britannica was disbanded.

In the first stages of the Roman invasion, and in the years following while the conquest was consolidated, the harbours and supply bases of Kent (Dover, Richborough, and probably Lympne) were of supreme importance, with their roads the vital link between them and the army. The discovery by Brian Philp of a ditch of Claudian date at Reculver goes a very long way to justify the long-held view that there must have been a fort there in those critical years. The importance of these discoveries cannot be over emphasized, for the firm and unequivocal establishment of early connections with the army or the Classis Britannica are central to this study. As inspection of the Ordnance Survey Map of Roman Britain shows, the status of Saxon Short Fort alone is insufficient to guarantee a road link.

If as a result of this recent work it can be said with some confidence that Reculver was an important early military base then we can be equally confident about the existence of a road to it.

THE ROUTE

The route that Codrington postulates lies on or about a minor 'modern' road that branches from the A28 just east of Sturry at Staines Hill to wind its way in the general direction of Reculver, some six and one half miles to the northeast, via Knaves Ash, Maypole, Maystreet Cross and Hillborough.

This route is the most obvious and on the face of it the most promising for it skirts the marshy inlets of the Wantsum economically, deviating as little as possible from a direct line between the point where the branch begins and the terminus at Reculver. Further, it incorporates two long straights of the Hoath/Herne Bay parish boundary, an occurrence generally accepted as a favourable indication of the antiquity of a feature on the grounds that a parish boundary is likely to follow a pre-existing marker.

If the route thus outlined does indeed perpetuate the course of a Roman Road then it would seem to have been laid out in three main alignments:

Alignment   1 Staines Hill – Ford.
            2 Ford – Hillborough.
            3 Hillborough – Reculver.

Alignment 1
STAINES HILL – FORD (3½ miles)

No structural evidence of the road is recognisable but the remarkable straightness of Hoath Lane when it leaves Staines Hill, and its general, if not exact, alignment with Maypole Road point very strongly to a Roman origin. The modern road departs briefly from the alignment at Hoades Court, and again at Buckwell, and although it might have been hoped, even expected, that some evidence of it would have turned up in the intervening farmlands, none has done so to date.

The modern road rejoins the alignment at Rushbourne, and the parish boundary joins both at Knaves Ash, so from this point through Maypole to Millbank all three coincide. In 1966 Post Office engineers laying a duct at the junction of Maypole Lane and Maypole Road, near the Prince of Wales Inn, found immediately below the modern road surface a sophisticated road

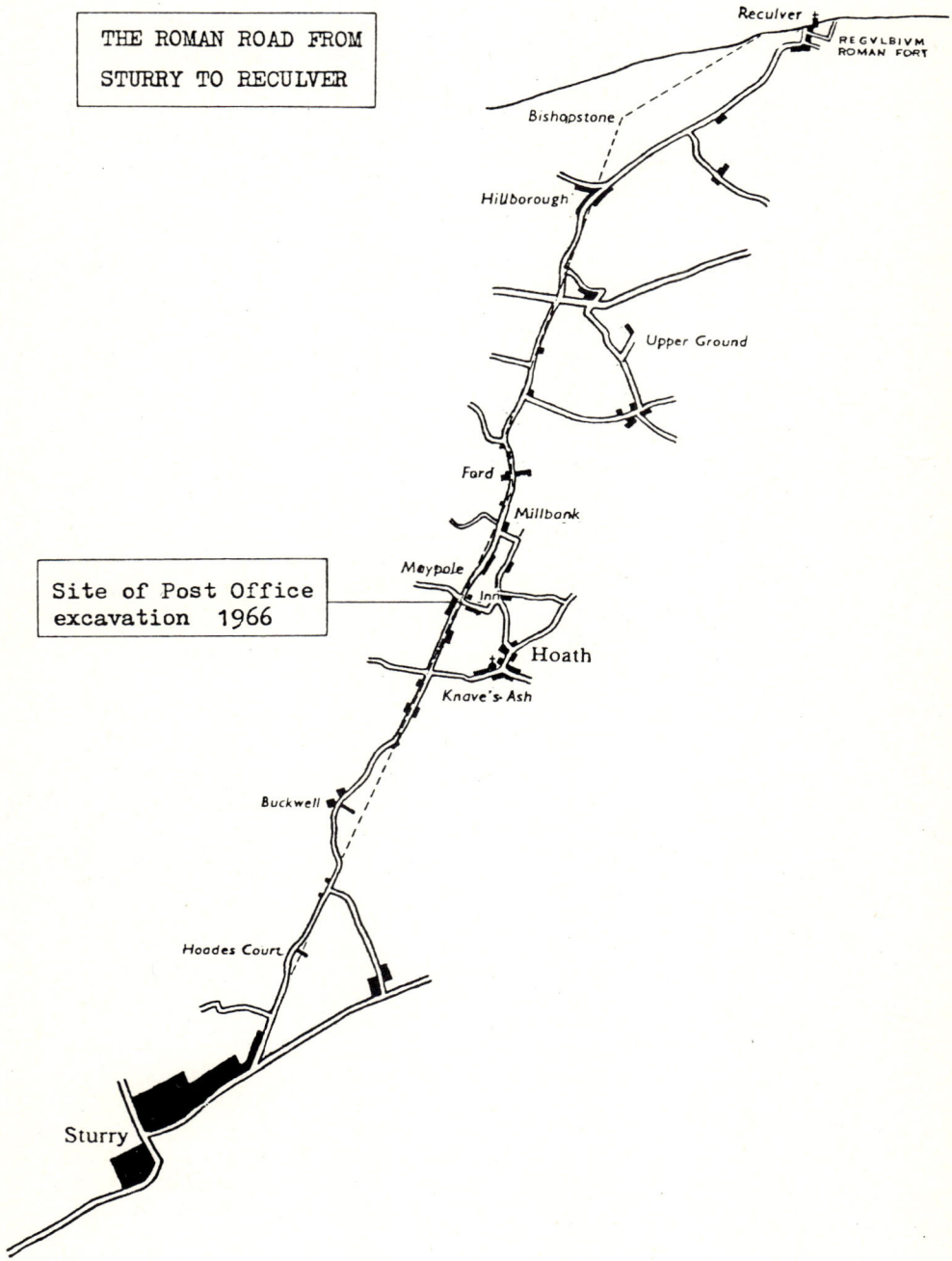

THE ROMAN ROAD FROM STURRY TO RECULVER

Site of Post Office excavation 1966

Reculver

REGVLBIVM ROMAN FORT

Bishopstone

Hillborough

Upper Ground

Ford

Millbank

Maypole

Inn

Hoath

Knave's Ash

Buckwell

Hoades Court

Sturry

foundation comprising four inches of hogging, eighteen inches of flint and chalk, and six inches of clay (information and diagram supplied by Dr. Frank Jenkins); the width was eighteen feet, which falls within the accepted limits for a Roman Road. Although it is tempting to accept this as the Roman Road its position beneath a modern road militates against unreserved acceptance. Nonetheless it is one piece of evidence that is something more than circumstantial and it occurs in exactly the right place.

Millbank sits above a steep and narrow little valley with the hamlet of Ford at its foot. The present road system suggests a deviation was necessary to negotiate this valley with a fresh alignment laid out from Edgehill on the far side. It is significant that the parish boundary also follows this deviation, indicating once again the antiquity of the route.

Relevant finds from the close vicinity of the above route include mid-second century cremations from Maypole, and an inscribed stone and coins from Ford Manor House; but Mr. Gough, Curator of the Herne Bay Records Society, thought the stone, which is part of a tombstone or memorial tablet, came from Reculver or Canterbury along with other building material used in the building of the Archbishop's Palace at Ford (OS Record Card).

Alignment 2
FORD – HILLBOROUGH/BISHOPSTONE (2 miles)

From the top of the escarpment at Edgehill above Ford a reasonable alignment can be proposed, still followed in part by the parish boundary, to Maystreet Cross (a significant name bearing a 'street' element), thence through Sweech Hill to Hillborough. Between Sweech Hill and Hillborough another steep little valley has to be crossed and here the modern road deviates some fifty metres west of the alignment, which is now masked by a sewage works.

The precise termination of the alignment depends very much on the identification of alignment 3 into Reculver (qv) but the topography strongly suggests the alignment angle occurred about 500 metres N of St. Mary's Church, on the top of the ridge which runs down into Reculver.

Alignment 3
HILLBOROUGH/BISHOPSTONE – RECULVER (1 mile)

This alignment poses the biggest problem of all for there are three plausible alternatives.

The first is represented by Reculver Lane which leaves Hillborough near St. Mary's Church and makes its way into Reculver by a very direct route along a shallow re-entrant. The depth of the cutting it occupies in places suggests it is of some antiquity.

The second is the route of 'The King's Highway', shown on Hill's map of 1685, which was a coastal road obviously of considerable importance, and presumably represented by the track that exists today between Reculver and Bishopstone.

The third is the spine of the ridge that lies between the first two. This has the advantage of gaining the high ground at Hillborough by a gentle but commanding route and with no need for deviation until the chosen point for the alignment angle was reached. The route crosses arable but nothing is visible.

It might have been hoped that the stretch of Roman Road found by Brian

12

Philp during his Reculver excavations, running for at least 350 metres south-westwards from the west entrance of the fort, would have resolved the problem. Unfortunately this stretch could provide the starting point for any of the three possible routes suggested above and the question must remain open. It comprised a band of pebble and gravel, some 12-16 inches below the ground surface, which was destroyed when the cliff collapsed. It was seen in two places on the cliff and Philp interpreted the course as having left the fort by the west gate, crossed the ditches by means of a causeway, and continued straight for another 100 feet or more before bearing some 15/25 degrees to the south. It should be noted that Philp considered the metalling that survived was put down not earlier than the end of the second century.

CONCLUSIONS

The paucity of supporting evidence for this road suggested at one time that the course should be sought elsewhere, but a suitable alternative is not easy to identify. If the route is moved too far to the east the problem of negotiating the Chislet Marshes is encountered, and moving too far to the west gives no recognisable advantages. The foundation of a road found by the GPO engineers at the Prince of Wales Inn, which looks as if it is Roman (a view endorsed by Dr. Jenkins), strengthens Codrington's route, certainly as far as Ford, and probably to Hillborough too; so although some doubt remains about the exact course from there into Reculver, on balance it can be said that Codrington's statement still stands, and is likely to do so until evidence to the contrary is found elsewhere.

References
a.   Roman Roads in Britain 1905 (T. Codrington).
b.   The Place Names of Roman Britain 1979 (A. L. F. Rivet).
c.   Plan of Reculver 1685 (Hill).
d.   The Roman Fort at Reculver 1969 (B. J. Philp).
e.   C.B.A. Research Report, The Saxon Shore 1977 (Ed. D. E. Johnston).

SEPTARIA IN EXTERNAL WALL OF HERNE CHURCH
Reproduced, with kind permission, from 'Kentish Architecture as influenced by Geology' by John Archibald, published by the Monastery Press, Ramsgate, 1934.

THE EARLIEST CHURCH AT HERNE

by

Nicholas Brooks, D.Phil., F.R.Hist.S.

The present parish church of Herne has fragments of re-used romanesque masonry in its walling, but has no indication of the existence of a church before the twelfth century. However, in 1976 traces of the foundations of an earlier church were found beneath the present Lady Chapel in excavations directed by Mr. B. Philp of the Kent Archaeological Rescue Unit. Though the foundations were much disturbed by later graves, it was possible to recognize that they had formed a small and simple two-cell structure (nave and semi-circular apse) comparable to the earliest Anglo-Saxon churches in Kent at Rochester, Canterbury, Reculver, Lyminge and elsewhere.[1] Whether this building was indeed a church of the seventh or eighth century, or was rather a lord's private foundation of the tenth or eleventh century remains uncertain. But it is tempting to associate it with a mysterious record in the *Domesday Monachorum* of c.1100; there, in a list of the Kentish churches which before Lanfranc's reorganisation had owed various ecclesiastical renders to the cathedral church of Canterbury, we find a certain *monasterium æt Hyrnan* ('minster at Herne').[2] Nothing else is known of an early monastery or 'minster' at Herne, and there is no trace of it in a surviving eighth or early ninth-century list of 'monasteries' in Kent.[3] It is perhaps most likely that the foundation of a corporate church at Herne should be attributed to the tenth century when attempts were being made to recover from the devastation of the Viking incursions.

1. B. Philp and H. Gough, 'Early Church discovered at Herne', *Kent Archaeological Review*, 44, (1976), 86-91.

2. *Domesday Monachorum of Christ Church Canterbury,* ed. D. C. Douglas, (1944), 79.

3. W. de Gray Birch, *Cartularium Saxonicum*, (1885-99), no.91.

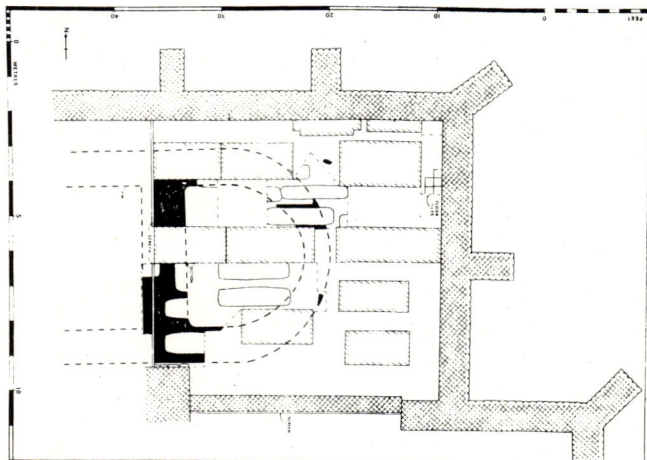

EARLY FOUNDATIONS

PRESENT CHURCH

TOMBSTONES

GRAVES

St. Martin's Church, Herne Plan showing earlier structure underlying Lady Chapel floor. Drawn by John Willson. Reproduced, with kind permission, from the Kent Archaeological Review, No. 44, Summer, 1976.

DOMESDAY AND MANORIAL MATTERS
by
Margaret Sparks, M.A.

In the other books in this series it was possible to show a Domesday entry for the village under its own name, such as Sturry or Chislet; but Herne is not mentioned in the great survey of 1086. Herne existed as a settlement, for there was a church there, as noticed above, but it was only one of the chapelries of the great estate of Reculver. From 669 there was a monastery at Reculver which received various grants of lands from Saxon kings. The remarkable stone church was built within the Roman fort and until some time in the late eighth century the monastery, dedicated to St. Mary, prospered. For reasons unknown, perhaps due to its exposed position and to Danish invasions, the abbey failed. Its lands were handed over to the Archbishops of Canterbury in 949, a transfer which was ratified by a charter in anglo-saxon defining the boundaries. Several attempts have been made to work out these limits, but although a few names can be recognised the terrain has changed a great deal. The area included a coastline to the north, much of which is now eroded away; marshes near the Wantsum Channel, now used as agricultural land; a great woodland to the south and arable land in the centre. A note was added to the Charter boundaries pointing out that the Reculver estates also included 'land within the water' (Stourmouth) and land in Thanet which with the main holding amounted to twenty-five sulungs, and there was also a small den at Chilmington in the Weald near Great Chart 'for the purpose of repairing the church' i.e. a source of good building timber. The Domesday Book entry for Reculver probably describes the parishes which are now Reculver, Herne and Hoath, while other parts of the old Reculver Abbey estate appear to come under the adjoining heading of Northwood, such as Makinbrook, Stourmouth and land at the west end of Thanet. These were lands let out to the Archbishop's knights. For the purposes of administration the Archbishop's clerks continued to regard the Reculver estate as a unit which included the demesne land of the home farm, the sulungs of farmland let to free tenants, cotland let to tenants who performed special services, and the more distant tenants of the areas under the control of the knights.

Between 1283 and 1285 a survey was made of the Archbishop's estates and the customary duties and payments of the tenants in each estate. It was carefully written up in a rental book, now alas lost; fortunately, however, a fifteenth century copy remains in the Cathedral Library at Canterbury. From the description of the Reculver lands the state of affairs two hundred years later can be compared with Domesday. There were still eight 'sulungs', the farmlands of the free tenants or villeins, divided up for the purposes of taxation, although it is probable that they may not comprise the same areas as the eight mentioned in Domesday, since two are said to be in Northwood. The manor farm or demesne arable land is still about 300 acres (3 ploughlands); the pasture has been increased from 33 acres to 81 acres. There are 59 acres of wood, but no acreage is given for the Domesday wood, so there can be no comparison here. There are four mills, said to be windmills, against one in Domesday. Churches are not mentioned in the estate book, and their mention in Domesday is haphazard, but by 1285 and for many years before there were four chapels, Herne, Hoath, St. Nicholas at Wade and All Saints (north-east of St. Nicholas) in addition to the great church of Reculver.

The Archbishop's estate book lists the duties of cotlanders who lived near Reculver and Bishopstone, a planted settlement about a mile to the west in a slightly less exposed position. They were to help with the harvest and haymaking, and with harrowing if they owned horses. Other tenants had to go to outlying portions of the estate to summon people to work or for a meeting. The old Reculver possession of Shottenden near Faversham, and Chilmington near Great Chart had to be visited, also Bereham (site unknown) and Stourmouth. Yet other tenants had to assist with the impounding of distrained animals, when the owners were in debt to the lord of the manor. One group were to go to Stourmouth, and two other groups took care of distraint in the main Reculver/Herne area – at Chelde, Strode, Underdown and Beltynge, and at Hoath, Risselle, Hawe and Broomfield.

These names from the survey of 1285 are perhaps the earliest examples of a list of the borghs or small hamlets of Reculver and Herne. Those of Herne were later known as Thornden, Strode, Hampton, Beltynge and Hawe. It seems reasonable to suppose that Chelde in some way equals Thornden: Chelde was a name associated with the south or wooded part of the estate, and it may be that the settlement was moved to a new site or clearing in the wood and thus acquired a new name. In the same way Underdown was succeeded by Hampton, a settlement a little to the north west. The borghs or boroughs remained as a feature of Herne local administration: they occur in the medieval churchwardens' accounts, and in the seventeenth century rentals of 'Reculver Rectory and Herne and Chapels' which remain at Lambeth.

From an ecclesiastical point of view the Reculver estate was carved up in 1310, when Archbishop Winchelsey ordained that there should be three perpetual vicarages under the Rector of Reculver, one for Herne, one for St. Nicholas at Wade and its chapel of All Saints, and one for Reculver with the chapel of Hoath. The Rector of Reculver had frequently been non-resident, and even if he resided, the rector and one vicar could not minister to the parishioners who numbered over a thousand under Archbishop Peckham, and were constantly increasing. In the past the rector had appointed as vicar an ignorant priest removable at his will, as was noted in the preamble to the deed of 1310. Under the new plan the chapelries would be as it were separate parishes, but their relation to the mother church was to be remembered on Whit Monday, when all were to come in processions to Reculver, and also on September 8th when the patronal festival of the Reculver church was kept, the feast of the Nativity of the Virgin Mary. Some tithes were to be paid to the Rector, others to the Vicars.

This new arrangement was only the final stage in a long drawn-out altercation between the parishioners of Reculver and its chapelries and the Archbishop. Since the area of the parish was so large and the tithes were many, the Rectors of Reculver were rich men. The stipend had been used to pay some high-ranking ecclesiastic in the service of the archbishop or the king, who had appointed a vicar to run the large parish on a small salary. The parishioners complained bitterly, and in the end their complaints were heard. So far as can be known the new arrangement worked satisfactorily, though in a sense it helped to bring about the ruin of the ancient church of Reculver, while those of Herne and St. Nicholas at Wade continued to flourish. But the sea, of course, was the greatest agent of its ruin.

Sources

1.   W de Grey Birch, *Cartularium Saxonicum,* 880.
2.   Domesday Book. *Victorian County History of Kent,* II, p.211.
3.   Archbishop's Estate Book C.A.L.C. Lit. MS E 24.
4.   Division of Reculver parish. Rose Graham, 'Sidelights on the Rectors and Parishioners of Reculver from the Register of Archbishop Winchelsey', *Arch. Cant.* lvii (1944) pp.1-12.

RECULVER AND THE CINQUE PORTS

by

Frank Jenkins M.A., Ph.D., F.S.A.

     The aim of this inquiry is to determine when Reculver became a limb of Sandwich in the Confederation of the Cinque Ports, and also the length of time it shared the burden of ship service to the King. As a starting point it is necessary to turn to the testimony of Stephen de Pencestre, Constable of Dover Castle and Warden of the Cinque Ports. In 1293 he was asked to give the names of the five ports, the names of their members (limbs), and the ship service they each owed to the King. His answers to these questions were written down in the Red Book of the Exchequer *(21st Edward I).* These reveal that Sandwich, one of the five head ports, had three limbs, namely, Fordwich, Sarre and Stonar. Less than a decade later, evidently before 1303, Deal appears as an additional limb in an Exchequer record of that year *(31st Edward I).* When Letters Patent were granted in 1359 *(33rd Edward III)* for the inspection and exemplification of that record, it was confirmed that there were four limbs of Sandwich, namely, *'Stonor, Fordwiz, Dale et Serres'.* Hence it is clear that Reculver was not a limb in 1303, and possibly the reason for the application to inspect the official records in 1359, was that the time had come for the list of the limbs to be brought up to date.

The Limbs of Sandwich.

Red Book 1293	Exchequer Record 1303 1359	Romney Version *c.* 1300	Sandwich Custumal 1353	White Book 1460-1469
Fordwich	Fordwich	Fordwich	Fordwich	Fordwich
Stonar	Stonar	———	Stonar	Stonar
Sarre	Sarre	Sarre	Sarre	Sarre
———	Deal	Deal	Deal	Deal
———	———	Reculver	Reculver	———
			Walmer	Walmer
			Ramsgate	Ramsgate

The Romney version of the so-called Ports' Domesday probably contains the earliest extant reference to Reculver as a limb of Sandwich. It is generally agreed that this was written *c.* 1300, so the precise date when it was appointed is not known. However, there are two other pieces of evidence which are probably significant. First, it is known that at the outbreak of the war with Scotland in 1332, writs were directed to Stonar which was already a limb of Sandwich, and also Reculver, which by implication must have been admitted prior to that date. Second, Reculver is listed as one of the limbs of Sandwich in an extract taken from the Ports' Domesday, which was copied into the Custumal of Sandwich *'per manus Willielmi de Burle anno regis Edwardi vicesimo septimo'*, evidently 1353. This tells us that Reculver, Fordwich, Sarre, Stonar, Deal, and the *'novo concessu'* Walmer and Ramsgate were the limbs of Sandwich, and they shared the burden of ship service by providing goods *(catallis)* for the five ships that Sandwich, their head port, owed to the King. As Reculver is not listed with these *novo concessu* it follows that it became a limb of Sandwich after 1303 but before 1353.

It is quite possible that Reculver was admitted to the Confederation before the outbreak of the Hundred Years War with France in 1337, when each head port was required to assemble its quota of ships, men and supplies for active service with the King's fleet. The embargoes and arrests of foreign ships which followed so seriously disrupted the trade of the Portsmen that they strongly protested to the central government. The situation was so bad that their representatives were summoned to Westminster in 1337 to discuss all of their problems. As the representative of Reculver attended the meeting, there seems no reason for doubting that it had been admitted to the Confederation as a limb of Sandwich prior to 1337.

During the long war the five ports took the full brunt of sporadic sea-borne invasions by the French and their allies. In 1339 the Mayor and Commons of Sandwich instructed the men of the limb town of Sarre to join the ships of their head port, set out to sea, and rendezvous with the rest of the King's fleet. It is not clear whether Reculver received the same order, but it is almost certain that it was obliged to provide its quota of goods for the expedition.

During a violent attack by the French in 1377, Rye was sacked and burnt to the ground. Three years later the men of the Castilian fleet attacked New Winchelsea and partly destroyed the walls of the town. Accordingly, strong measures were taken to restore and strengthen the defences of the Cinque Ports. One of these measures was the imposition of a tax to pay for the work. This was rated at 3d on every noble's worth of fish landed, that is, on every 6s 8d worth. As Reculver was one of the places taxed, it seems that it was still liable to be called upon to discharge its duties as a member of the Confederation.

It seems that thereafter there is no record of the participation of Reculver in the affairs of the Cinque Ports. There is certainly no reference to it in the minutes of the Courts of Brotherhood (Brodhull) held at New Romney during the period 1432-1571, as recorded in the White Book of the Cinque Ports. On the other hand there are a few references to Sarre to show that it was still a limb of Sandwich between the years 1460-80. It is also known from another source that in 1498 Sarre, as a corporate member, had the right to put up two candidates for office, who were sent to Sandwich for the Mayor to select one of them *(13th Henry VII)*.

One can only conclude that the complete absence of Reculver from these later records means that it had long ceased to be a limb of Sandwich. The probable reason for this was that it had fallen into decay, owing to the drastic coastal erosion, and the consequent silting up of the Wantsum Channel between Sarre and the North Mouth. However, the channel still remained navigable for some time later between Sandwich and Sarre, to give access up the River Stour to the port of Fordwich. For that reason Sarre and Fordwich remained active limbs of Sandwich, and retained the right to send their representatives, when especially invited, to the Courts of Brotherhood at New Romney, whereas Reculver, no longer a member of the Confederation of the Cinque Ports, had lost all of its privileges.

BIBLIOGRAPHY

K. M. Murray, *Constitutional History of the Cinque Ports, (Manchester U.P.)* particularly pp. 240-4.

William Boys, *Collections for a History of Sandwich (1792) pp. 528-9,* for extract of Ports' Domesday in the Sandwich Custumal.

White Book of the Cinque Ports 1432-1571 (H.M.S.O. 1966) edited by Felix Hull, pp. 42, 60, 79, 83 and 85.

THE CURE OF SOULS AT HOATH

by

Harold Gough

Hoath has never been an ecclesiastical parish in its own right, but was known as the Borough and Chapelry of Hoath, dependent upon Reculver parish church until 1960.

The ancient parish of Reculver comprised the considerable area of the monastic estate founded in 669 A.D. by King Egbert, and by the tenth century included the later parishes of Herne, and St. Nicholas-at-Wade (Thanet) and the Chapelry itself.

The wide distances between these peripheral settlement-hamlets and the parish church led to the establishment of chapels-of-ease where Masses could be heard daily. There seems to be no record of the names of the priests who served the Church and its chapels in the early days, but about 1284 we find that the people of St. Nicholas and All Saints in Thanet were complaining that the Vicar of Reculver was failing to send a chaplain to them for Mass (*Note 1*). These clergy were under the overall control of successive Rectors of Reculver, men of considerable substance, but with little local interest, such as John de Langton, Chancellor to Edward I, and Nicholas de Tyngewick, the same King's favourite physician (*Note 2*).

The only burial ground for the whole parish was at Reculver, and the problem of finding a priest to minister to a dying parishioner and then to convey the body anything up to six miles for burial, in a bleak north Kent winter must have been as distressing as it was formidable.

In 1310, Archbishop Winchelsey recognised these difficulties, and propounded a solution. He pointed out that the population of this sprawling parish had now passed the three-thousand mark, and was thus beyond the scope of a single priest employed by an absentee rector, and he divided the area, appointing three perpetual vicars, in charge of parishes based on Reculver Church and the chapels of St. Martin, Herne, and St. Nicholas, Thanet.

There were two other small chapels in the district, one dedicated to All Saints, just north of St. Nicholas, and the other at Hoath, then dedicated to the Virgin Mary and the Holy Trinity; the former was to be united to St. Nicholas, while the latter remained an appendage of Reculver itself. The old parish was thus divided into three new ones and the Chapelry, and three Vicars were appointed to the cure of souls. The Vicars were to be supported out of the income from their respective parishes, and each might have a suitable priest to assist him, at his own expense; all the parishes were to contribute to the upkeep of the church at Reculver, whose Vicar was to be regarded as taking precedence, and entitled to due honour and reverence (*Note 3*).

Between 1354 and 1360 Thomas Nyewe, Vicar of Reculver, founded three chantries, two in Reculver Church and one at Hoath Chapel, with a priest for each to sing Masses and pray for the souls of various benefactors. He showed the subordinate position of the Chapel, by rendering the priest there liable to assist the Vicar if required, and even to desert his own chapel to serve at Reculver if there was a lengthy vacancy at one of the chantries there, but clearly the presence of a priest at Hoath was intended to relieve the Vicar and his successor of the personal responsibility to see that the Chapelry was served (*Note 4*).

The inhabitants of the Chapelry however, retained a sense of grievance. Apart from the physical distance involved – the Chapel is almost 3½ miles from the mother church as the crow flies – Hoath is intersected by a stream in a steep-sided valley. The main road to Reculver runs down one side of the valley and up the other, crossing the stream beside the Archbishops' manor house at Ford, which doubtless gained its name from its function as a crossing point. Though originally laid down by the Romans, the road had become neglected, and the inhabitants found it difficult to use, especially in winter, when the swollen stream flooded the sandy bottom of the valley. The locals therefore successfully petitioned Archbishop Arundel (1396-1414) for the right to bury their dead at Hoath, but their inferior status was once again stressed, for to protect Reculver's position, they were to hand over half the burial fees to the sexton of the parish church, while half of any legacies intended for the upkeep of the chapel must be directed to Reculver's fabric fund.

At the time of the suppression of the chantries, the return for Hoath, made in 1546, set out the history of its foundation as follows: 'the said Vicar was bounden to come or to send his Curate to the foresaid chapell every sunday and festivall day and other tymes to minister the Sacraments . . . . . and bycause it was tedious to the said Vicar' (Nyewe) 'to do the premisses, And also grevous to the Inhabitants of the said Borough to send for the Vicar or his deputie when any neede was to come a Visitac'on, and soe many tymes prevented with Death departed without Sacrament bycause of soe long distance between the said Chapell and Reculver which is ii Miles and more'; the Vicar therefore founded the Chantry to ensure the presence of a priest there; the Return stated that 'the profits of the said Boroughe is nothing able to Fynde a Preist without the said Chauntrie' so the foundation had been beneficial to the local people, who could not otherwise have afforded to maintain a priest – the net income was only just over £6 a year, and there were no plates, jewels or ornaments (*Note 5*).

So with the suppression of the Chantry, the responsibility for the cure of souls at Hoath reverted to the Vicar of Reculver, and the custom evolved for the Vicar to visit Hoath in person or by a curate, one Sunday in four, with the Parish Clerk reading the service the other three weeks; at the same time the Vicar was supposed to be 'on call' for baptisms etc., as required.

One of these post-Reformation Vicars, Robert Hunt, was himself apparently born at Hoath about 1570, and so he grew up in full knowledge of the local problem. There are no reports that he neglected his duties there while Vicar from 1595 to 1602, but his successor, Barnabas Knell, who came from Heathfield to exchange parishes with Hunt, was a very different man. During his long incumbency he was the cause of much strife and ill-feeling in many ways, not least in his persistent neglect of the Chapelry.

Knell very soon refused to go to Hoath, and required his flock there to attend Reculver Church, or go without spiritual comfort. The villagers appealed direct to the Archbishop, who as an occasional resident at Ford was regarded as one of themselves. The Vicar was summoned to the manor house in March 1607, where he pleaded that he could not find the time to go to Hoath, and as a poor man with a wife and many small children, could not afford to pay a curate. But he agreed to resume the old custom of one week in four at Hoath, with a lay reader for the other three with the Archbishop's consent. His Grace had in fact been insistent that Hoath should be served, and put the onus on Knell to make some decision in the matter (*Note 6*).

The Vicar seems to have observed this procedure faithfully for 30 years; a new Archbishop, the zealous William Laud however objected to a layman conducting three-quarters of the services at Hoath, and forbade the practice in 1636. Knell continued his monthly visits for a year, until the 'new broom' made another sweep: Knell was told he must not leave his parish church unattended,

HOATH, 1983   A Watercolour by Jennifer Evans

even once a month! On the other hand, no solution to Hoath's problem was proposed – it was seen as Knell's problem (*Note 7*).

So, for three years, apart from an occasional Communion Service, Knell left the Chapel alone, and the villagers had to hire an unattached curate at their own expense. In 1640, they sent several petitions to the Archbishop, an enquiry was ordered, and a meeting of all parties took place in May. It was then agreed that the inhabitants might apply the value of the small tithes of Hoath to the stipend of a curate, and to paying Knell £18 a year to compensate him for the loss of the tithes. The Vicar was to get his £18 in quarterly instalments, payable on his attendance there to preach and celebrate Holy Communion 'at the four usual quarters of the year'. On these occasions the Hoath curate should take his place at the mother church (*Note 8*).

On the face of it, this seems a reasonable settlement, but the locals later claimed that Knell had gone behind their backs to the authorities with the outline of the scheme, which had then been imposed on them without their real approval. They showed their resentment by withholding the quarterly instalments of the Vicar's £18, and in January 1641 they petitioned the Parliamentary Committee of Religion for a better settlement.

Knell counter-attacked by appealing in turn to both Church and State for support for his claim for the £18. His petition to Parliament, by way of the County Member, Sir Edward Dering, is a model of unctuous grovelling. He stated that he was now 67 years of age, and had spent 39 of these years 'peicably, honestly and painfully in his well approved ministry at Reculver and Hoath'. He was now destitute of means to sustain himself, his wife of nearly 60, a sister of 74, two sickly daughters and an orphan grandchild of 9, and was in daily danger of imprisonment for debt. He claimed that the church at Hoath was not entitled to a regular minister, as it was in reality only a chapel erected for Mass and other superstitious ceremonies at the burial of the dead.

The inhabitants, in turn, sent in a comprehensive summary of the history of the chapel and of the controversy, for submission to Parliament, pointing out that their anxiety for church services was leading them to other nearby churches, whose parishioners were justifiably annoyed by the resulting shortage of pews (*Note 9*).

Laid before a Parliament deeply involved in a constitutional crisis, the petitions sank almost without trace, and matters remained much as they were (*Note 10*).

In 1646, Barnabas Knell's career was brought to an end by the changes in the religious climate of the country. He was sequestered by the Committee for Plundered Ministers, for 'swearing, observing ceremonies, and, in sermons and otherwise, expressing great malignancy against Parliament'. Deprived of his incumbency he withdrew to Canterbury and died soon afterwards. (*Note 11*).

After the Restoration, Knell's successors seem to have come to amicable terms with their divided responsibilities, and despite the 'foundrous' and sometimes impassable roads, the often pluralist, absentee Vicars of the 18th century discharged their duties with the help of curates. In the 19th century, some Vicars actually lived at Hoath rather than at Reculver, and one served both churches from his residence at Herne Bay.

The physical presence of the Thanet Way (A.299) cutting through the southern part of Reculver parish, suggested a convenient adjustment of the boundaries in the area, and in 1960, by Order in Council, Hoath was at last detached from its 1300-year connection with Reculver, and formally linked to Chislet which embraced it on three sides; more recently still, the two have become united with St. Nicholas-at-Wade, so that, since 1971, the Vicar of St. Nicholas and Sarre has also been Curate-in-charge of Chislet with Hoath.

NOTES

1. R. Graham, *Sidelights on the Rectors and Parishioners of Reculver from the Registers of Archbishop Winchelsey* (Archaeologia Cantiana, LVII, 1944, pp.1-12).

2. Ibid.

3. J. Duncombe, *The History and Antiquities of the two parishes of Reculver and Herne in the County of Kent* (Bibl. Top. Brit. XVIII, 1784) p.135-38, prints the Latin text of the ordination of the vicarages. R. Graham (*op. cit.*) gives a summary in English.

4. Sections of the foundation deed are printed in K. Wood-Legh, *Perpetual Chantries in Britain* (C.U.P. 1965) from *Reg. Whittlesey,* fo. 45-46v.

5. The Chantry Return is printed in C. Cotton, (ed.) *The Canterbury Chantries and Hospitals* (Kent Archaeological Society, Records Branch, vol. XII Supplement, 1934) pp.58-60.

6. A. Hussey, (ed.) *Visitations of the Archdeacon of Canterbury* (Arch. Cant. XXV, 1902, pp.11-56).

7. *Proceedings in Kent in connection with the Committee of Religion appointed 1640* (Camden Society, 1862, pp.133-140).

8. As note 6.

9. As note 7.

10. As note 6.

11. A. G. Matthews, *Walker Revised,* (1948) pp.220-221.

HOATH, 1983   A Watercolour by Jennifer Evans

CHURCH LIFE IN MEDIEVAL HERNE

by

Margaret Sparks, M.A.

There is no need for more than a brief description of St. Martin's in this volume, since Mr. Harold Gough has written an excellent and well illustrated guide which is for sale at the church. This does however present an opportunity for bringing together some additional material which sheds light on the medieval community, information gleaned from church wardens' accounts, chantry certificates, wills and other records.

The ancient chapel of St. Martin was probably on the same site as the north aisle of the present church. An apse has been found under the floor of the north chancel, evidence which takes the old chapel back to at least the eleventh century and possibly earlier. About the time of the making of Archbishop Winchelsey's new parochial arrangements in 1310, the tower at the west end of the chapel site was built, and shortly afterwards the nave was set alongside it and the old chapel demolished to make the new north aisle. The south aisle was soon added so that within perhaps thirty years the old chapel had been replaced by a large fourteenth century church of nave, chancel and north and south aisles with chapels, in which the furnishings were many times altered but the structure remained virtually unchanged. The archbishops were regarded as 'founders' of the church and it is probable that they assisted financially in its building.

Until thirty years ago Herne was unusually fortunate in possessing medieval churchwardens' accounts for 1339, 1396, 1397, 1447. These were destroyed in the flood of 1952/53 at Herne Bay; but by a piece of good luck they had been translated and printed by C. E. Woodruff in the Appendix to his *Canterbury Diocesan Records* (1922).

In the heading to the earliest set of accounts (1339/40) there are names of four men who are described as 'wardens of the lights and fabric of the church at Herne'. Later accounts give only two names, 'wardens of the goods of the church at Herne'. Their income came from the letting of workshops and houses, and from stock. Parishioners gave sheep and cows to the church as gifts or legacies, and it was the wardens' task to make money as they could. In 1339 they started with 11 cows, 42 sheep, 29 ewes and 7 yearling lambs. They let out some of the cows for milking, and sold others. From the sheep there was an income from sales of wool, skins and animals; but sheep were liable to die of murrain and must have been an anxiety for the wardens and their shepherd. 2d. a head was paid out for pasture. Even so, the sheep were the largest source of income, bringing in 43 shillings in 1339/40, out of a total of just over £7. This total included the special sum collected each year from the borghs towards the cost of the Paschal Candle at Easter.

Running expenses were much as usual for churchwardens. They did not pay the priest, but there was the stipend for the parish clerk, expenses for church cleaning, and expenses on the bells (which always figure largely in church accounts). As in the halls of larger houses, the church floor was 'strewn' or carpeted with straw at Martinmas, Christmas and Easter, and with rushes at Midsummer. In addition to such ordinary expenses, the wardens were much concerned with lights and oil and wax. Special consignments of wax were bought, out of which candles were made for Christmas and Easter; and the special Paschal Candle which would be lit on Easter Eve as a symbol of Christ's Resurrection, as it still is during the darkness of the Easter Vigil, and lit again at all services during the forty days from Easter to Ascension Day. The wardens were also responsible for sustaining the small lights about the church before statues or paintings of the saints; the light before the great cross on the rood screen; and the light before the Reserved Sacrament which hung in a silver pyx near the high altar. Parishioners left small sums for these lights in their wills, so that the wardens became their trustees to use the money and sustain the lights.

In some years there were special expenses: in 1340 the church porch was being built; in 1397 a roof was being repaired with new timber and lead, and in the following year there were repairs to the workshops and houses which were let. A new handcart was bought, costing 10d. It is only possible to recapture glimpses of church life in medieval Herne because of the survival of documents such as these accounts, a list of church goods in 1341, and an excellent collection of wills of parishioners, beginning in 1396. These add to the material evidence which survives in the fabric of the church and create a picture of people at work and prayer in their medieval setting.

As well as the churchwardens' accounts there was also a roll of accounts of the Warden of the Chantry of St. Mary in Herne Church for 1359. The Chantry was endowed with land in the parish, and two houses, one being next the church. Like the churchwardens, the priest had sheep and cows to augment the chantry finances out of which he had a salary of £5 a year. The task of the chantry priest was to sing mass daily on week days in prayer for the soul of his founder

JOHN DARLEY, 1446, HERNE
Detail — Animal at Feet

and the souls of others designated by the founder. A perpetual chantry of this kind was a freehold like that of a rector or vicar, to which the chantry priest was instituted and inducted, and his name listed in the bishop's registers. When chantries were to be valued and dissolved in 1546 and 1548 accounts had to be drawn up and declarations made about chantry property and its use.

These chantry certificates provide between them further information about the chantry of St. Mary at Herne. It was founded by Thomas New (Niewe) in 1355 with the intention that prayer should be offered for the souls of the Archbishops of Canterbury, who were founders of the parish church at Herne, and it was endowed with scattered lands which brought in about £7 a year in 1548. Thomas New had formerly been Vicar of Reculver and at the same time as the founding of the chantry at Herne, he had endowed two chantry priests at Reculver and one at Hoath. One of the chantry priests at Reculver was to sing a mass of the Blessed Virgin daily on the south side of the church at an early hour before the parishioners went to work. On Sundays and feast days the two priests should assist the Vicar at high mass. Presumably there was a similar arrangement at Herne. There is no direct evidence for the position of the Herne chantry of St. Mary. It was partly enclosed by a screen with a door: two parishioners asked to be buried 'at the door of the chancel of the Blessed Mary' (1401 and 1476). It is probable that, as at Reculver, the chantry was in the south chapel at the end of the south aisle. A priest's door gives easy access from the chantry lodging across the churchyard, and there was a small sacristy, perhaps a lean-to building, beneath the east window. Bequests to the church indicate that until about 1510 there were only three altars in the church, the high altar of St. Martin and those of St. Mary and St. John Baptist.

The chapel of St. John Baptist was that on the north side, where members of the Phillip family asked to be buried, and where a brass to one of them does remain and may possibly be in its original place. The family were apparently prosperous farmers at Greenhill; but one of them, Matthew, went to London and became a goldsmith. He died in 1475. His brother and nephew, both called William, left money in 1459 and 1471 for masses to be said at St. John's altar, but this was for a different form of chantry. There was no formal foundation with endowment, but money was left by parishioners for masses to be said for two years, or a year or half a year, and the executors or the church authorities hired a priest for the specified time. During the second half of the fifteenth century there were many such bequests, and the staff at Herne would usually consist of the Vicar or his deputy, the chantry priest, and the soul priest who sang mass in St. John's chapel, and used the 'squint' which remains there.

The list of 'ornaments' in Herne church in 1341, before the St. Mary chantry was founded, implies that the Vicar had assistance and that there was more than one priest at the church. There are vestments and copes, sets of necessary books for mass and choir offices at different seasons, three chalices, a censer for incense, and many candlesticks. Fifteenth century wills mention a silver pyx for the Reserved Sacrament, promised in 1466 by Thomas Bysmere, who also left 3 shillings and 4 pence towards an organ; vestments; an altar frontal; a missal and of course the many lights to be sustained before altars and saints. In the 1460's the church was paved and provided with pews, for which bequests were made.

Many of the parishioners who left wills were small farmers, some of whom had fish weirs on the shore as a sideline. James Shipman (1461) had a boat as

CHRISTINA, WIFE OF MATTHEW PHELIP, 1470. HERNE

well. John Cobb, John Bates and the Phillip family were more prosperous and in each case household silver is mentioned in wills. From the Phillip family came Matthew the goldsmith, sometime Lord Mayor of London and Warden of the Goldsmiths' Company. Although he was a citizen of London, he did not forget his native parish, since he bought Hawe Manor as his country house. His second wife Christina was buried in St. John's Chapel, where her brass remains. Another brass in the same chapel records William Bysmere who died in 1456, another citizen and goldsmith of London, also a former Warden of the Goldsmiths' Company. Bysmere left kinsmen in Herne, Thomas and Alexander, but whether he was himself a son of the parish, and whether it was through him that Matthew Phillip went to London is not recorded.

Two among the many medieval Vicars of Herne have memorials in remaining brasses, and both are of interest, providing connection between Herne and the University of Oxford and perhaps the civil service. John Darley (Vicar 1432-1446) was an academic. He went to Oxford, most probably to Queen's College, from Carlisle diocese, a district with which the College is closely linked. He persisted with his studies and became a Master of Arts, a qualified university teacher, in 1414, and at the same time Principal of Edmund Hall, a near neighbour of Queen's College, where he was in charge of the students who lodged at the Hall. In 1421 he became a Fellow of Queen's College and was ordained to the title of his Fellowship. He took full part in college life and was the equivalent of junior and senior bursar. A Long Roll or college account kept by him in 1428/29 is among the muniments. Meanwhile he studied Theology, becoming a Bachelor of Theology in 1431: presumably this was a matter of pride, since he is portrayed on his brass in his Bachelor's robes, and the degree is mentioned in the verse inscription. But he must have quarrelled in some way with the other Fellows, as he was forced to resign in 1431, and was not provided with a college living (a parish in the college's gift). Darley probably appealed to Henry Chichele, the Archbishop of Canterbury, who had Oxford interests, and he was rewarded with the parish of Herne, where he appears to have resided for the rest of his life, retiring a few months before his death. His career is not unusual: Fellows often remained for ten years or so in their colleges and afterwards settled in a college living, except for the few who remained in Oxford as senior university teachers.

Andrew Benstede (Vicar 1511-1531) is an example of a different sort of ecclesiastic. He was a Wykehamist, that is to say a member of William of Wykeham's two foundations, Winchester College and New College, Oxford. He came from Hambledon in Hampshire and was elected a Scholar of Winchester College in 1467. When his school days were over he went as a Scholar to New College in 1472. He became a Fellow from 1474-1484, and in due course a Master of Arts. He did not proceed to a further degree, and from his ordination as priest in 1477 he held a bewildering array of benefices in which he clearly did not reside. In addition to various parishes he held prebendal stalls in the cathedrals of Lincoln, Wells and Chichester. These were usually given to provide an income for men teaching in universities or acting as 'civil servants' in royal or episcopal service. The information provided about Benstede is not sufficient to explain what he really did, but since he appears not to have been at Oxford, a 'civil service' post is a probable answer. By 1511 when he obtained the parish of Herne from the Wykehamist Archbishop Warham, Benstede was about 55 and had perhaps 'retired'. There is evidence that he was sometimes at

Herne, and it is possible that he resided regularly for part of each year, though he also held the New College living of Great Horwood, Buckinghamshire, and a prebendal stall at Chichester.

Benstede's period at Herne was one of great activity in the fabric and ornaments of the church, when church life was apparently flourishing. Restoration had started under his predecessor, John Caton. Just at the end of Caton's time in 1510, a Jesus Altar was set up in the church and a Brotherhood or parish guild of Jesus was formed. The Feast of the Name of Jesus grew in popularity in England in the late fifteenth and early sixteenth centuries. In cathedrals and large parish churches a Jesus Altar was set up in the nave, near the rood screen, since the feast was associated with the Passion of Jesus and with the crucified figure on the cross in the chancel arch. Special masses were said on Fridays, and anthems were sung after Compline on Fridays. At Herne the altar was perhaps on the south side of the church in front of the screen, where there is a piscina. In 1510 legacies were left for the altar light, for a chalice, and for chantry masses to be said at the Jesus Altar. In the years following books for use in the choir and vestments were given to the church. The chapel of St. John Baptist had new windows, and there were repairs to St. Mary's Chapel in 1526 (the chantry priest's house was in need of repair in 1511 and perhaps the chapel walls were also crumbling). Andrew Benstede himself paid for the restoration and redecoration of the choir. The stalls on the south side remain from this work, having beautifully carved misericords beneath the hinged seats, displaying angels, birds and flowers and St. Andrew's crosses which recalled the Vicar's christian name. Visually the crowning glory must have been the new rood screen, running right across the church, which was built and ready for gilding by 1522. Of this screen the northern section remains: it has intricately carved tracery, and very 'advanced' or modern motifs in the doors, Renaissance ornament such as was beginning to appear at the time in, for instance, the panels of the Christ Church Gate at Canterbury (finished in 1521). This ornament is a visual testimony to the presence in Herne of men such as Sir John Fyneux and Andrew Benstede who belonged to the world of the Court and of London, an interaction of town and country which is a feature of Herne's history.

This survey of church life in Herne suggests that the large church was well used and loved by the parishioners who regarded it as part of their life. Money for its support came from land and stock, with which many were concerned. On feast days it was decorated with carpets and coverlets, once their prized possessions, and the lights in it were sustained in memory of their relatives. Often there were three priests to offer worship to God and prayer for the living and the dead. Not least in the years before the Reformation the interior of the church was well kept and furnished as was fitting for the apparently flourishing community in the village and scattered farms of the parish.

Sources

Accounts: C. E. Woodruff, *Canterbury Diocesan Records* (1922), pp.224-235.

Chantry
Certificates: C. Cotton, *The Canterbury Chantries* (1934), pp.62-63.
              A. Hussey, *Kent Chantries* (1936), pp.146-154.

Wills: *Archaeologia Cantiana*, XXVlll (1909), pp.83-114, and XXX (1914), pp.93-126.
              Testamenta Cantiana (1907), pp.160-164.

Clergy: A. B. Emden: *Biographical Register of the University of Oxford* (1957-59).

SIAMESE TWINS AT HERNE, 1565

An entry in the Herne Burial Register, reproduced below, records the birth and death of two girl babies who were joined together. At this time such united twins were known as monsterous. They lived half a day, and one died almost an hour before the other.

A ballad was written about them in 1565 which was published as a broadside 'Imprinted at London/in Fletestreet by Thomas Col-/well; For Owen Rogers dwelling/ at S. Sepulchers Church door'. This broadside, entitled 'The true discription of two monsterous chyldren', is No. 6774 in the *Short-Title Catalogue of books printed in England, etc. 1475-1640*, London (1926). There is only one known copy in existence and this is in the Henry E. Huntingdon Library, San Marino, California, and the editors are greatly indebted to Mr. Alan H. Jutzi, the Curator of Rare Books, for the opportunity of seeing a xerox copy of it. It begins:

The Monsterous and unnaturall shapes / of these Chyldren & dyuers lyke brought / foorth in our dayes (good reader, ar not / onelye for vs to gase and wonder at, as / thyngs happenyng either by chaunce, or / els by naturall reason, as both the old, and our Phy / losophers also holde now a dayes: and without anye / farther heede to be had therto, or els as our common / custome is, by & by to iudge god onely offended wyth / the Parentes of the same, for some notoryous vyce or / offence reygning alone in them: But they ar lessons / & scholynges for vs all (as the word monster shewith) / who dayly offende as greuously as they do, wherby / god almyghtye of hys great mercy and longe suffe-/ raunce, admonysheth vs by them to amendmente of / our lyues, no lesse wycked, yea many times, more then / the parentes of suche mysformed bee.

ANNO 7mo ELIZABETHAE REGINAE
John Jarvys had two woemen children twynes
baptized at home, ioyned togeather in the belly
& havynge each the one of theyr armes lyinge
at one of theyr owne shoulders, & in all other p(ar)ts
well p(ro)portyoned children, buryed Augusti.

Herne Burial Register entry for August 29, 1565

THE CHURCH OF HOLY CROSS AT HOATH

by

Canon Derek Ingram Hill, M.A., D.D., F.S.A.

This small building in a quiet country village had always had close connections with the mother church of Reculver some four miles away but today is (after a period of time linked with Chislet) under the care of St. Nicholas-at-Wade in Thanet. It must originally have been, like many churches in East Kent, a building consisting of just a simple nave and quire or chancel built to serve a small farming community who did not wish to have to travel all the way to Reculver for their worship and the satisfaction of their spiritual needs.

In 1303 Pope Boniface VIII allowed the parishioners the right to have a churchyard of their own and also a font in their church, but the rights of the Vicar of Reculver were safeguarded a century later when in 1410 Archbishop Arundel consecrated the church building with rights of burial on the express understanding that the Vicar of Reculver was not to be prejudiced in his rights to offerings from the daughter church; nor would he be obliged to find a chaplain to serve the church of Hoath, which by this time had acquired a chantry foundation by a benefaction between 1354 and 1360 when Thomas Niewe, Vicar of Reculver, founded a chantry dedicated to Holy Cross to be served by a resident priest, who, besides the duty of serving the chantry with its regular masses and offices, would officiate parochially in the church of Hoath and would have a house and glebe provided by the parishioners. Under the Chantries Act of 1547-48 the chantry was dissolved, but the title of Holy Cross seems to have stuck to the church itself. Alas, the chapel was then allowed to fall into neglect, the Vicars of Reculver claiming that the foundation of their predecessor, Thomas Niewe, had relieved them of any obligation to care for the church of Hoath or its people. This was in fact upheld both by the visitors of Mary Tudor and later in the time of James 1 by Archbishop Abbot.

How long this neglect lasted is not clear, but by the time Hasted was engaged in his famous work it was possible for him to write: 'The Vicar of Reculver has for years now past constantly shared the care of this chapelry (Hoath) and received the endowments of it. In his time the Archbishop paid over yearly a sum of forty shillings from his manor of Forde in the parish.' The tithes of Hoath were only £14 per annum in the XVIIth century, but the number of communicants at Easter was 140.

Quite a lot of information about the parish or rather the chapelry of Hoath in mediaeval times can be gleaned from documents that have survived. Archbishop Winchelsey (Register) ordained that there were to be three perpetual vicars; one to serve Reculver and Hoath, one for St. Nicholas-at-Wade and All Saints (Birchington) in Thanet, and one for Herne, all three to serve their cures under the Rector of Reculver who was entitled to all the oblations and tithes including those on flax, hay, wool etc. and the land on which the rectorial house stood. But the vicar of Hoath had to maintain a suitable resident priest. In the Archdeacon's Visitation of 1502, Hoath is described as being in the Deanery of Westbere but exempt from the jurisdiction of the Archdeacon and only subject to the Archbishop. (Arch. Cant. XLVII page 40, Woodruff). Holy Cross remained in the parish of Reculver until on 1 November, 1960 it was linked

31

officially with Chislet, the Vicar of that parish looking after both churches. On 20 May, 1975 these two were added to the parish of St. Nicholas-at-Wade where the parish priest now resides. When we visit the church today we must always be aware of the heavy restoration of Joseph Clarke in 1867. Clarke had a considerable practice as an architect in East Kent and in 1876 was to build the present church at Reculver, to do a lot of restoration work at St. Peter in Thanet as well as adding the tower and chancel to Holy Trinity, Sittingbourne. Here at Hoath, as at St. Catherine's, Preston-by-Faversham, he restored the mediaeval building and added a north aisle including most of the fittings we see today.

The mediaeval chapelry of Holy Cross must have been dominated in the later Middle Ages, like so many churches all over the land, by its Rood Screen which would have been demolished soon after the Reformation. It must have effectively cut the little church in two but added a sense of mystery to the place with its loft surmounted by a tall crucifix and attendant figures of Our Lady and St. John the Apostle. A series of wills published in Arch. Cant. XXXII (1917) by Arthur Hussey suggest considerable devotion to their church on the part of the parishioners. Agnes Bery in 1484 gave twelve pence for the repair and renovation of a pair of silver shoes for the Holy Cross in the chapel of Hoath (presumably on the feet of Christ). Lawrence Hob gave 3/4d. in 1509 to the rood-loft, Richard Spencer in 1516 for its repair 6/8d., Nicholas Ive in 1518 gave 6/8d. for its painting and a similar sum was given for its gilding by Robert Kennett in 1519. Bequests to lights suggest several tapers or hanging lamps burning constantly in the little church. Agnes Bery left 'a croft of land to "Thomas Knoller my son" at Blean on condition he provide one pound of new and pure wax to the support and renewing of a taper burning in the chapel of Hoath for ever'. (How long did this last, one wonders, with the Reformation little more than half a century away?). William at Berye, her husband, left a bushel of barley for the lights of Holy Cross, St. Mary and the light called 'Hoklight'. Both he and their son William Bery in 1484 left bequests for a chaplain to celebrate requiem mass for their souls and those of their families. Both Robert and Richard Bysmer left legacies to the High Altar and the Rood light with bequests for requiems and Richard wills that 'his wife keep his son Bartholemew, if he will be so content, but if not he is to be ruled and guided by Sir William Dawkyn, chantry priest of Hoath'. Sometimes bequests to buy liturgical books occur – an antiphonal or a manual. Well into the reign of Henry VIII these bequests to the church continue, one of the greatest and latest being recorded in the will of Thomas Brooke third son of the sixth Baron Cobham and husband of Susan, niece of Archbishop Cranmer then in high favour with the King. Thomas Brooke had leased the parks of Ford and Chislet from the Archbishop and no doubt had an affection for the chapelry of Hoath since in his will of 5 January, 1545 he had desired to be buried in the quire of the chapel, leaving to the archbishop 'my great black horse and signet' with a bequest of forty shillings, 'at my burying to priests, clerks and poor people.'

The Rev. T. S. Frampton, who spent much of his time in the valuable research work of recording the names and details of the careers of the parochial clergy of the diocese of Canterbury, made a list of the chaplains of the chantry of Holy Cross at Hoath. (Arch. Cant. XXXII pages 85 and 86). Between 1393 and 1547 he recorded the names of eighteen chaplains from the archbishops' registers of whom one William Hyghmore was appointed in 1501 during the

THE CHURCH OF HOLY CROSS AT HOATH

vacancy of the archiepiscopal see (following the death of Cardinal Morton) by the Prior of Christ Church, Canterbury, Thomas Goldstone II. In the Valor Ecclesiasticus of 1534 William Deacon (Dawkyn) is mentioned as chaplain of Hoath, and, after the suppression of the chantry, he was paid a pension of £6 per annum which he was still receiving in 1556. Two years later George Knowler of Herne, yeoman, in his will proved in 1558, died 'seized of the chantry house and lands in the parish'.

The church plate here consists of a cup and paten cover dating from 1562 and 1578 respectively; the latter was remade and a silver alms dish was provided in 1818 by the Rev. C. B. Naylor, the Vicar of Reculver who has the unenviable reputation of having been the priest who pulled down the great Saxon church of Reculver in 1807 because his mother fancied that the church was used for 'a puppet show'.

The nineteenth century saw a restoration of the little chapel which has given it the appearance familiar to its congregation today. The shingled spire was probably reconstructed in 1842 – the date on the wall plaque. Not only was the north aisle added but the roof was covered in by timbers and the walls were plastered, though the chancel arch and much of the nave remains of the original XIVth century chapelry including a window of Perpendicular date in the south wall which has a triangular aperture cut out of the sill – was this a piscina?

The altar stands under a carved reredos of oak which is in fact a Rood – crucifix and figures of the Blessed Virgin Mary and St. John – in view of the old dedication of the chantry chapel an appropriate memorial to the dead of two World Wars. On either side of the chancel arch are plain boards with the Ten Commandments of XIXth century date. In the chancel a handsome ledger stone in the floor commemorates Vincent Varham who died aged 68 on 13 May, 1803, and Sarah his widow.

The church has a pleasant modern porch with an ancient holy water stoup by the south door and the churchyard is entered by a lych-gate.

Small though the chapel must have been before the enlargement in Victorian times, there was more than one altar, for a bequest of Richard Hoode, chantry priest, who died in March 1500 and was buried in the church quire, left two cruets to the altar of St. Margaret; while Robert Hunte in 1542 desired to be buried in the church at the end of the Trinity altar. Perhaps these two altars flanked the rood screen on either side. The most original bequest seems to have been that of Richard Lowes, who in 1499 left 3/4d. to the altar of Hoath and 42 sheep of the age of two teeth for the new bells to be bought for the church of Hoath. Mr. Lowes seems to have been a well-to-do and pious farmer for this will contains several clauses endowing 'dirge and masses' for a year's obits and a curious clause – 'if Alice my wife die within twenty-two years and also her daughter then her twenty marks serve to buy a cope for the church at Hothe . . and ten marks to a priest to sing for our souls in the church at Hothe'.

In the eighteenth century the church was obviously much neglected and when Sir Stephen Glynne visited it between 1829 and 1840, i.e. just before the restoration, he described it as small and mean with a nave and chancel and a wooden turret over the west end. There are some lancet windows; at the east end is a double lancet with a circle between the heads. The West window was Curvilinear of three lights but the tracery has been sadly mutilated. There are a few others of Curvilinear character and some of Rectilinear date. The arch to the chancel is pointed. The editor of the 1877 edition of Glynne's Notes on the Churches of Kent adds a footnote; 'The church has been restored and reseated'.

Like most of the churches in this part of Kent, Holy Cross is built of flint and is set in a spacious churchyard with a large yew outside the south door and many gravestones in the churchyard. The registers begin in 1554 and since 1975 have been deposited in the Cathedral Library. The earliest registers are in composite volumes, the first containing baptisms from 1554 to 1687, marriages from 1559 to 1683, and burials from 1559 to 1680. It is a mark of the disorder to ordinary life caused by the Great Rebellion and the proscription of the Church of England thereafter that no baptisms are recorded between 1649 and 1651, no marriages between 1645 and 1664 and no burials between 1642 and 1658. This volume is composed of sheets of vellum in its original cover. On the last page the vicar has signed thus: 'Theophilus Beck, Master of Arts, Vicar of Reculver and Hoath'. The same signature appears on the first page of Register II which runs from 1677 to 1728. Register III from 1695 to 1706 has also in it a list of chapel wardens, sidesmen and overseers and parish briefs for this period. A note of the cost of Register IV (thirteen shillings) bought in 1728 can be found in it; this goes up to 1781. The last composite register ends in 1812 and thereafter there are separate registers for baptisms, marriages and banns, and burials down to modern times; the marriage register bought in 1837 is still in use.

Statistics for the early years recorded in these registers are illuminating. Usually five or six infants were baptised annually in the reign of Elizabeth I, rising occasionally to seven but never more than nine. Weddings in this reign

A group outside Hoath Church including the curate (Allan Shields) the Vicar (Mr. McPherson, Assistant Chaplain to the Forces) Florrie Chapman, Jim Wilson, Percy Wilson, Madge Fuller, Mrs. Tarrant, Jim Chapman, Charlie Hubbard, Jessie Gough, Marjorie Rose, Louisa Amos, Norman Palmer, Jane Amos, Annie Chapman.

Photograph by courtesy of Miss A. Chapman

35

averaged two a year with three or four recorded occasionally. Weddings diminished in number in the reign of Charles I, there were none in the years 1632 to 1634, one in 1635 and none in 1636 to 1638 while the average number of burials in the reign of James I was six to seven. In the churchwardens' accounts we learn that the population in the early part of the twentieth century was 397 persons and the acreage of the parish was 915. In 1866 the parish got a loan of £200 for the repair of the church roof and in August 1896 a faculty was granted for the extension of the churchyard. Another faculty was issued on 28 November, 1905 for the placing of two stained glass windows in the north wall and one in the east wall of the north aisle. A faculty for the War Memorial Reredos was granted in 1920.

EPILOGUE

The Church of Holy Cross at Hoath, like the countryside in which it stands, still retains an air of remoteness, of belonging to a quiet rural world far away in spirit from the bustling seaside towns of Thanet across the fields and marshes of this, part of East Kent, and equally far from the crowded streets of Canterbury with the streams of tourists and shoppers that invade the ancient city now all the year through. Long may this little church remain undisturbed among its yew trees as a link with a way of life now fast disappearing.

THE ARCHBISHOPS' MANOR HOUSE, FORD, HOATH

by

Harold Gough

Certainly the largest and most imposing complex of building in the medieval landscape of Herne and Hoath was the Archbishops' manor-house at Ford, on the Hoath side of the road which formed the boundary between the two former chapelries which were part of the manor of Reculver. Today almost every obvious trace of the house has gone, but the farm-yard on the site retains a large early-Tudor barn, and there are pieces of brick and stone-work which may be identified with parts of the building.

The site is in a little valley on the Roman road from Canterbury to Reculver, and would seem to have little to commend it for an important house. The soil is mainly sand and gravel, and the road has carved a cutting in the hillside over the years. The little stream at the bottom must have been crossed by means of a ford in early times, to give the site its name – today it is spanned by a brick bridge. Springs on each side of the road would have provided a water supply, but the whole area must have been damp and chilly in winter, though providing a pleasant sun-trap in summer. Its winter condition may be judged by the fact that in 1398 the inhabitants of Hoath obtained their own graveyard, because the 'foundrous' state of the road prevented them from taking their dead to the mother-church for burial.

Just when the earliest version of the manor house (popularly but wrongly called 'the Palace') was built is unknown, but its presence in the middle ages is attested by documents dated from Ford in the 14th and 15th centuries. The oldest work of which any evidence existed until recently was built of stone, probably obtained by quarrying the ruins of the Roman fort at Reculver, 2½ miles away.

CHS

? PASSAGE

CHAPEL
75' × 25'
(stone)

52' TOWER
48' × 30' (Brick)
5 LODGING CHAMBERS OVER

PANTRY,
CELLARS
(1 WINE 3 BEER)
UNDER,
DRAWING RM
OVER

LARGE CHMBR OVER

4 LODGING
CHAMBERS
4 FAIR CHBRS
OVER

LONG GALLERY 82' × 15'

COMPASS WINDOW

2 CHS

3 CHS

CH

PORTER'S LODGE, 5 LODGING CHBRS

6 CHAMBERS OVER

TURRET
OVER

BUTTRESSED

GREAT HALL
52' × 27' (stone)

INNER
COURT
52' × 49'

CH

INNER
(GREAT)
COURT
89' × 80'

SCREENS

PASSAGE
3 CHAMBERS OVER

LDGNG CHMBR

CH

CH

GREAT GATE

PANTRY PASSAGE

BUTTERY
2 CHMBRS OVER

BASE
COURT
52' × 30'

CH

BAKE
HOUSE
(TWO
OVENS)

CH

? PASSAGE

2 LODGING CHAMBERS
3 CHAMBERS OVER

GREAT
KITCHEN
30' × 22'
F.P.16'

LESSER
KITCHEN,
WET
LARDER,
2 OTHER
ROOMS

CHAMBER
OVER

BOULTING
HOUSE,
WASHHOUSE,
FOLDING RM,
3 LODGING
ROOMS OVER

2 CHS

| Metres | O | 10 | | 30 |

→ stairs up

| Feet | O | | | 100 |

CH chimney

| Metres | O | 1 | 2 |
| Feet | O | 1 | 6 |

A

C

B

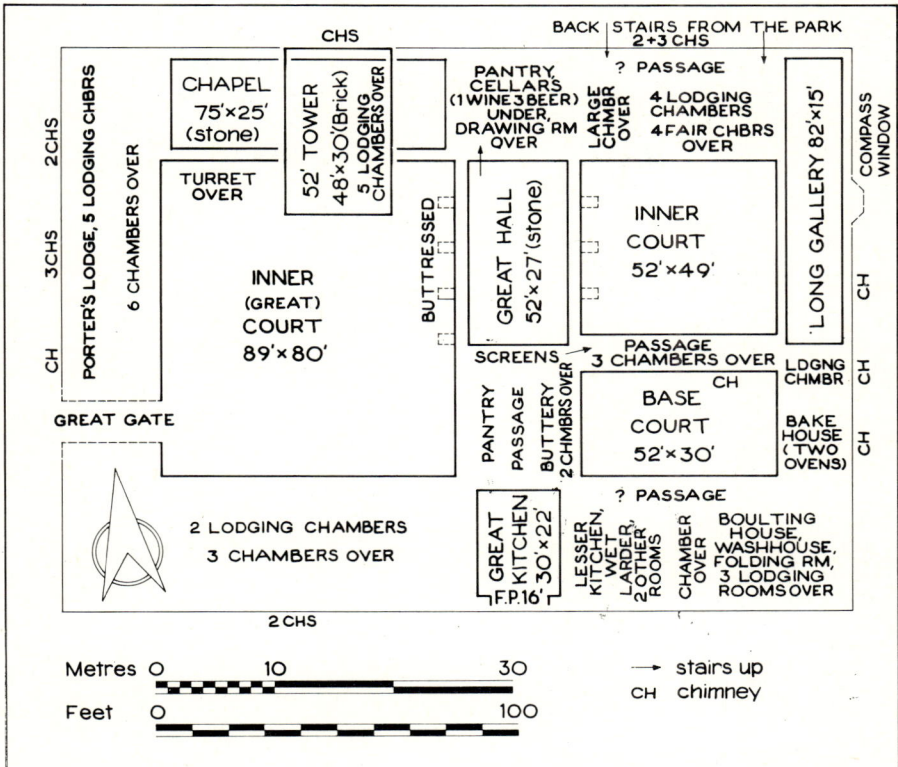

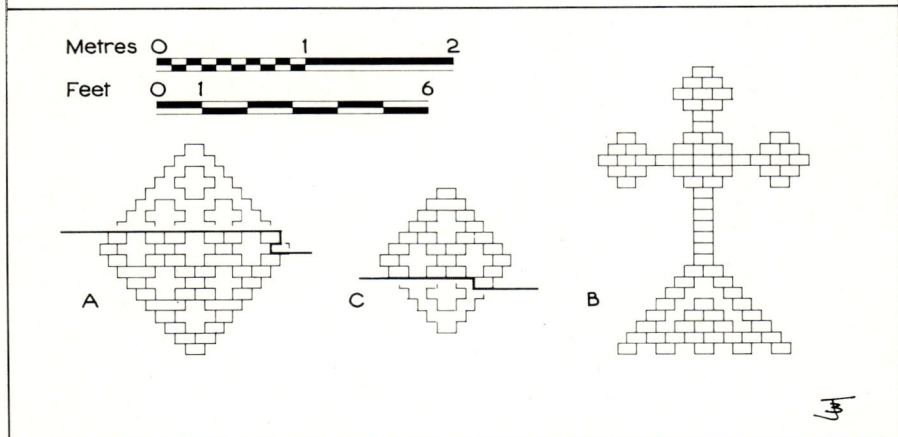

Drawn by John Bowen

At the end of the 15th century, however, Archbishop Morton set about a massive programme of improvements and rebuilding on his numerous manors in the South-east, and according to John Leland, writing less than 50 years later, 'he made almost the hole house at Forde'.

One of Morton's great contributions to English building tradition was his generous use of brick, and certainly the barn which survives at Ford could be his work. A Survey in 1647 says that 'most of the premises were built with brick', but it is clear from the detailed text that much stonework of earlier construction remained unaltered.

The little stream which runs by the site feeds into the once-broad Wantsum Channel between Kent and Thanet, and Archbishop Henry Dean, in his will of 1502 asked that if he died at Lambeth, his body might be brought to Canterbury for burial, by barge, either to Faversham or to his manor of Ford, before completing its journey by road. In the event Faversham was selected, and it is possible that the silting of the Wantsum, which was already the subject of legislation, made Ford less conveniently accessible.

Thomas Cranmer was evidently fond of Ford, and frequently made it his residence in the summer, and when he entertained Henry VIII there in 1544, the King's journey by barge terminated at Gravesend; he then rode on horseback to Ford to dine with the Archbishop before continuing to Dover to embark for France.

Cranmer's connection with Ford is linked to his part in the story of the English Reformation, when he appointed his chaplain Nicholas Ridley to be Vicar of Herne, so that the two men could be close neighbours for discussion and debate on matters of the changes involving the Church. The first copy of Thomas Matthew's version of the Bible was studied there; the Forty-two Articles were drafted there; and the Archbishop was there when he received the summons to appear before the Privy Council, which led to his arrest and execution at the stake.

Archbishop Parker was not so fond of Ford, and wanted to demolish parts of it in 1573, in order to repair the Canterbury Palace, and enlarge his preferred house at Bekesbourne; however, he died before he was able to do so.

In 1627, Archbishop Abbot was suspended from his duties over his refusal to licence the printing of a sermon by the Vicar of Brackley which supported Charles I's belief in the Divine Right of Kings, and he was ordered to withdraw to Ford for some months, while the future Archbishop Laud took over the management of the See. Abbot later described Ford as a 'moorish (i.e., marshy) Mansion-place' and was clearly not very pleased with it. In the last years of Abbot's life he carried out a programme of repairs on his manors around Canterbury, and a total of £11 15s 6d was spent on Ford between November 1631 and October 1632.

Following the execution of Charles I (at least partly the result of his belief in his Divine Right to rule) Parliament abolished the office of the Archbishop and the powers of the Church of England, and took over the Church's valuable real estate. Commissioners were appointed to survey those properties through-out the country, and in 1647 Ford came under scrutiny. From the report drawn up by the Commissioners we learn almost all we know of the physical form of the manor house, which stood at the entrance to a deer park of 166 acres.

We find that the house formed an open block of buildings around three courtyards. The Great Hall and Kitchen formed a block across the middle, looking west across the Outer Court to the entrance gate, and across the inner Courts to the Long Gallery overlooking the Park to the east. On the north of the Outer Court was the Chapel, and a brick tower-block of five storeys of guest-rooms, which being of brick was probably one of Morton's additions to the complex. There were many other rooms providing accommodation on the main frontage, and domestic offices at the rear; when the Archbishops were in residence the house must have sheltered a considerable population.

In all, the complex around its courtyards formed a rectangular framework of buildings about 160 feet by 210, set nearly 300 feet back from the road, where the main outer gate is now represented by the present farmhouse. Along the north side of the 'driveway' between the two gatehouses was the stable yard, and the stable and hay-store, 182 feet long and 37 feet wide, built of brick and covered with tile. Today about half of this great building survives as a barn, five bays and a half, 113 feet long, showing clearly at its eastern end how it has been shortened and a later wall inserted to close it.

The barn is indeed built of early brick, and its late crown-post roof supports a covering of tile; it is almost certainly Morton's work.

What may perhaps be evidence of an earlier moated site can be seen to the south of the present farmyard nearer the stream, but its true history is unknown; a large pond fed by a spring still exists close to where the back of the house must have been and probably served as the water supply.

Following the 1647 Survey, the greater part of the building was demolished for the sake of the materials, and after the Restoration Ford became again an

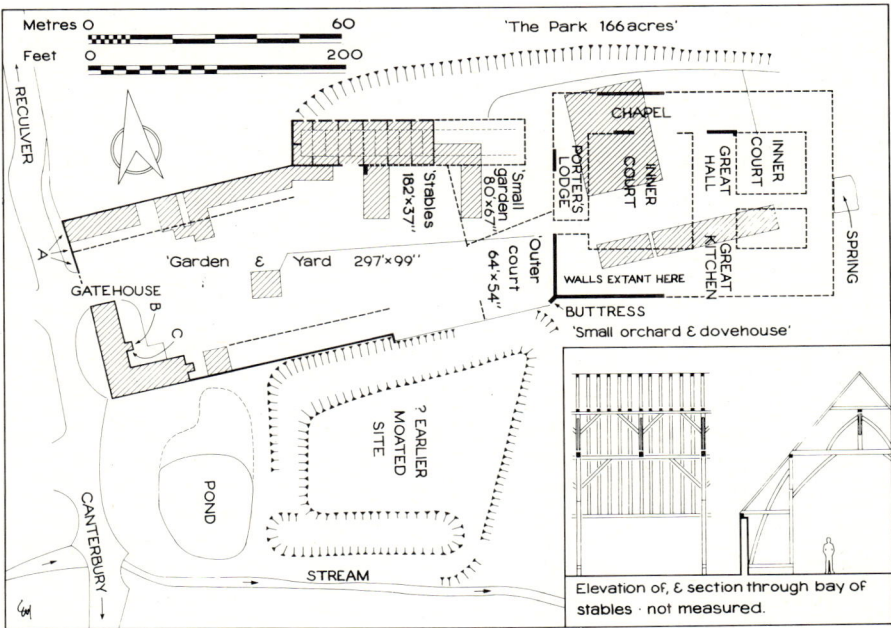

Drawn by John Bowen

archiepiscopal property but was never again an official residence. The land and such buildings as were left were leased to tenant farmers.

Over the years the ruins, originally quite substantial, fell into further decay and were themselves used as a source of building material. Near the end of the last century, part of a Roman inscription too fragmentary for interpretation, was found during a search for stones to make a rockery. The presence of Roman burials close by along the road could well account for its being on the site, and does not prove Roman occupation where the Archbishops later located their house. Oasthouses built about the same time led to the discovery of massive foundations, then assessed as Roman, but their position shows that they were more probably medieval.

In 1963 the Church Commisioners sold the farm, and shortly afterwards the remaining fragments of standing wall, apparently parts of the Great Hall and the Chapel, were demolished to clear the area for later buildings. Today, little can be identified as original traces of the stone buildings, and only a piece of brick garden wall, and the truncated brick and tile barn, remain as evidence of the great medieval manor house whose story was closely linked to important events in national history, despite its secluded and unpromising position.

SIR JOHN FYNEUX: A Herne Worthy

by

Margaret Sparks, M.A.

In the seventeenth century when antiquarians such as William Somner began to make serious studies in local history, there was a parallel interest in what might now be called 'potted biographies'. Thomas Fuller (1605-1661) laboured for years at what he called his 'Worthies', which were eventually published in the year after his death. The 'Worthies of England' were subdivided under county headings, and among those for Kent was Sir John Fyneux of Herne, Lord Chief Justice of the King's Bench.[1] He had died in 1525, but his relatives still lived in the county so that stories about him were handed down from one generation to another, and Leland on his journeys had noticed his house at Herne and written of it. Fuller could afford Fyneux only a few paragraphs: today it is possible to learn much more about him. His story is set out here in order to preserve the memory of a remarkable Herne Worthy.

John Fyneux's ancestors can be traced back to the early fourteenth century, when Robert Fyneux held 1½ knight's fees in Swingfield, on the downland north of Folkestone. Swingfield belonged to the Hundred of Folkestone and the duty of the knights there was to provide a force to guard the castle at Dover. Thirty years later, Robert son of Robert Fyneux had only a third of his father's holding, which had been divided between seven people, as often happened at that time. Robert II paid 20 shillings for his share, which was probably Northcourt where the Fyneuxs lived as poor but respectable country gentlemen.[2] Tradition, recorded by Thomas Philipot, son of the seventeenth century herald, told that John Fyneux, perhaps Robert's son, saved the life of Nicholas Criol at the battle of Poitiers in 1356, and received as a reward the neighbouring half fee of Boynton (now Bovington Court), thus increasing his holding to the value of 40 shillings.[3]

Attempts have been made to trace the Fyneux family in France but without success, although the form Fénioux occurs as a place name.[4] At some time the family took as their arms a shield of green and gold 'vert a chevron between three eagles displayed or': this coat is to be found in the west walk of the cloister at Canterbury Cathedral.[5] Its presence there among the shields of many local families, and of more illustrious persons from elsewhere, suggests that the Fyneux family was sufficiently prosperous in the early fifteenth century to make a donation to the rebuilding of the cloister.

John Fyneux was born at Swingfield, probably in 1441. His father was William Fyneux, and his mother a member of the Monins family, centred on Dover, whose christian name has not been preserved. John had two brothers, William and Richard. Richard lived in Dover (where he was mayor) and died in 1520, leaving two sons, William and Thomas. William (John Fyneux's brother) was settled at Hougham Court on the cliffs west of Dover. He died without issue and made his nephew William his heir. William II remained at Hougham where the name of Fyneux continued for several generations up to 1664. Although John eventually inherited his father's land as if he were the eldest brother, he was clever and made his own way in the world. In his time common law was a fashionable education for the landowning classes and ambitious young men so that the Inns of Court in London flourished as a school both for potential lawyers and for administrators. A poor boy could not study there, as the fees were high, but, providing the family could pay, the Inns of Court gave a clever and industrious young man the means to achieve a high position and great wealth.

The admiring notices of Sir John Fyneux preserve no account of his schooling or early days in London. He would go to a grammar school in Dover or Canterbury, and then to one of the Inns of Chancery such as Staple Inn where 'the originals and something of the elements' of law were learned.[6]

 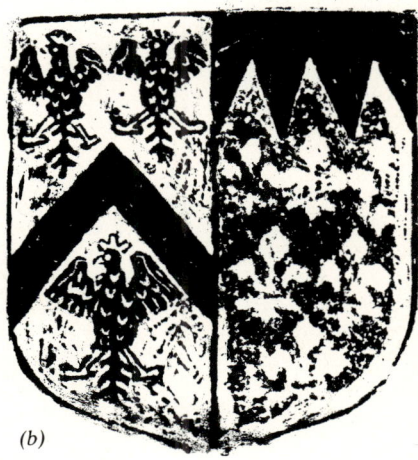

(a)   (b)

HERNE, KENT ELIZABETH FYNEUX 1539

Shields:-
    (a) Fyneux – vert a chevron between three eagles displayed or.
    (b) Fyneux impaling or a chief indented and six fleurs de lis azure.
        The two other shields are for paston and Fyneux.

41

From the Inns of Chancery successful students went on at say the age of 20 to one of the four Inns of Court, Inner and Middle Temple, Lincoln's Inn and Gray's Inn. Fyneux went to Gray's Inn, but the dates of his sojourn there have not been preserved. After about another seven years' study the students attained the status of senior members of their Inns, being called to the Bar as Utter Barristers. It is probable that Fyneux was called in 1469, aged 28: tradition in his family noted that year as of special importance, but mistakenly supposed that he began his legal studies then. From this time he was a busy practising barrister, taking his share of the duties of his Inn, and gradually becoming known in the world outside. He is recorded as the Reader at Gray's Inn, whose task was to give lectures to the members, but again without the date being specified.[7]

Fyneux's work was becoming known in his own county of Kent, and in 1472 he began a long association with Christ Church Cathedral Priory at Canterbury. The income of the monks at the Priory was largely in the form of rents from their estates scattered all over this and other counties. As now with the laws of taxation, there were then endless disputes about payment concerning who owned land and tenements and how much rent should be paid, with frequent recourse to law. It had been the ancient custom of the Priors of Christ Church to have a council of advisers in such matters, gentry who gave support and were knowledgeable in the customs of the county, and lawyers. Some lawyers were retained to look after the Priory's affairs in particular courts, others advised at Canterbury, and others, such as Fyneux were causidici, advocates who could plead on particular occasions. His name appears in the first Prior's Account Roll of William Sellyng of 1472/3, chosen perhaps on the recommendation of the Prior's relatives, the Tyll family at Sellindge.[8]

In 1473 his name begins to occur in the royal patent rolls. In that year and the next he was chosen as a commissioner for Walls and Dykes for the coast between Tenterden and Lydd, and Robertsbridge and New Romney. With him were William Brent and John Nethersole, fellow lawyers of the Prior's Council, and Sir John Fogge, Sir William Haute and Sir John Scott, leading men of the county, with whom Fyneux worked for many years. In 1475 a similar group were commissioned to enquire into bales of wool which had avoided customs duties.[9]

His ability and knowledge were recognised in his appointment by Prior Sellyng as Seneschal of Manors in 1475. Here he had charge of legal affairs for all the Priory's Kentish manors. He was confirmed in his appointment for life in 1477, but gave it up in 1486 when he became Serjeant at Law and was presumably too busy in London. He was later succeeded in 1507 by John Roper (his son-in-law) in partnership with John Hales.[10] Three items in the Priory letter collection give a vivid picture of his activities as Seneschal.[11] All are addressed to Prior Sellyng and seem to date from 1478/9: they perhaps owe their preservation to a chance bundle of correspondence being put aside at that time. The first is from Fyneux himself and concerns a commission of Walls and Dykes from Appledore to Folkestone in 1479. The Archbishop, the Prior and the Abbot of St. Augustine's were included in this commission, presumably because of their possessions in Romney Marsh. At the time when Fyneux wrote his letter the commissioners had been conferring together about the behaviour of the men of Walland Marsh. Fyneux and Nethersole were laying plans and would tell Master Fogge and Master Gifford and meet together again at Ashford, but the Prior need not trouble to come. If he has thought of any new points since the last meeting he is to 'send word to Ashford on Tuesday betimes'. The letter is written in a neat old fashioned hand, but may well have been dictated.

The other two letters are from a monk, Reginald Goldstone, a trusted lieutenant of Prior Sellyng's. In both cases he is in London, engaged on legal matters. He says that Master Fyneux requires more money to spend on lawyers in a particular case, and also reminds the Prior that the retaining fee for Master Jeny must be paid at once. In the second letter the law term is ending, and Goldstone and Fyneux are coming home. They will take the barge at 6.00 a.m. on Thursday and hope to be in Canterbury on Friday afternoon. Goldstone will spend Thursday night with Fyneux at Lynsted.

The mention of Lynsted requires explanation. About 1477 Fyneux married Elizabeth, daughter and heiress of William and Mildred Apulderfield of Badmangore, later called the Lodge and now Lynsted Park. The Apulderfields were an ancient Kentish family who took their name from Apperfield in Cudham in West Kent and had bought Badmangore from the Cheneys before 1354. By Fyneux's time the Lodge was a courtyard house with separate kitchen and offices, dovehouse, gardens and orchards, large enough both for the Apulderfields and the growing Fyneux family. There was a son John, who went into religion as a Canon of Leeds Priory, under the name of Bartholomew Lynsted, [12] and three daughters: Jane who married John Roper from another legal family, Mildred who married James Digges of Barham, and Anne who went into religion and became sub-prioress of the Dominican Nuns' house at Dartford. [13]

[97]

HISTORY OF HERNE,

BY JOHN DUNCOMBE, M.A.

HERNE, or HEARN, is fituated in the North part of Kent, fix miles North of Canterbury, 12 Weft of Margate, and 14 Eaft of Feverfham, in the Weft divifion of the lath of St. Auguftine, and Eaft divifion of the county, in the upper half-hundred of Blengate, the deanery of Weftbeer, and diocefe of Canterbury.

This parifh, which is bounded North by the German ocean, North-Weft by Swacliff, or Swalecliff, Weft by Whitftable, South and South-Eaft by Chiflet and Hoath, and North-Eaft and Eaft by Reculver, is in length from North to South about two miles, and in breadth from Eaft to Weft about fix miles. It is divided into five boroughs, viz. Hampton, Thornden, Stroud, Haw, and Beltringe, each of which has a borfholder fubordinate to the conftable of the upper half-hundred of Blengate, who is chofen at the court-leet two years from this parifh, one from Reculver, one from Hoath, and one from Stourmouth. It is in the arch-bifhop's manor of Reculver, whofe fteward holds a court-baron there every year.

It probably derives its name (as does alfo Herne-hill) from the number of herons that ufed to frequent thefe parts; and the family of Knowler, who have been fettled in this parifh fome centuries, have that bird for their creft.

P   Places

43

William Apulderfield died in 1487 leaving the Lodge to his wife, and after her to Fyneux, Fyneux settled it on his daughter Jane who brought it to the Roper family on her marriage. Her third son Christopher inherited the house, which became eventually the seat of the Barons Teynham. Jane's eldest son William married Thomas More's daughter Margaret, and has a different niche in history.

As well as a share in the Lynsted house, Fyneux had a house in London, said to be in the Strand, and a house in Canterbury at the end of Best Lane beside the churchyard of All Saints Church, with a yard or garden running down to the Stour. Fyneux was much respected in Canterbury: from c.1480 onwards he occurs frequently in the City Chamberlain's accounts. In association with William and Roger Brent, John Nethersole, and William and Richard Haute, he acted as arbitrator in the City's altercations with St. Augustine's Abbey about boundaries, a long continuing problem. With Sir Edward Poynings he was lavishly entertained for three days in 1497 when coming to investigate the proper procedure for electing the mayor. In 1501 he and Poynings are described as 'patrons of the City'. Presents of wine were often given to him, and in return he gave a benevolence 'of his charity and goodness' towards the building of the new Fishmarket.[14]

In the meantime his legal career continued. From 1480 the Patent Rolls show him increasingly concerned with legal matters outside the county and in August 1484 he was given an annual grant of £53.6s.8d. at the King's pleasure.[15] The King was Richard III. Some of Fyneux's associates in Kent, William Haute, John Fogge and Edward Poynings had been attainted in 1483 after Buckingham's Rebellion;[16] but Fyneux seems to have been an example of a lawyer who was skilful enough to remain neutral in such difficult times, though he eventually flourished in the reign of Henry VII. In July 1486 he attained the degree of Serjeant-at-Law, a position somewhat like that of attaining a doctorate in Divinity or Canon Law at the universities. As with the doctors, much money was needed for the feasts and presents which accompanied the event. It was customary that gold rings were given by the new serjeant: Fyneux had his engraved with a motto *Suae quisque fortunae faber:* Every man hammers out his own fortune. One of his rings was still extant in 1863 in the possession of his descendants, the Strangford family.[17]

Judges were chosen from the ranks of the serjeants, and in February 1494 Fyneux was appointed a Judge of Common Pleas. Cardinal Morton opposed his appointment on grounds of Fyneux's recent activity in parliament, where he had spoken against the King's demands for money for war in France, and was reputed to have said 'Before we pay anything, let us see whether we have anything we can call our own to pay'.[18] In time Morton forgave him: they became friends and Fyneux was an executor of Morton's will. In November 1495 Fyneux became Lord Chief Justice of the King's Bench, a recognition of the skill, judgement and immense industry which had brought him to the top of his chosen profession.

About this time Fyneux moved house. His daughter Jane married John Roper, so that the Lynsted house was settled on her. In 1494 Fyneux bought land in Herne, Reculver and Hoath from William Philip,[19] which presumably included Hawe Manor, where he planned and built a great house in brick in the most modern style. Hawe still is a moated site: it had been a prosperous house since the late fourteenth century and was probably an ancient settlement, giving its name to the Borough of Hawe, one of the five sub-divisions of Herne parish. The old house was probably of some size and of stone and timber-framing, smart enough to serve as the country house of Sir Matthew Philip, Warden of the Goldsmiths' Company and Lord Mayor of London; but Leland says that 'Old Finiox builded his fair house',[20] so presumably he took down most or all of it and started again. His building was a courtyard house with the gatehouse range lying east, lodgings to the south, probably the chapel and chambers to the north, and the hall and chambers on the west, facing the gatehouse across the court. Parts of the gatehouse and the lodging ranges remain, but a modern house has been built on the site of the west range and the north side of the court is open. There was probably an additional court, and the farm buildings were to the south. Cardinal Morton built in brick at Ford Manor about a mile away across the fields, and Fyneux's friends the Priors of Christ Church built in brick in Canterbury and at Chartham. A house on such a scale would take time to put up and it is to be hoped that the Fyneux family stayed at Lynsted until the new lodgings were ready for them.

When they first went to Herne Fyneux's wife, Elizabeth Apulderfield, may still have been alive. The date of her death is unknown. Her arms are in Herne church, although she seems not to have been buried there, but most likely at Lynsted near her parents.[21] By about 1512 Fyneux had remarried to another Elizabeth, who was cousin to Sir Edward Poynings, his associate for many years. She was born Elizabeth Paston, daughter of Sir John Paston the younger and Margery Brus his wife. Sadly she does not figure in the Paston Letters, being a generation too young. She had married William Clere of Ormsby, one of the Pastons' Norfolk neighbours, who died in 1501. When she married Fyneux she was probably about 28 and had already a daughter who subsequently (before 1525) married Henry Hubbert. There were two children of Fyneux's

PART OF HAWE FARM, HERNE

45

new marriage; a son William who inherited Hawe Manor and passed it on to his own son John in 1556; and a daughter, confusingly called Jane or Joan, who married Anthony Sondes of Throwley and had four or possibly five children. William's descendants (through his grand-daughter) became the Lords Strangford. Joan Sondes' descendants became the Barons Sondes, and Jane Roper's grandson became the 1st Lord Teynham, so Fyneux's family did well.

Fyneux's public life continued. He was knighted in 1503 and is often referred to as Sir John Fyneux of Herne. One of his predecessors as Lord Chief Justice, Sir John Fortescue wrote that justices had more leisure than serjeants, since the King's Courts were only held in the morning; but Fyneux no doubt more than filled his time.[22] Two of his sayings were remembered, one being 'Today I have not lived' if no work was accomplished, and the other 'We should not complain that we have little time; but that we spend much either in doing nothing or doing evil, or doing nothing to the purpose'.[23]

He continued his interest in the City of Canterbury and in the affairs of Christ Church Priory. An official of the Priory wrote to William Roper their counsel probably in 1497 about valuations for paying the King's Aid.[24] The valuation for the Christ Church property in Canterbury had been made by Fyneux, but it was 'like to be countervayled' by some in the city. He also had influence at St. Augustine's Abbey: in 1506 a letter to the Prior of Christ Church asks that Fyneux should speak to the Treasurer at St. Augustine's on behalf of John Hales who desired to succeed John Nethersole as Steward there.[25] For many years Fyneux had been a trusted executor, from Prior Sellyng's kinsman Richard Tyll in 1485 and Sir John Fogge in 1490 to Cardinal Morton in 1500 and Henry VII himself in 1509. The shields on the Christ Church Gate facing the Buttermarket in Canterbury are a permanent reminder of Fyneux's relations with Henry VII and with the great men of the county: the shields of Henry VII, Prince Arthur and Katherine of Aragon occupy the centre of the frieze, but at the left are Sir William Scott and Sir John Fyneux and others, and Sir Edward Poynings is among those on the right.[26]

As well as his industry and success in pleading cases, and his skill as a judge, Fyneux was remembered for his devotion to religion. Two of his children (including his eldest son) had chosen the religious life. He was a generous donor: the memory of one of his gifts, a grant to the Austin Friars in Canterbury, was preserved by publication in the Appendix to Somner's *Antiquities*.[27] He had spent £40 on repairs to the Refectory, Dormitory and walls of the White or Austin Friars' house, whose site is now occupied by the Whitefriars Shopping Precinct. In return the Friars promised to pray for Fyneux and his wife Elizabeth, and the souls of Henry VII, Cardinal Morton, William and Mildred Apulderfield, and they drew up an agreement for that in 1522. He was a devout churchman of the old fashioned school who was fortunate to die in 1525 before the ordered world into which he fitted was overturned.

Fyneux made a will on 7 August, 1525, and died on 17 November.[28] He had arranged for burial near the altar in the Martyrdom in the cathedral, in the entry of the passage to the crypt. His friends Prior Sellyng and Prior Goldstone were buried in front of the altar, and at the altar his name was to be remembered daily. He left money to the Friars, the Hospitals, the parish churches and St. Gregory's and St. Sepulchre's Priories in Canterbury, and of course to Christ Church Priory. Beyond Canterbury there were legacies for 'the most poor parish churches next where I was born', and to Herne and Lynsted

ELIZABETH FYNEUX NEE PASTON 1539, HERNE

churches. Money was left to be administered by the Prior of Christ Church for charitable causes, and it so happens that an account for this has been preserved.[29] The Prior, with the agreement of Lady Fyneux, expended the money on mending the highway from Canterbury to Sturry; mending St. Peter's Street near the Blackfriars' Gate; scholarships at Oxford and Cambridge for young Blackfriars; and doles given to poor men seeking help at the Christ Church Almonry. Fyneux left money specifically for mending the highway between Ospringe and Boughton: in the days before official road mending, legacies of this kind were greatly to the public good.

The many servants at Herne were remembered. All were to remain for a year after his death so that they 'may provide in that mean time for their further living as they shall think best', and each could take a cow or 10 shillings. Fyneux's collar of gold (worn across the shoulders, as seen in Holbein's portraits of the period) was to be kept for his son William when he reached the age of 24; but all his 'other apparall' was to be sold and the money shared among the servants 'by the discretion of my wife'. Part of the Fyneux family assets was in plate, such as salts, standing cups, basins and ewers and so on of silver and silver gilt. These were shared out among members of the family. Money was specifically left for young Joan's marriage.

The land was divided into two parts, that which Fyneux had inherited from his father and purchased over the years, and that which he had inherited from the Apulderfields. The Lynsted land 'all such store and other stuff' as Fyneux had from Mildred Apulderfield was to go to Jane Roper, recently widowed, and to one of her sons. Out of it she should give an allowance to her sister Mildred Digges, her sister Anne in religion at Dartford, and her brother John in religion at Leeds Priory, and also pay for a chantry mass in Lynsted church for her parents and grandparents. The remaining land at Herne, Reculver, Hoath, Chislet, Seasalter, Hackington, Harbledown, Swingfield and other places was left to Fyneux's son William, though his mother was to have the profits of it until he came of age. She had been left all the household stuff except the plate, and was given a choice of 'my manor place at Hawe' or one of his other houses to live in. Money was provided for a chaplain to attend her. As might be expected the will is a clear and business-like document. It was proved on January 19, 1525/6.

Elizabeth Fyneux stayed at Herne. She died 22 August, 1539 and was buried in Herne church where her brass remains.[30] Her will is very different and more personal, suggesting a clear-minded but bustling person, at the centre of a large family and household, concerned with the division of goods such as feather beds and pillows, gowns and kerchiefs, spoons and standing cups. From the will it is clear that there was a chapel at Hawe, to which Elizabeth left a chalice, a mass book, a vestment of crimson damask, and a crimson and green altar cloth and altar linen. In the chambers at Hawe there were large beds with featherbeds, bolsters, counterpanes and curtains, and sheets of various widths. Amongst the silver were thirteen precious spoons, 'whereof one beareth the pretence of Christ and the others of the apostles'.

Elizabeth had several grandchildren and many godchildren, who are remembered by name: John Fyneux, William's son; Jane Roper's daughter Elizabeth and Joan Sondes' daughter, also Elizabeth, who was specially favoured, and Elizabeth and James Hubbert, probably the children of her 'daughter Clere'. Anthony Sondes and Henry Hubbert, two sons-in-law, were executors.

Gifts were made to Herne church, and the church at Ormsby where Elizabeth's first husband had been buried. Master Nicholas Ridley, then parson at Herne, was left four marks, and Richard Tyndall the chaplain and William Bowker the parson at Tunstall were given their bedding and small sums of money. A group of dispersed nuns from Dartford who were lodging at King's Langley had £10 as a group and 3s.4d. each, a generous donation towards their precarious existence.[31] John and Anne Fyneux are not mentioned. They do not occur in the pensions lists of Leeds Priory and the Dartford nuns, so probably they had gone abroad before the dispersal of their houses.[32] Servants at Herne were remembered, and the residue left to Elizabeth's son William who had inherited the Fyneux land, all except the goods in the house at Canterbury which were to be sold 'for the comfort and relief of poor persons and other charitable deeds'. Nicholas Ridley, looking back before his death by fire at Oxford wrote of his time at Herne 'I bless God in all that godly virtue and zeal of God's word, which the Lord by preaching of his word did kindle manifestly in the heart and in the life of that godly woman there my Lady Fiennes (Fyneux).'[33] He had only known her as a parishioner for a year, but the imprint of her strong personality remained.

The story of John Fyneux moves across Kent from the bare windy uplands of Swingfield where the snow lies long in the spring to the law courts of London and to the noisy small world of the City of Canterbury. Throughout his life he travelled a great deal, up and down from London, and through the Kentish lanes to the houses of his friends, Fogge at Ashford, Haute at Bishopsbourne, the archbishop on his manors. But towards the end of his life the family seems settled at Hawe in the handsome moated brick house where they might long have remained had there been sons to continue the line. By the time that Thomas Fuller wrote of his Worthies, the house was part of the possessions of the Lords Strangford; but he records that Fyneux's motto still remained in the windows at Hawe: *Misericordias Domini cantabo in aeternum* – I will sing of the mercy of God for ever.[34]

FOOTNOTES

1. Thomas Fuller, *The Worthies of England*, new edition ed. J. Nichols (1811), I, p.500.

2. List of Knight's Fees in *Archaeologia Cantiana*, X, (1876), p.129.

3. E. Hasted, *Kent*, III, (1790), p.350.

4. C. R. Councer 'Heraldic Notices of the Church of St. Martin, Herne', *Arch. Cant.*, LIII, (1940), p.88.

5. A. W. B. Messenger, *The Heraldry of Canterbury Cathedral*, (1947), p.90.

6. For the organisation of legal studies, cf. Sir John Fortescue, *De Laudibus Legum Anglie*, ed. S. B. Chrimes, Cambridge, (1949), pp.117-121.

7. W. R. Douthwaite, *Gray's Inn, Its History and Associations*, (1886), p.46.

8. C.A.L.C. Prior's Roll 12, Prior's Roll 14.

9. *Calendar of Patent Rolls*, 1467-1477, pp.428, 463, 571.

10 C.A.L.C. Register S. fol. 275; *H.M.C.* Appendix to IX Report, (1883), pp.118, 120.

11. Ed. J. B. Sheppard, *Christ Church Letters* (Camden Society 1877), XXII and XXVIII; and C.A.L.C. Christ Church Letters, III, 198. These letters are variously dated by Sheppard but seem to belong to 1478/79.

12. W. E. Flaherty, 'A Help toward a Kentish Monasticon', *Arch. Cant.*, II, (1859), p.64.

13. The will of John Roper, Esq., *Arch. Cant.*, II, (1859), pp.153-174; Anne Fyneux p.169; the Lodge granted to Ropers by Fyneux p.157.
14. *H.M.C.* Appendix to IX Report (1883), City Chamberlains' Accounts, 1480-1520.
15. *Calendar of Patent Rolls,* 1476/1485, p.513.
16. A. E. Conway, 'The Maidstone Sector of Buckingham's Rebellion', *Arch. Cant.* XXXVII (1925), pp.97-120.
17. Edward Foss, 'Legal Celebrities in Kent', *Arch. Cant.,* V, (1863), p.21.
18. David Lloyd, *State Worthies* (1766 edition), I, p.91.
19. *H.M.C.,* Appendix to IX Report (1883), p.170, Cant. City Records, Register A.2. 1494.
20. Leland's passage (*Itin.* vi. p.6) is quoted at length in E. Hasted, *Kent,* III, (1790), p.617.
21. C. R. Councer, 'Heraldic Notices of the Church of St. Martin, Herne', *Arch. Cant.* LIII (1940), pp.88-90.
22. Sir John Fortescue, *op. cit.* p.129.
23. David Lloyd, *op. cit.* p.96.
24. C.A.L.C. Christ Church Letters, III, 129.
25. Ed. J. B. Sheppard, *Christ Church Letters* (Camden Society 1877), p.70, dated by the resignation of Sir Richard Guldeford as Controller of the Household (1506).
26. Philip Blake, *Christ Church Gate, Canterbury Cathedral* (1965), pp.17-27.
27. W. Somner, *The Antiquities of Canterbury,* ed. N. Battely (1703), Appendix p.18.
28. Fyneux's will is at the P.R.O. PROB 11/22, p.6; his death is recorded in C.A.L.C. MS C11 (Dom William Ingram's Account Book) fol. 63 b; his funeral expenses in 'The Sacrist's Rolls of Christ Church Canterbury' ed. C. E. Woodruff, *Arch. Cant.* XLVIII, (1936), p.71.
29. C.A.L.C. Christ Church Letters II, 130, 141.
30. Elizabeth Fyneux's will is at the K.A.O., PRC 32/18/26.
31. M. D. Knowles, *Religious Orders,* III, (1961), p.440.
32. Pensions list for Leeds, *L. & P. Henry VIII,* XV, 359 p.551; Dartford, *L. & P. Henry VIII,* XIV (1), item 650.
33. G. Ridley, *Life of Dr. N. Ridley* (1763), p.638.
34. T. Fuller, *The Worthies of England,* new edition ed. J. Nichols (1811), I, p.500.

NORTH STREAM BY RECULVER

Reproduced with kind permission from, A DETECTIVE IN KENT by Donald Maxwell, published by John Lane, The Bodley Head (1929).

CHISLET MARSHES IN THE 15th, 16th AND 17th CENTURIES, THE EVIDENCE FROM EARLY MAPS

by

Tim Tatton-Brown, B.A.

In the Marquess of Salisbury's Library at Hatfield House there is a remarkable vellum map that was probably made in 1548[1]. This shows the whole of the Isle of Thanet and its surrounding areas including Sandwich Bay, Pegwell Bay 'Sandewiche' (as it is called), Richborough, and the Chislet Marshes as far as Reculvers (sic), and the North Mouth. The map, which is endorsed 'The plat of Sandwiche', and was drawn at a scale of 3 inches to 1 mile, was clearly made to show the works already carried out (largely apparently by Cardinal Morton, Archbishop of Canterbury, 1486-1500) and the works projected to improve the tidal flow in the river Stour and channels to the North Mouth. The map is a very valuable and uniquely early record of the Chislet Marshes and proves once and for all that all the drains (or sewers, as they were called), sea walls, droves, salt mounds, etc., date from before *c.* 1486 as the new channel cuts across them.

State Papers and Sandwich Borough records[2] tell us that in 1548 the mayor and jurats of Sandwich were trying to obtain government support for a project to improve Sandwich Haven. They petitioned the Lord Protector (Edward VI was still a boy) complaining that 'by the ... covetousness of one cardynall Moreton... who... stopped up, muryd and insetted in such sorte the same haven at a place called Sarre, as by a platt thereof made... more at large may appere,... the same haven at this present is utterly destroyed and loste'. They

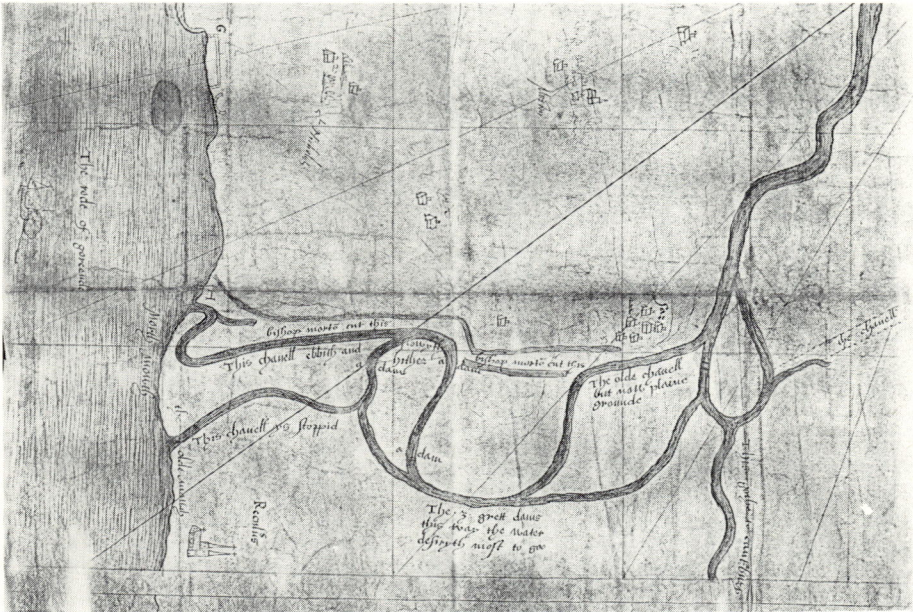

Reproduced by courtesy of the Marquis of Salisbury

CHISLET MARSHES

then went on to request authority to make a 'newe cutt' east of Sandwich. The new channels cut by Cardinal Morton are shown clearly on the map and marked 'bishop mortō cut this'. These channels can still be located on the ground, and are marked as 'Old Channel' on pre-war Ordnance Survey 6 inch maps, though unfortunately the central section of the channel has now been filled in and virtually ploughed out. It is also clear from the modern maps that Morton was making short cuts to iron out bends in the river Wantsum and thus to allow a greater tidal flow to Sarre. This was partly achieved (the 1548 map says of the northern part of Morton's channel from North Mouth, 'this channel ebbith and flowyth hither') though almost certainly at the expense of the flow in the Stour to Sandwich, hence the citizens' complaints. The harbour in Sandwich was by this time silted up, and a large flow of water was needed to flush out the silt. A little bit earlier than this, in Henry VIII's time, Leland says in his *Itinerary* that 'at Northmuth, where the estery of the se was, the salt water swellith yet up at a creeke a myle and more toward a place cawled Sarre'. This creek was Morton's channel, and we know also that the first bridge (replacing earlier ferries) across the Wantsum to Sarre was built at the same time (An Act of Parliament was passed in 1 HENRY VII i.e. *c.* 1486 to allow a bridge to be made at Sarre ferry).

One may well ask how the great Archbishop, Lord Chancellor, and Cardinal, John Morton, came to be involved in so mundane a scheme. The short answer is that we do not really know, but it is known that as Bishop of Ely, Morton was involved in Fenland drainage (there is still Morton's Leam between Peterborough and Wisbech), and he may well have studied 'drainage and embanking' when he was in exile in Holland in 1483-5. Morton also owned the land through which the new channel passed (the manors of St. Nicholas at Wade and Down Barton, the latter perhaps having a small quay), and not far away to the west was his great Palace at Ford (see article by H. Gough p.36).

A second map at Hatfield entitled 'Ryver of Stoure betwixt sandwych and fordwych' which probably dates from 1562[3] shows a 'Newe hauen' at 'Normouth' and 'The Newe cutte' on the Stour between 'Groue ferry' and Sarre. It also shows the 'New Stowre' as the name of a new series of straight cuts (just called the Little Stour today) leading from the 'Ickhm valeye' to Plucks Gutter. All the writing on this map is in Sir William Cecil's hand and State Papers of 1562[4] tell how Cecil and the Commissioners of Sewers were involved at this time in another abortive attempt at scouring Sandwich Haven by an increase or inflow from side valleys on the west, especially 'Chislet water', and for widening and deepening the Stour. Originally the Little Stour ran into the Great Stour just below Grove Ferry where there was a mass of meanders still marked today by parish boundaries, and the New Cut (now the Mile Cut beside the Railway line) and New Stour were certainly major engineering works for the time. They too were clearly cut to increase the flow of water through Sandwich and were the last successful cuts to be made. Work east of Sandwich was never completed.

One other early map of Chislet Marshes also exists[5], this time in the Kent Archives Office. The map, *c.* 1675 and endorsed 'Plan of the sewers between the River Stour and Reculver sluice', is no more than a sketch plan but virtually all the features on it are clearly marked and annotated, and it is therefore easy to fit it to the modern Ordnance Survey maps. The map is also very useful in showing all the channels and sluices, and the supply of fresh water to the Chislet area (and the 'scotts' or taxes payable) before the great Northern sea wall was built in 1808, effectively sealing the area from the sea on the north. The map also shows diagramatically areas of streams that were then partially blocked. For example, at the point where the modern Thanet Way crosses the Wantsum, the map says 'At this place last winter flood was the Weeds lodg'd by reason of bushes growing 'cross the Channel that there was almost a Stoppage, the expenditor[6] was sent to three times before any notice taken of itt...'

With all this material it is possible to show in great detail how the area between the Isle of Thanet and the mainland to the west evolved between *c.* 1450 and the present day. Detailed documentary evidence in the 'Black Book of St. Augustine's Abbey' allows us to go back another stage to the 13th century and it is hoped that the present writer may be able to complete a full study of these changes in due course.

References

1. CPM I.61 and No. 40 in R. A. Skelton *'Catalogue of Manuscript Maps in Hatfield House'* (1948-9).
2. Boys, *'Collections for a History of Sandwich'* (1792) appendix F, 732-40.
3. B/Saxton, f.22 and No. 41 in *op. cit.* above (note 1).
4. S.P. 12/23/35, Thomas Wotton to Cecil 3 June 1562.
5. K.A.O. S/EK P32, F. Hull (ed.) *'Catalogue of Estate Maps 1590-1840 in the Kent County Archives Office.'* (1973), 24.
6. A charge per acre was made to the 'General expenditor' to pay for keeping the drains in good order, e.g. the map records that for the area south of the Sarre Wall, 'The Marsh from Cutend to Grove Ferry which formerly paid 4 pence per acre to the Stour but now are in South Chislet Scott' – Stour and South Chislet are here administrative areas.

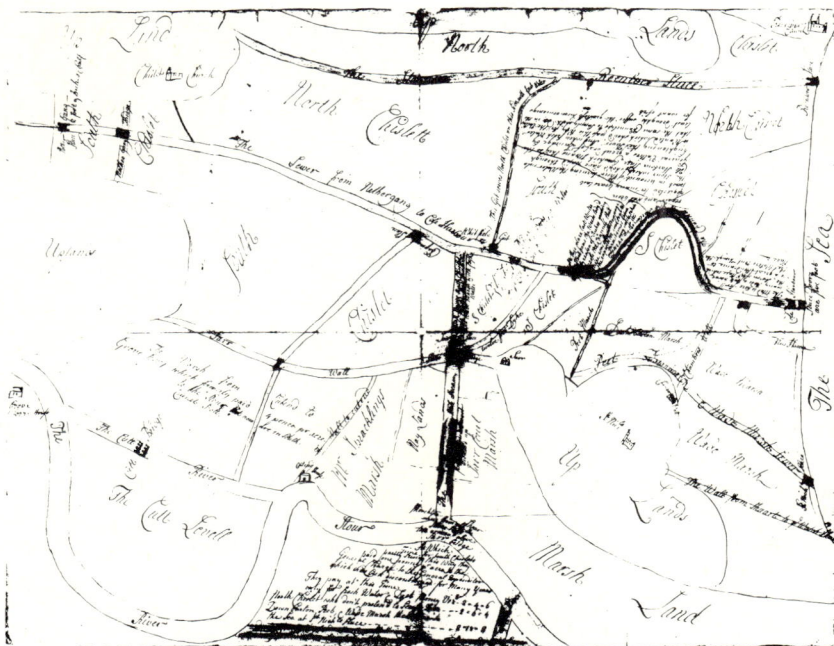

Plan of Sewers between the River Stour and Reculver Sluice, c.1675

THE MONUMENTAL BRASSES OF HERNE AND HOATH

by

Leslie A. Smith

The brasses in Herne Church have long excited the interest of the antiquarian; other Kent churches can claim superiority of numbers but Herne may boast a selection of such diversity as to merit special attention. All current catalogues show a series of nine brasses dating from c.1430 to 1605 but recent finds have extended that to physical evidence of eleven and revealed a tradition of monumental brass memorials lasting some 300 years. Even this does not constitute the total picture since antiquarian and testamentary sources point to the likelihood of further memorials of which all trace has long since disappeared. One must treat such sources with some caution because of possible errors, and executors did not necessarily precisely comply with instructions.[1] These provisos notwithstanding, there is fairly strong evidence of Herne brasses which have disappeared over the centuries.

Thomas Philipott in the seventeenth century notes a gravestone, possibly of Sir Matthew Phelip who died in 1475, from which the brass had been torn off.[2] Duncombe in his *History and Antiquities of the Two Parishes of Reculver and Herne* in *Bibliotheca Topographica Britannica* (1784) quotes an inscription – Hic iacet Wilhelmus Fineux fil & heres Johannis Fineux militis qui obiit . . . regis Henrici VII – which Cozens[3] confirms as a brass plate in a slab in the chancel 'but now gone' so it must have been lost in the intervening nine years. Cozens describes an associated brass shield which then remained with the arms (vert) a chevron between three eagles displayed (or) for FYNEUX impaling (sable) a cross (or) voided for APULDERFIELD.[4] Cozens also notes three brass plates under the gallery at the west end of the nave:

Iohn Terry yeoman housholder was
buried ye 24 of September in ye year
of our Lord 1615.

Here lyeth buryed the body of Richard
Terry yeoman who deceased ye . . day
of . . . A° Dni . . .
(he died in 1615)

Here lyeth buried the body of Iohn Terry the
you'ger who deceased the 8th of August 1603
being of the age of twenty six yeres.

This evidence may be regarded as reasonably accurate so we have five lost brasses although Buchanan in his *Memorials of Herne* (1887) clouds the issue by saying that some of the brasses mentioned by Weever, Hasted and Greenwood[5] cannot now be found whereas they contain no references to other than extant brasses.

As for wills I know of none for Herne which specifically ask for a brass but *Testamenta Cantiana* (K.A.S. extra volume 1907) lists nine wills between 1401 and 1541 containing requests for burial within Herne church and it seems probable that brasses figure in that number.

Let us now survey what is left to us, beginning with the discovery that has pushed back the date of the earliest Herne brass by about 100 years.

In the south chancel is a very worn Bethersden marble slab of roughly coffin shape on which can just be discerned the indents of four separate inlay Lombardic letters and six round stops, pairs of which, in colon form, separate the words. On the sinister side of the slab the word 'DE' can be identified; this does not assist in ascertaining the language used as it is of course common to Latin and Norman French which are both found on slabs of this date, i.e. early 14th century. The 'DE' may form part of a name and a possible attribution is Hugh de Godynestre, first vicar of Herne from 1310 to 1321.[6] There are similar slabs to Kentish ecclesiastics at Adisham, Brasted, Cranbrook, Ickham, Sutton Valence and Wingham, all associated with crosses but the Herne slab is too decayed to be definite about the possible existence of a cross.

The Lombardic letters were not engraved but cast in moulds and inlaid in separate indents cut round the perimeter of the slab. Remaining letters and indents can therefore be classified and Blair (*Specimens of Lettering from English Monumental Brasses,* with Badham & Emmerson, 1976) has identified a main group of three sizes, Herne belonging to size III. The earliest examples are associated with the Cosmati mosaic pavement of 1268 in the presbytery of Westminster Abbey but the main group dates from about 1290 to 1350.[7] The use of Bethersden marble instead of the more usual Purbeck suggests that the letters were supplied, probably from a London lattoner, to a local marbler for placing in the slab; the letters were not fixed as such but merely laid in pitch, which accounts for their low survival rate.

A second find occurred during the 1976 excavations in the Lady Chapel[8] when a slab was uncovered a few inches below the Victorian tiled floor. About 10 cm thick and originally 88 x 140 cm the slab had been considerably damaged on the dexter side and showed signs of severe weathering. The surface had been eroded but eight rivets still within their lead plugs and a further four distinct rivet holes indicated a lost brass. The position of these rivets showed that there had been three figures, each approximately 52 cm in length and fixed by three equally spaced rivets, above a foot inscription which extended beyond the outer edges of the flanking figures. This bottom plate measured some 59 x 5 cm suggesting a two or at most three line inscription which would tend to indicate a 15th century date. The slab was reburied on consolidation of the present wood block floor.

PETER and ELIZABETH HALLE, engraved c.1430 (M.S.I.)[9]

The effects of the 1976 dig answered a question which had been awaiting resolution for many years. The bottom of the slab of the brass of Peter Halle and his wife Elizabeth, engraved c.1430, had been covered by a wooden platform under which was thought to be a shield of arms for HALLE – barry ermine and gules three escutcheons or. During the re-ordering of the Lady Chapel the slab was fully uncovered to reveal only a rivet which may have held the shield. Recent close examination of the slab has found a line of lead plugs without rivets about 6.5 cm apart stretching across the slab 20 cm below the bottom edge of the foot inscription. These plugs, fourteen in all, are very flush with the stone and it appears that the slab has been refaced at some time. Some 10 cm below the row of plugs is a faint trace of a short straight line cut in the stone and one may conclude that the slab was re-used for the Halle brass but its original use remains a puzzle.

The brass shows Peter Halle in full plate armour minus misericorde and gauntlets; the sword is missing from the hilt. He is holding Elizabeth's hand but it looks more like a formal handshake than a gesture of affection, and his free hand, as does his wife's, rests on the chest. There are a number of examples of this pose (a closely related design is that of Thomas, Baron Camoys, 1421, at Trotton, Sussex) and it does at least provide some animation in an otherwise very stiff composition. The dog on which Peter's feet rest is portrayed gazing up at his mistress but again the attempted expression of sentiment is singularly unsuccessful. Rowel spurs are on the heels which Buchanan, inter alia, describes as 'guarded', ascribing them to a possible court appointment. This is one of those misconceptions to which Victorian antiquarians were prone; it is more likely that the circle of brass round the spur is no more than a particular workshop's attempt to strengthen an inevitably vulnerable part of the brass.

The figure of Elizabeth is a fine example of the dress of the period. She wears a tight fitting kirtle and a sideless surcoat, over which is a loose mantle fastened by a cord held by two clasps. An elaborate crespine head-dress adorns her head, its side cauls extending far beyond the side of the face, and a veil hangs in folds behind, which in life no doubt provided a background to set off her necklace. Both figures have prayer scrolls, for Elizabeth – Mater dei memento mei, and for Peter – Miserere mei deus. The figures stand above a two line Latin inscription:

Hic iacet Petrus Halle Armig' et Elyzabeth uxor eius filia dñi Willi Waleys Militis et dñe Margarete / uxis ei' filie dñi Johîs Seynclere Militis quor aîabs filior et filiar pdcōr petri et Elyzabeth ppiciet de' amē //.

(Here lies Peter Halle, Esquire, and Elizabeth his wife, daughter of Sir William Waleys, Knight, and Dame Margaret his wife, daughter of Sir John Seynclere, Knight, on whose souls and those of the sons and daughters of the aforesaid Peter and Elizabeth, God have mercy, Amen).

The remaining shield bears the arms of HALLE impaling 1 and 4 gules a fess ermine for WALEYS and 2 and 3 azure a sun resplendent or for SEYNCLERE. The brass is set in a slab of Bethersden marble.

JOHN DARLEY, engraved c.1450 (M.S.II.)

The brass of John Darley, vicar of Herne from 1432 until he resigned in 1446, is partly covered by the choir stalls in the chancel. It now bears no date but may be assumed to date from c.1450. The figure is complete but the marginal inscription is much mutilated; only one of the original four roundels containing an evangelical symbol (St. John) now remaining; the foot inscription is intact although its original form was that of an unrolled scroll. John is attired in academic rather than ecclesiastic robes with the cappa clausa, which has two slits for the arms, worn over his subtunica (cassock). The cappa was a gown and hood combined but in this instance the hood (caputium) is shown separate. On the head is a round skull cap, mistaken for a tonsure by Buchanan and which Belcher,[10] in his often misleading fashion, illustrates rising to a slight apex like a pileus, a case it seems of the mind deceiving the eye. The absence of colour and a frontal only view makes difficult any positive identification of a particular academic Faculty but we can be reasonably certain that this is the dress of a Bachelor of Sacred Theology.

The figure stands on a ground of grass with three leaf clovers and other trefoiled plants. The animal at his feet has for long been described as a lion and as such is unique on a brass to an academic though featured on some ecclesiastic

PETER and ELIZABETH HALLE, HERNE

brasses. However Norris[11] suggests that it is some type of medieval poodle and certainly the upturned smiling face and almost playful attitude could admit such an interpretation but I still favour the established opinion that it is a lion.

Only three pieces of the marginal fillet have survived with an inscription, interspersed with trefoils, quatrefoils, roses and other motifs, to which may be added, in brackets, parts now lost but recorded by Cozens:

Hic iacet Magister Johēs (Bacalarius in Sacra) Theologia quondam Vicarius . . . . . Secundo Idus . . . (aetat 31°).

Cozens must have misread lxxxi as xxxi for the age since Darley was granted a pension of £10 a year when he resigned in 1446 on grounds of age and infirmity (Buchanan, p.46).

The foot inscription has some intricate line end decoration and is in very obscure Latin verse for the translation of which I am greatly indebted to Mrs. Margaret Sparks. In the original it reads:

Siste gradum videas corpus iacet ecce Iohannis
Darley qui multis fuit hic curatus in annis
Iste pater morū fuit Et flos philosophorum
Dux via norma gregis patrie lux anchora legis
Pagina sacra cui dedit inceptoris honorem
Hinc memor esto tui precibs sibi dando favorem.

And in translation, somewhat free to give the sense:

Stop and look: here lies the body of John Darley, who for many years was vicar here. He was guide to conduct, flower of philosophers, leader, path and pattern for the flock, light of his country, support of the law, who was granted the honour of being a teacher of Holy Writ. And so remember him by granting him the favour of your prayers.

WILLIAM BYSMARE 1456 (M.S.III.)

This inscription brass is not recorded by Duncombe or Cozens but is by Buchanan as 'lately recovered'. It has lost its right hand edge and reads:

Hic iacet Willm̄s Bysmare quondm̄ civis et Aurifaber Londîn . .
Anno dn̄i Millm̄o cccc° lvi et Elizabeth Agnes ac Margareta uxo . .

(Here lies William Bysmare citizen and goldsmith of London (who died . . .) 1456 and Elizabeth Agnes and Margaret (his wives)). A prayer for the soul would have ended the text. It is likely that the brass was laid down before Bysmare's death as the 'lvi' of the year was added after the initial engraving. This was not unusual, some wills specifically mentioning burial under a pre-prepared stone,[12] and was designed to remind the eventual occupant of the transitory nature of life on earth.

The brass is now mounted on a board in the Lady Chapel.

DAME CHRISTINE PHELIP, 1470, (M.S.IV.)

This unique figure lies on the floor of the Lady chapel. As she was the wife of Sir Matthew Phelip, mayor of London in 1464, and, like William Bysmare, a goldsmith,[13] its singular features have traditionally been explained by ascribing it to her husband's workshop. Emmerson[14] challenges this by attributing it to a London workshop and stylistically there are elements, particularly in the shape of the face, which support this view. However, the sumptuous treatment of the dress and accessories, plus the excellence of the engraving, does not lie easily alongside contemporary London products and other influences seem to have come into play. There are similarities to East Anglian design, as in the treatment of the hands[15] but it cannot be said that Dame Christine is recognisable as a product of any known workshop. It may be that the brass was a special commission executed by London craftsmen to a goldsmith's design.

Dame Christine wears a horned head-dress, a later derivation of the crespine in which the side cauls gradually curved upwards until, as here, they formed horns above the head. The cauls are richly worked with suns and roses and two layers of veil hang down the back of the head. Her full length low cut gown has a high waistband from which hangs a rosary of six decades and six pater nosters. Buchanan notes the absence of a cross but I know of no rosary on a brass during the brief period when they were incorporated in the design, i.e. late 15th and early 16th centuries, to feature one. Slightly below the waist emerge the somewhat disembodied fur trimmed cuffs of the gown with the hands spread palm outwards, the fingers together and thumbs bent back, as though depicting the wings of a bird (?or angel). Over the gown is a heavy furred mantle the bottom of which lies in folds completely obscuring the feet. It is secured by two long tasselled cords held by a large decorated round slide and fixed to the mantle at four petalled flowers. This remarkable figure stands on a ground of grass with spiky leaved plants at the corners and below is a very well engraved raised letter inscription which reads:

Orate specialit p Aîa Dñe x̄pine dudū uxoris Mathei Phelip civis
& aurifabri ac quondā Maioris Civitatis Londîn que migravit ab hac valle miserie xxv° die maii A° dnî Millm̄o CCCC° LXX° cuius Aîe ppiciet de' Amē.

(Pray specially for the soul of Christine Phelip late the wife of Matthew Phelip citizen and goldsmith and one time Mayor of the City of London who departed from this vale of misery the 25th day of May 1470, on whose soul may God have mercy, Amen).

Above the figure is a scroll of a most pleasing form, but unfortunately incomplete, again in raised letter and decorated with an oak leaf motif. Complete it would have read, with missing letters in parenthesis,

Miserere mei deus secundum mangnam misericordia(m tuam).

(Have mercy on me, O Lord, according to Thy great mercy).

The engraver has misspelt magnam.

The composition is completed by four shields of which only two now remain bearing the arms, at top dexter – Sable a lion rampant crowned or between eight fleurs-de-lis argent for PHELIP impaling a bend indented; at lower sinister – as the impalement.

Fragments of Inscription from Brass to John Darley, c.1450, Herne

Cozens notes one shield lost and gives a third bearing the same arms as at top dexter. Councer tentatively attributes the bend indented to LENTHAL which family bore arms, sable a bend lozengy argent, in which form they appear on the roof of the Great Cloister Vault of Canterbury Cathedral.

ANTHONY LOVERICK, 1511 (M.S.V.)

We find this brass on the floor of the Lady Chapel, the shield lost but with an inscription as follows:

Hic iacet antonius Loveryk armiger & constancia uxor eiu' qui qdē atoniu' obiit sextodecimo die oc
tobr āno dñi M°V°XI quorum aiabus propicietur de' amen.

(Here lies Anthony Loverick, Esquire, and Constancia his wife the which Anthony died the 16th day of October 1511, on whose soul may God have mercy, Amen).

The crude style of lettering, the odd splitting of words between lines and the confusion over contractions are all indicative of a brass of local manufacture and it is likely to have been made in a workshop in or around Canterbury which produced some very inferior work in the early part of the 16th century. The missing shield no doubt bore the arms of LOVERICK, argent a chevron sable, three leopards heads or, which appear on the early 14th century font in the church and on the brass of Anthony's grand-daughter Elizabeth Engham, engraved c.1573, at Goodnestone-next-Wingham.

ANDREW BENSTEDE, 1531 (M.S.VI.)

Mounted on the board in the Lady Chapel is a further inscription which was in a slab in the south chancel but in view of its text, supported by evidence from Cozens, was removed thence from the choir. Unnecessary confusion over its interpretation was caused by Buchanan being led astray by his versifying churchwarden Henry Gray who misread it and compounded his error by rendering it in free translation which is a complete nonsense.[16] Following publication a correspondence (preserved in Herne vicarage) ensued between Buchanan and Mill Stephenson who, in consultation with St. John Hope, assistant secretary of the Society of Antiquaries, supported the reading which Haines had published in 1848.[17] This gave the inscription as:

Hic chorus indecorus fuerat nu(n)c valde decorus
Andreas is sum qui decoravit eum.

Which may be translated thus:

This choir was unsightly, now it is very seemly,
I am that Andrew who adorned it.

The exchange of letters was passed to Mr. Gray for comment and he was clearly piqued, making pointed references to dog and doctors' Latin. Initially he sticks to his guns with 'I am not *yet* sure that with all due deference to so high an authority as St. John Hope his reading is correct' but follows with a partial concession of 'possibly we are all wrong' and then a grudging acceptance; 'If "Andreas is sum" is correct I should feel inclined to render it as follows, roughly of course:-

The quire required restoring. Now d'ye laud it?
I Andrew am the man who has restored it'.

Which only proves that Mr. Gray's ability to mislead was totally unimpaired by his skirmish with 'authorities'. Haines not only correctly deciphered the inscription but also found a likely candidate for the Andrew in Andrew Benstede, vicar of Herne from 1511 to 1531. Stephenson therefore dates the brass as 1531 but this need not necessarily be the case as it may be that it was laid down on completion of the work, perhaps prior to Benstede's death and we do not know that this was 1531 for that was the year of his resignation. However, since the brass was set in a grave slab the two events may have been nearly contemporaneous or the restoration may have been as a result of a bequest in Benstede's will (I am mindful of the brass in St. Alphege, Canterbury, for Thomas Prude, 1468, which commemorates the building of a column under the terms of his will).

Looking again at the inscription, at the end of the second line is a skull and cross bones which Harold Gough, in his guide to the church, reasonably hypothesises is a rebus on the name Andrew, alluding to the cross of St. Andrew.

In 1970 the brass became dislodged from its slab and broke where two pieces of metal had been joined by a lead solder wipe. One piece was blank on the reverse but the larger part was found to be palimpsest bearing a portion of a slightly different version of the obverse inscription and reads:

. . . e decorus nu(n)c e(st) valde decorus
. . . sum qui decoravit eum.

The skull and cross bones are replaced by a fairly standard space filler in the form of a decorated reversed letter S. Precisely why or by whom this was rejected is not clear but it was never laid in a stone and thus falls into the category of a workshop waster. In re-using the metal certain of the engraved lines coincide which has now caused holes to appear. A facsimile of the reverse is also mounted on the board.[18]

ELIZABETH FYNEUX, 1539 (M.S.VII.)

Again on the floor of the Lady Chapel this is another locally manufactured brass of a higher standard of design than most Kentish 'locals' but still inferior to contemporary London work. Elizabeth is shown in a rounded head-dress with veil and falling lappets which may be a transitional style between the pedimental and the French hood. The head is too large for the body as is the neck at which is seen a gathered and embroidered partlet with on top, an undergown with slashed sleeves and frills at the wrists. Over all is a short sleeved, fur trimmed gown with an ornamented belt round the waist from which hangs a pomander on a braided cord. The oddly worded foot inscription, engraved in a peculiarly spiky script reads:

The xxv daye of the moneth auguste the yere after the Incarnacyon / of owr lord god to reken Juste A thowsand fyve hundreth forty save one / Dyed thys lady whych under thys stone lyeth here buryed Elysabeth by name / The wyfe of S(ir) John Fyneux late gone The whych in thys world had ev(er) good / fam(e) Whose soll I p(r)ye Ihū throwgh hys grace In heven maye have a restyng place //.

There is in this a rather fractured attempt at verse which is not immediately apparent.

There are four corner shields; one for PASTON – or a chief indented and six fleurs-de-lis azure; two for FYNEUX – vert a chevron between three eagles displayed or, and one with the two coats impaled.

Haines, in his *Manual of Monumental Brasses* of 1861 compares the figure with one, now lost, at Hockwold, Norfolk, 1532 whereas Norris[19] regards it as being wrongly associated with the Norfolk series and rather as imitating London work 'with little success'. Elizabeth does have Norfolk connections, being the daughter of Sir John Paston, and another 'local' at Upper Hardres to Dorothy Hardres, 1533, another daughter of Sir John, could point to a link between the Norfolk and Kent groups but neither brass corresponds with the styles of Norfolk engraving identified in recent research, principally by Greenwood.[20]

The 'Kentish School', if it can be so called, produced brasses from c.1510 to c.1540 and sixteen surviving examples have been identified. Fourteen fall between 1520 and 1535, the two Herne examples being those outside that period and their inscriptions bear no stylistic resemblance. It must be conceded that some of the 'locals' have been so classified by default because their style does not match other contemporary work.[21]

JOHN and MARGARET FYNEUX, 1592 (M.S.VIII.)

This inscription plate, to Elizabeth Fyneux's grandson, was found by Buchanan in about 1884 on a window ledge with on the back the chalk written message 'Key to sandpit at Mr. Roote's'. Now fixed to the board in the Lady Chapel it has suffered some damage to the right hand edge and a few letters are missing but it read:

> Here lieth Iohn Fyneux late of this pish of Hearne
> Esquier and Margaret his wife, daughter of Thomas Morley
> sometyme of Glyne in the countie of Sussex Esquier
> wch Margaret deceassed the nynth day of December
> 1591 and in the fower & thirtith yere of the reigne
> of our sovaigne ladie Queene Eliz. and the said Iohn
> Fyneux departed this life ye last day of Iuly following
> 1592 in the said XXXIIIIth yere of the queenes matie leving
> behind them one only daughter and heir named Elizabeth
> who maried Iohn Smith Esquier soñe and heir of Thomas
> Smith late of Osnighanger in this countie of Kent Esquier.

The place name in the last line seems to have confused the engraver, the first letter n being engraved over a letter t. The correct name is Ostringhanger as it appears in Thomas Smith's will of 1542 and is the present day Westenhanger.

The brass is a typical plate of the period, rather thin and flexible and the engraving is stereotype Roman capitals.

JOHN, MARTHA and SARA SEA, 1604 (M.S.IX.)

The last in this fine series, also in the Lady Chapel, is for John Sea and his two wives. Each figure stands on a round dais, John placed centrally full face flanked by his wives in semi-profile. He is in civil dress, a buttoned doublet with a neck ruff over which is a long plain cloak with false sleeves, in this case mere strips of material hanging from the shoulders. As in most civilian and military brasses of the time the hair is worn short and he sports a beard and moustache. His wives are identically attired but Capes[22] surely goes too far in suggesting that the second wife 'not only stepped into the first wife's shoes but . . might have appropriated to her own use the entire wardrobe'. It can be said that a London workshop pattern has been used as the same arabesque design appears on the petticoat of Mary Rust, 1596, at Necton, Norfolk. The ladies wear the Paris hood, sometimes referred to as the Mary Queen of Scots bonnet, and a stiff circular neck ruff; the sleeves are quilted and the bodice has a peaked stomacher. The skirt is a farthingale, precursor of the hoop petticoat and the crinoline, with the front open to display the finely embroidered petticoat. The shoes are round toed and have a low heel.

The three effigies stand over an inscription (it is most surprising to see that the Victoria and Albert Museum catalogue plate[23] has tidied up the composition so that the flanking figures do not overhang the edge of the inscription) which reads:-

Here lieth interred John Sea of Underdowne in the parishe
of Herne Esquire, who tooke to wife Martha Haṁond daugh:
ter of Tho Ham: of S. Albans in East Kent Esq: by whom he had
Issue vj.sonnes & iij.daughters, & after her decease maried
Sara Boys eldest daughter unto Thomas Boys of Barfreston
Gent: by whom he had one sonne & one daughter he lived and
died in peace. Obijt 23 Februarij.Anno Dñi 1604.

The eleven children mentioned were shown on two plates – nine on the left under Martha and two on the right under Sara – both of which were lost. The smaller plate was rediscovered when a row of cottages adjacent to Herne Vicarage was demolished in 1962. This plate, now in private possession, shows a boy and girl in semi-profile turned in the same direction as their mother and in similar, but plainer, costume to that of their parents.[24] The slab originally had four corner shields but one had gone by 1793 (Cozens). At some time around the end of the last century the lower shields had been wrongly positioned upside down where the children once were and this was corrected during the 1974 repairs. The three shields are: at top and bottom dexter – argent a fish hauriant azure between two flanches azure charged with bars nebuly argent for SEA impaling argent on a chevron sable between three ogresses each charged with a martlet of the field, as many escallops or, all within a bordure engrailed vert for HAMOND; and at bottom sinister SEA impaling or a griffin sergeant sable within a bordure gules for BOYS.

This description of the Herne brasses has of necessity been confined to the physical aspects of the memorials and lack of space precludes any attempt to place the commemorated in their social context but it will be observed that we have three brasses to ecclesiastics, a goldsmith, the wife of a goldsmith who was Lord Mayor of London and the others here recorded represent families of some substance and influence, e.g. Elizabeth Fyneux was the widow of a chief justice of the King's bench. From this it could be surmised that monumental brasses were the memorials of the privileged but this would be a false impression; one need only recall the brass, lost from St. Mary Magdalene, Burgate, Canterbury, of Christopher Elcok, 1492,[25] who was a draper to realise that they encompass a wide cross section of society. One must not, therefore read too much into the pattern displayed in one particular parish but it is still worth emphasising that even the upper strata did not necessarily buy from the large London 'store' but were prepared to patronise their neighbourhood 'shop' and we see this repeated at Hoath.

THE BRASSES OF HOATH

There are only two brasses in the small and much restored church of Holy Cross at Hoath, one from a London workshop and the other a local product.

ISABELLA CHAKBON c.1430 (M.S.I.)

This now headless figure stands above a short inscription in a slab in the chancel. Hasted[26] does not note the beheading but inexplicably says, 'the date obliterated' when no date ever existed as the complete inscription reads:-

Hic iacet Isabella chakbon cuius
Anime ppicietur deus Amen.

(Here lies Isabella Chakbon on whose soul may God have mercy, Amen).

She is dressed in a kirtle, the close fitting sleeves appearing at the wrist, and a high waisted gown with deep full sleeves known as devil's receptacles as they were capable of hiding a large amount of stolen goods. Needless to say such a connotation should not be applied to Isabella. The engraving is typical of London work of c.1430 with many similar examples as at Aylesford, Kent, 1426, Bookham, Surrey, 1433 and All Hallows, Barking, 1437. Many brasses of this style of dress have the horned head-dress and from the indent of the missing head it looks as though this was also worn by Isabella, with a veil over the horns. The brass has been relaid in its original slab most probably during Victorian restorations.

ANTONY and AGNES MAYCOT, 1532 (M.S.II.)

The slab lies where Antony requested to be buried in his will, 'in the middle path before the quire'. Newman, in *Pevsner's Buildings of England, North East and East Kent,* describes the brass as 'crude little figures' but they do have a certain appeal and it is in these small figure brasses that the work of the local engravers shows some consistency of style. Their main features are in the treatment of the hair and the fur linings of the gowns, the less than subtle shading and the badly proportioned figures. Comparable figures are at Mersham, c.1520; Canterbury, St. Gregory (formerly in St. Mary, Northgate), 1522; Goodnestone next Wingham, 1523; Selling, c.1525; Ash next Wingham, 1525; Capel-le-Ferne, 1526; Chartham, 1530; Ringwould, 1530; Canterbury, St. Paul, 1531 and West Malling, 1532. The Hoath brass is the most pleasing of the series.

Antony is in civil dress, a fur lined wide sleeved robe over a tunic, and broad toed shoes. His hair is shoulder length and the hands touch only lightly, and the mound of grass he stands on is but sketchily engraved. He stands in semi-profile, a convention dictated by his wife's head-dress which can be shown to best advantage at that angle. This is a transitional style with the veil of the butterfly and lappets, one lost, of the pedimental, or kennel head-dress; by contrast her daughters wear the pedimental which was introduced from about 1490 so Agnes is in a style which was some years behind the fashion. Her gown, with fur trimmed cuffs falls to folds at her feet and at the waist is a girdle whose pendant end almost reaches the ground. The two figures stand above an inscription:-

Prȳ for the soules of Antony Maycot & Agnes his wife the which
Antony decesyd the first day of February A°dni M°V^c xxxii
On whos soules & all xpēn Iħu have marcy AMEN.

ISABELLA CHAKBON, HOATH

Beneath Antony are two sons in square necked knee length gowns portrayed in a most odd bent kneed stance and under Agnes five daughters, now rather worn, with their hair falling down the back. They wear long gowns and the two outer figures have a distinct lean towards the rest of the group.

Justin Simpson in his *List of the Sepulchral brasses of England* (1857) states that the wife is palimpsest, which is repeated by Haines although he gives no details, and no illustration is known.

I gratefully acknowledge the assistance of Mr. Harold Gough on aspects of the Benstede and the lost Fyneux brass.

NOTES

1. R. H. D'Elboux, M.C., F.S.A., *Testamentary Brasses* in *Antiquaries Journal*, 29, (1949) pp.183-191, which quotes many Kent wills. Although there are no brasses or indents in Chislet church (see *Chislet and Westbere, Villages of the Stour Lathe*, 1979), the will of William Consant, 1527, requests burial 'in the chancel of our Lady and Joseph in the Church of Chistelett, from the pillar head unto the foot of the step where I used to sit commonly and a tomb to be made at my cost with a picture of my body upon it'.

2. C. R. Councer, *Heraldic Notices of the Church of St. Martin, Herne,* in *Archaeologia Cantiana, Vol. LIII.*

3. Z. Cozens, *A Tour Through the Island of Thanet and other parts of East Kent,* (1793).

4. Philipott also notes the inscription and arms but does not mention it as a brass. The photograph published by Councer (op. cit. note 2) of ff.34b – 35 of Harleian MS 3917 shows the regnal year as what looks like 27 but as there is no such year for Henry VII it is probably 21, giving a date of 1505/6 for the brass. Councer compiled a family tree of the Fyneux, based mainly on Hasted, stating that Sir John Fyneux had only one son, William, by his second wife Elizabeth Paston but the date and arms on the lost brass indicate that there was also a son by his first wife Elizabeth Apulderfield and that this William predeceased his father.

5. John Weever, *Ancient Funerall Monuments* (1631); Edward Hasted, *The History and Topographical Survey of the County of Kent,* 2nd Edn. Vol. IX, (1800), and C. Greenwood, *An Epitome of County History,* Vol. 1. Kent (1893).

6. Duncombe, p.159, citing Archiepiscopal Register, Winchelsea, f.30.

7. John Blair, English Brasses and Indents before the Black Death; a summary list, Part IV, Kent, in *Monumental Brass Society Bulletin* no.28 (1981).
See also *Collectanea Historica* (K.A.S. 1981).

8. *Kent Archaeological Review*, no.44, 1976.

9. The letters M.S. followed by Roman numerals indicate the Mill Stephenson reference in his magnum opus *A List of Monumental Brasses in the British Isles,* 1926 and *Appendix,* 1938.

10. W. D. Belcher, *Kentish Brasses,* Vol. 1, p.65, fig. 126, (1888). Mill Stephenson reviewed this volume in *Monumental Brass Society Transactions*, Vol. 2, p.137 in scathing terms, e.g. 'many of the illustrations are unreliable' and Vol. II, (1907) attracted similar critical comment.

11. Malcolm Norris, *Monumental Brasses – The Memorials,* (1977). Vol. 1, p.90.

12. e.g., Richard Galon, Ash next Wrotham, 1465, 'corpus meum in monumento preparando' and Thomas Propechaunt, Canterbury, St. Paul, 1493, 'buried in the church under the stone that lieth afore the door of the high chancel the which stone I have paid for'.

13. Councer, op.cit.note 2, states that 'the position at Herne is complicated by the fact that in the later Middle Ages, as now, numbers of Londoners seem to have settled in the parish on retirement from business or to have established country pieds à terre'. John Goddard, 1399, goldsmith of London desired his executors to pave the chancel of Herne church and it seems probable that once one goldsmith had set the fashion others in the Guild would follow.

ANTHONY and AGNES MAYCOT, 1532, HOATH

14. Robin Emmerson, Monumental Brasses – London Design, c.1420-1485 in *Journal of the British Archaeological Association,* Vol. CXXXI (1978).

15. See particularly Lucy, first wife of William, Fourth Baron Willoughby d'Eresby, c.1400 at Spilsby, Lincs., and Anne Herward, 1485 at Aldborough, Norfolk.

16. Buchanan, *Memorials of Herne,* p.44.

17. Herbert Haines, *A Manual for the Study of Monumental Brasses,* published for the Oxford Architectural Society, 1848.

18. The brass was repaired by Mr. Bryan Egan in 1974, together with parts of other brasses in the church. Details are in *The Repair of Monumental Brasses,* Egan and Stuchfield, 1981.

19. Norris, op.cit.note II, p.191.

20. Roger Greenwood and Malcolm Norris, *The Brasses of Norfolk Churches,* The Norfolk Churches Trust, 1976.

21. For discussion of the ?Canterbury workshop see Griffin and Stephenson, *A List of Monumental Brasses remaining in the County of Kent in 1922,* Ashford, 1923, pp.44-45.

22. George Capes in *J.B.A.A.,* Vol. XII, p.80. There are a number of instances of wives in identical dress, e.g. Richard Allarde, 1593, at Biddenden has three almost identical spouses and the petticoat design of Aphra Hawkins, 1605, at Fordwich is repeated in smaller scale but greater number on the dress of Florence Windham, 1596, at St. Decuman's, Somerset.

23. Victoria and Albert Museum, *Catalogue of Rubbings of Brasses and Incised Slabs,* 1929, pl.51(4).

24. Illustrated and described in Arch.Cant. Vol. LXXVII, (1962).

25. Illustrated in Belcher, Vol. II, p.24, no.65.

26. Hasted, Vol. IX, 1800, p.100.

The photographs of Dame Christine Phelip and Peter and Elizabeth Halle are reproduced by kind permission of Malcolm Norris from his book *Monumental Brasses, The Memorials,* Vol. 2, Phillips and Page (1977).

DEATH AT THE STILE

Anecdote relating to the death of Anne Weatherly, late of Whitstable, A.D. 1775

Anne Weatherly, a young married woman, about a month or six weeks ago, accompanied her father to Hearne, a village about five or six miles from Whitstable. On their return home, she asked her father twice if he did not see Death standing before them; once in the path-way in the field, another time at a style where they were to get over. He for some time endeavoured to laugh her out of it, as a mere whim. She continually asserted that she had actually seen Death: soon after which she became blind; the disorder then fell into her legs, so that it was with great difficulty she got home, was put to bed immediately, and died in a very few days.

This I had from her own brother.

from *The Olio* by Francis Grose, 1796

RUSHBOURNE MANOR

by

Tim Tatton-Brown, B.A.

South-west of Hoath village is a large block of land of about 250 acres which has been separate from the other surrounding manors (and parishes) since at least the Norman Conquest. This land is called Rushbourne Manor and was a detached part of the Archbishop of Canterbury's great Hundred and manor of Westgate. From *c.* 1087, the tithes were given by Lanfranc as one of the many endowments for his newly founded St. Gregory's Priory. The first charter in the Priory's *Cartulary*[1] says:

Ceterum in Risseburnia de ducentis acris a possessoribus earum totidem garbas.

Translated: 'From two hundred acres in Risseburn the owners shall pay the same number of sheaves (in tithes)'.

Later charters in the *Cartulary* confirm this, especially after a law suit in 1218; and tithes were still being paid by Rushbourne to the owner of St. Gregory's, G. Gipps, Esq., (M.P. for Canterbury) in 1800[2].

This remarkable little estate, probably of late Saxon creation, can still be traced on the ground, and it is clear that much of it was assarted from the Blean Forest. To the north of Rushbourne Manor is an area of the Blean Forest that originally belonged to Chislet manor while to the west and south-west are parts of Sturry manor (the borough of Buckwell) which were also cut out of the Blean. To the south-east was the Abbot of St. Augustine's Deer Park at Chislet

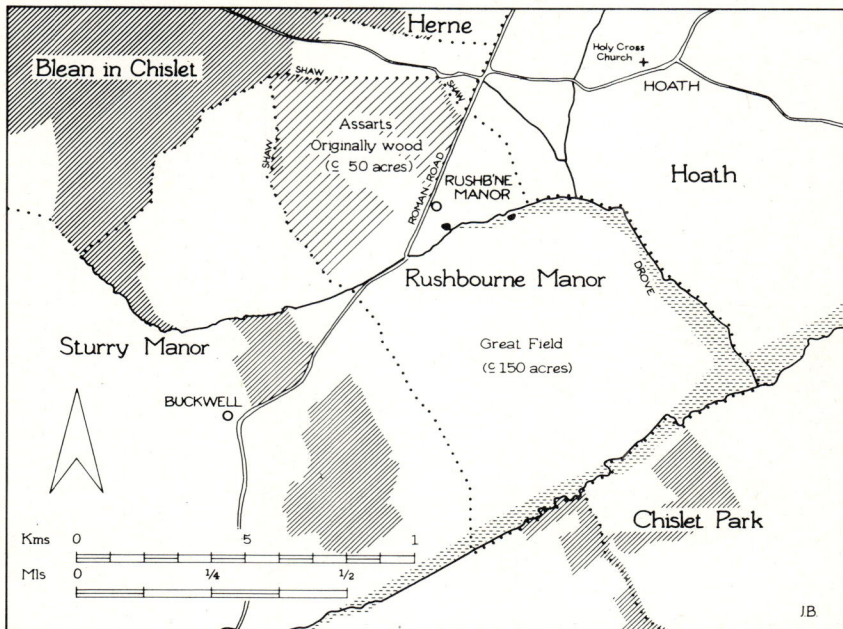

Drawn by John Bowen

(also cut out of the forest), and only to the north-east is there a more gravelly area of heathland (hence the name Hoath) which formed a large area of the arable land belonging to the Archbishop's manor of Reculver. The centre of Rushbourne Manor is still occupied by the Manor House (see below), which sits beside the Roman road at the head of Rushbourne Drove. Not far away the little stream which gives its name to the Manor (Old English *risc burna* – stream beside which rushes grow) comes out of the Blean, crosses the Roman Road and runs down beside the drove to join the Nethergong Penn. Rushbourne Drove must also be a very ancient feature of the Manor, and clearly was originally the route by which sheep were taken to graze on parts of what are now Chislet Marshes. West of the Drove is a large area of fields which rise up to just over 100 feet above sea level, which is called the 'Great Field' on the 1838 Tithe Map[3]. This was, until the late 18th century, one large field (as its name implies) of about 150 acres. Only with the late Georgian agricultural improvements was this field divided up and underdrained[4]. It is interesting that the Tithe Map still shows an area of one acre in the centre belonging to St. John's Hospital. This must be a last vestige of medieval strip cultivation and contrasts strongly with the 8 acres of Hops in the eastern part of the field which was relatively new then. The highest part of the field on the west was situated on the 100 foot gravel terrace and in 1976-7 this gravel was removed causing the top of the hill here to be sliced off. It is today arable once again.

Photographs by Melvin Pinnock

THE MONUMENT

THE CHIMNEY

70

To the north-west of the Roman road is another large area, also divided up into smaller fields. Several shaws (strips of ancient woodland) still survive here showing the origin of this part of the manor.

From at least 1218, Rushbourne Manor was part of Westbere Parish (it is still a detached portion of Westbere parish on the Tithe Map), and one can imagine some of the inhabitants objecting to having to travel about 3 miles there and back to church each Sunday instead of less than a mile to Hoath Church. But in fact the first owner of Rushbourne Manor of whom we know anything, Henry Twyman, has his monument in Westbere Church, as do some of his successors[5].

Henry Twyman, who died in 1677, was certainly the man who pulled down the old manor house and built the splendid brick structure that is still there. The house can be dated to 1659, as on the west side of the northern chimney stack is to be seen the following inscription:

T
H S
1659

The shaped gables at either end, in the 'Dutch' style are typical of the period and remains of the curved brick tops to the original windows can still be seen at both ends of the house, large ones on the north and three much smaller round-headed ones on the south, flanking the chimneystack. The house has a little shaped-gabled porch on the west, but this is in fact 19th century and dates from when the house 'was turned round'. At the back of the house on the north-east can be seen the remains of the two-storied original porch which was once

RUSHBOURNE MANOR

the original entrance. It is now partly buried in early 19th century additions to the house. Inside, much remains of the 17th century building including the roof and some timber internal portions and the house is beautifully cared for by the present owners, Mr. and Mrs. Brian Stephens, whose family have been here for the last 70 or so years.

References

1. A.M. Woodcock (ed.), *Cartulary of the Priory of St. Gregory, Canterbury* (1956), 2, 65.

2. E. Hasted, *The History and Topographical Survey of the County of Kent* XII (1801), 144.

3. Now in Canterbury Cathedral Library, part of Westbere parish.

4. The present owners kindly lent me a map of 1856, entitled Plan of Rushbourne farm that shows the newly inserted drains and underdrains in the fields. In other respects the map is almost the same as the Tithe Map.

5. K. H. McIntosh (ed.) *Chislet and Westbere* (1979), 44.

NICHOLAS RIDLEY (1500?-1555)
by
Roger Higham, B.A.

On 13 April 1538, Thomas Cranmer, Archbishop of Canterbury, instituted Nicholas Ridley to the vicarage of Herne. The previous year, he had become one of Cranmer's chaplains, and increasingly exerted a strong influence over the archbishop's religious opinions, since the latter had come to respect highly Ridley's learning and judgment.

This learning had been acquired over the last twenty years. Ridley was the second son of Christopher Ridley of Unthank Hall, near Willimoteswick in Northumberland, and Anne his wife, both of old border families; he had been first educated in Newcastle-upon-Tyne, then at Pembroke Hall, Cambridge. Excelling in Greek, he graduated in 1522. He continued his studies at Cambridge and was elected a fellow of Pembroke Hall with his Master's degree in 1526. Thereafter he studied abroad, in Paris and Louvain, but in 1530 returned to Cambridge and settled in Pembroke Hall as junior treasurer to the college.

These were the days when European Christianity was undergoing profound upheavals: frequent and vehement (although informed and judicious) criticism of the Church Universal had failed to alter its imperviousness to reform, and Martin Luther had long since embarked on his divergent course. Many churchmen, while condemning his extreme measures, were inclined to agree with him in principle, and the Reformation movement was under way. In England it received unintended encouragement when King Henry VIII, desperate for a male heir, failing to obtain permission from the Pope to divorce his wife and remarry, took the unprecedented step of denying the Supreme Pontiff's authority and establishing his own independent Church of England, with Cranmer, who was instrumental in the long and complicated process, as his archbishop. Henry's Church was still orthodox Catholic, but his churchmen construed his action as an avenue to Protestant reform.

In 1534 Ridley, now Proctor of Cambridge, helped to gain support for the king's position by procuring from the University a statement condemning the Pope's spiritual power; he was then appointed chaplain to the University.

72

In point of fact, until 1536 Ridley was still in two minds: he had not committed himself to the reformed faith in its entirety, but had by this time read deeply in it and had discussed the root questions with Cranmer. In 1537 Cranmer gave him the appointment as his chaplain, in 1538 the vicarage of Herne. However, Ridley continued to maintain a cautious line on reformed doctrine, still accepting transubstantiation, permitting auricular confession (although not insisting on it) and the principle of clerical celibacy: in fact he never married, himself. This enabled him in 1541 to become one of the king's chaplains, but by 1543 it was possible for the unswervingly Catholic Bishop Gardiner to bring a case against him for nonconformist practices. He accused Ridley of having doubts about confession, of having condemned some church ceremonies, and of directing that the *Te Deum* should be sung in English in his parish church at Herne. Ridley refuted all these accusations to the satisfaction of the king's commissioners who examined him, but the incident set him against the old dogma, and just before the king's death in 1547 he finally renounced transubstantiation, a conclusion at once adopted by Cranmer.

Young Edward VI's reign gave him his chance: on 4 September 1547 he was nominated bishop of Rochester, with permission to hold *in commendam* until Christmas 1552 his two vicarages (his college had presented him to the other, of Soham in Cambridgeshire) and his two canonries (of Canterbury and Westminster). From now on he was busy furthering Protestant reform, establishing it firmly at Cambridge, helping Cranmer to compile the first English prayer book, and serving on commissions for reforming ecclesiastical law and for depriving the Catholic bishops Bonner of London and Gardiner of Winchester of their sees. On 12 April 1550 he replaced Bonner as Bishop of London.

Ridley proceeded with his customary caution in his new diocese, but soon was ordering all altars to be replaced by communion tables and gave preferment

HERNE

to clergy of his own persuasion. He may be credited with at least one great humanitarian act, when he appealed to the young king early in 1553 for better provision for the destitute of London: the result was the foundation of Christ's, St. Thomas's and Bethlehem Hospitals, with funds from the king and the City of London. Somewhat less admirable was his conduct in respect of the nefarious Duke of Northumberland, who had assumed the government of the country on behalf of the king. He had encouraged the king's avaricious courtiers to help themselves to church property throughout the country, in the name of reforming zeal, thereby promulgating the spread of poverty through widespread dispossession. Ridley protested to Northumberland about it, causing the iniquitous Duke to view him with suspicion: he thereupon used his threat of disfavour as a lever to persuade Ridley to sign letters patent acknowledging the title to the throne of Lady Jane Grey, Northumberland's daughter-in-law. To mitigate the threat, Ridley was offered a bribe: a promise of the rich bishopric of Durham.

Ridley finally committed himself to Northumberland's unsavoury cause by preaching at St. Paul's Cross on Sunday, 9 July 1553, just after the king's expected early death, before the Lord Mayor and Corporation of London: he declared both the princesses Mary and Elizabeth illegitimate, and vigorously attacked Mary's Catholic opinions.

It was not long before he realised his error of judgment and tried to make amends. He went to Mary's camp at Framlingham in Suffolk and appealed to her for mercy. Adamantly unforgiving, Mary had him arrested and he arrived at the Tower of London on 20 July. Bonner was reinstated as Bishop of London, and Ridley accepted that his cause, being lost, must be defended with utmost conviction. He wrote to all his friends, insisting on the absolute necessity of standing resolutely by the reformed faith.

The spring of 1554 brought Sir Thomas Wyatt's rebellion against Queen Mary's proposed marriage to Philip of Spain, and the consequent execution, not only of Wyatt, but of the innocent and luckless Lady Jane and her husband. Ridley, with Cranmer and Hugh Latimer, lately Bishop of Worcester, were taken to Oxford for examination by scholastic disputation. Ridley defended himself before his hostile audience and was declared a heretic. A royal commission then called on him to recant: he refused, and was excommunicated.

At this stage England was not yet formally reconciled to Rome, and Parliament had not yet consented to enact laws against heresy. Both of these steps in England's recovered Catholicism came within the next year, and on 30 September 1555 Ridley was tried under the new law on the capital charge of heresy. Called to write out his beliefs, Ridley did so at length: the judges found his screed too blasphemous even to read aloud, and sentenced him to greater excommunication and formal degradation. Then they handed him over to the Mayor of Oxford for punishment.

On 16 October 1555 Ridley and Latimer, who had received similar treatment, were marched to a stake set up 'on the north side of the town, in the ditch over against Balliol College'. Ridley, with equanimity, gave his bishop's clothes away, and his brother-in-law tied a bag of gunpowder round his neck, to hasten the end. The fire was lighted. 'Be of good cheer, Master Ridley', said Latimer, 'we shall this day light such a candle by God's grace in England as, I trust, shall never be put out'.

The smoke overcame Latimer almost at once, but poor Ridley suffered atrocious torments before death released him.

MORRIS DANCING 1589
by
Philip Edmonds

The following are excerpts from statements in the records of the Quarter Sessions in the Cathedral Archives Library, Canterbury.

John Tinfrey (The vice in the daunce servant to George Ryder of Herne, 20 yrs.)
'John Lychefild, servunt with Jencke of Herne dyd, about 14 dayes past, as he thinketh, byfore may day last, hyr Henry Parkes the fydler and his men to serve them for the moryce dance tyll St. Peters day next, for syche dayes as they should wule hym. He gave hym 4s. a day for every day daunced.'

Nycholas Seynt, aged 20 yrs.
'On May day last they wer daunsyng at Herne with the company, and on Sunday last they also daunsed ther in the afternoon and a little in the forenoon.'

John Lychefyld (Servunt to Jencke of Herne, 19 yrs.)
'That on assencyon day last (8th May) were at servyce at Chyslet and their daunsed a lytle in the foornone and dansed at Hod in the afternoon.'
'. . . and further confessed that he did hyr the muster as was said.'

Nicholas Saynt
'and yesternyght beyng fryday they cam to Brydge [called Bourne by others] to the ale howse and ther laye and from thens cam to Canterbury and sayeth they were going to St. Stephens to Mr. Peter Manwood but that Mr. Manwood dyd not request and they went of ther on myndes. . . . . . they began at St. Georges Gate to daunse till they cam to the highe streate and ther they daunsed once or twyse agaynst Mr. Mayers dore.'

Henry Seers, aged 24 yrs.
'Tymothy Dunkyn one of the company of the moryce dauncers ys syck and lyeth syck without the town and that he (Henry Seers) was procured in his place and was not of tham byfore.'

James Barley (Barby. Barly, aged 20 yrs.)
'. . . . . and dyd turn to the George without Saynt Georges gate and ther dyd adresse themselves in the morrys dansis appere (apparell).'

Thomas Yong (Young) aged 12 yrs.)
'being dressed in womans apparell for mayd Marryon, without any breeches and with breyded here.'

Henry Parkes (musycion, 26 yrs.)
'. . . and put on ther bells and furnytur for the morryce dance with mayd maryon being a boy in womans apparell.'
'it was never merry with Ingland sens men wer to go with lycence.'
They were charged with not having a licence.

THE CLOCK, ST. MARTIN'S CHURCH, HERNE

by

Kenneth Stocker

Careful examination of the clock movement has revealed that whereas it was at one time thought that it was late 18c. there can be no doubt that it was made in the first half of the 17c. In the extract given below from the Church-wardens' Accounts a new clock is recorded as being installed in 1677/78, or rather Mr. Grinall was paid for it then. Judging from the delay in paying Mr. Grinall for maintenance in subsequent years, installation could have been a few years earlier!

The late Dr. Beeson, in his book 'English Church Clocks' claims that this type of clock, the 'birdcage' frame (so called because it is a simple rectangular box or cage formed by flat wrought-iron bars in horizontal and vertical assembly), dates, when the rope barrels were placed end-to-end, from early 17c.

Although these barrels are now side-by-side, there is clear evidence that they were originally end-to-end, since the holes in the vertical bars at each end of the frame, which would have carried one end of each of the barrel arbors, are still visible, now unused.

This is further confirmed by the movement having had additional vertical bars attached by nuts and bolts of 18c. appearance, in order to reposition the two trains at 90 degrees to the original, whereas the original bars and frame are held together by wedges, as was the custom before nuts and bolts came into use after mid-17c.

HERNE CHURCH CLOCK   Photograph by Kenneth Stocker

After the invention of the anchor or recoil escapement in late 17c., many clocks were converted from the earlier 'verge and foliot', for better time-keeping, and it is probable that, when at some time, the clock was converted, the trains were repositioned to their present arrangement.

At some still later date, a completely new 'going' train has been fitted, since the present one has brass wheels and steel pinions, machine-cut, while the original striking train is all iron in the custom of the earlier clocks, which were often the product of the blacksmith.

There are also clear signs of bearing mountings for the original verge; none of the now-unused pivot holes in the bars have, fortunately, been filled as was sometimes done after conversions, for neatness. This, of course, makes it easier to trace the original arrangement.

The following is an extract from the Churchwarden's Accounts 1663-1728, kindly supplied by Mr. S. T. Allen, Churchwarden, and thanks are due to him and the Vicar for permission to view and photograph the clock.

HERNE CHURCHWARDENS' ACCOUNTS: 1663-1728;
references to the CLOCK

Year		£	s	d
1677-78	It: pd to Mr. Grinall for a new Clock to the Church	14	0	0
1678-79	(To John Overy, clerk) for Looking after the Church Clock	0	10	0
	It: to Mr. Greenhill for one yeares repaires of the church clock due at Michall^S 1678	0	5	0
1679-80	It: to Mr. Greenhill concerning ye clock	0	5	0
1680-81	It: to Mr. Greenhill concerning the clock	0	5	0
1681-82	It: to Greenhill for the clock	0	5	0
1687	It: to Mr. Greenhill concerning ye clock	1	15	0
1693	Paid to Mr. Grinall for 6 years repaires for the clock til Michalmas last	1	10	0
1698-99	To Mr. Greenhill for 5 years Repair of the Church Clock due at Michalmas last			
	Itm: 5s for new lines as per Account	1	10	0
	pd. to John Buckhurst for Communion Bread & Oyl for ye Clock	00	7	0
1707-08	June 11. Paid for mending & cleaning ye Clock	0	14	0
	Paid for painting the diall of ye Clock Lamblack it, and Lowances	0	7	9
	June 13 for to Lines for the Clock and duson of trushes for the pues	0	13	0
1709-10	Nov. 22 Paid Mr. Greenhill Eight years at rears for the Church Clock	2	0	0
1710-11	July ye 10 for Cleaning ye Clock	00	5	00
	paid for Ile for ye Clock	00	00	07

1714-15	Apl. 20 Pd to Wm Badcock for Wages, washing the surplice & Keeping the Clock	3	10	0
	(Note: Badcock was Parish Clerk)			
	Apl. 20 More for bread for the Communion and oyle for the Clock	0	2	6
1715-16	Oct. 25 for a pynt and a Quarter of Oyle for ye Clock	00	01	03
	Feb. 4 Paid Goodlad for Cleaning the Church Clock	00	07	00
1717	Paid the painter for the Clock	02	10	00
	For a Clock Line for ye Church Clock	00	03	06
	Pd John Baret for Church Clock	02	00	00
1719-20	Mar. 22 Pd John barret for Cleaning of the Church Clock	00	10	00
1720-21	Sept. 26 pd Moyse for a Clock line	00	3	06
1722-23	June 7 pd (Jos. Reeve) for Cleaning the Clock	0	10	00
1724-25	July 9 pd for Cleaning the Clock	00	07	00
	Apl. 17 Oyle for ye Clock	00	01	00
1727-28	Oct. 16 Pd for cleaning the Clock		10	
	April 20 Pd for wiar for the Clock		0	4½

There is also 1694-95. To Richard Hearne.... for colouring of the diall post and the frame 4s 0d (this sounds like a Sundial?).

STURRY CHURCH CLOCK

THE BELLS OF ST. MARTIN'S CHURCH, HERNE

by

Richard Offen

The fine North-Western tower of St. Martin's Church contains an interesting ring of six bells. The ring, which is hung in an eighteenth century bell frame, is the work of founders from three different centuries.

The oldest bell in the ring is the fourth, which was cast by Joseph Hatch in 1621. It is not certain how many bells formed the ring when Joseph cast this bell, but by the middle of the seventeenth century we find references to a ring of five which seem to have been augmented to six sometime prior to 1700.

There is still some doubt about the original home of the Hatch family, but Thomas Hatch, the first of the bell founders, might have come from Tenterden. There is now only one of Thomas's bells left, at Langley, near Maidstone. Soon after the marriage of Thomas the family seems to have moved to Roses Farm at Broomfield, near Maidstone, and it was there that the bell-founding business was based. At the turn of the seventeenth century the business was taken over by Joseph, who may have been Thomas's son or younger brother and it was under Joseph's management that the foundry became one of the most prolific foundries in the South-East of England at that time. Joseph died in 1639 and the foundry went into the hands of his nephew William; but these were troubled times, those of the Civil War and Cromwell's usurpation, and business was very poor – only twenty five or so bells seem to have been cast by William. The death of William in 1664 brought this foundry to a final close.

ST. MARTIN'S CHURCH, HERNE   Photograph by Kenneth Stocker

79

During the first part of the eighteenth century the two smallest bells were recast by Samuel Knight of Holborn. The Churchwardens accounts for 1724/25, when the second was recast, add further evidence to prove that there had been at least five bells at Herne for some time, as the following two entries show:-

Year								£	s	d
"Jan. 15	Spent	when	we	took	down	the	bell	00	05	00
Mar. 26	Paid	for	new	casting	ye	bell		04	10	00"

The treble is dated 1737 and, again, was probably a recast of an earlier bell.

The other three bells are recasts of original Hatch bells, this work having been done by the famous Whitechapel Bell Foundry. The fifth was recast by William Chapman, who was responsible for casting 'Great Dunstan', the three-ton service bell at Canterbury Cathedral. He, in partnership with various others, reigned over the Whitechapel firm from 1769 to 1784. The other two were recast by Robert Stainbank in 1867/8, who had bought out George Mears and taken over the firm in 1865. During the first few years of his proprietorship bells were inscribed with just his name, but after that the firm became known as Mears and Stainbank and continued trading under that name until it became a limited company in the late 1960's.

The bells are rung regularly by a keen and enthusiastic band, but are now unfortunately in need of restoration, the state of the bell frame and fittings making them rather difficult to ring.

Bell	Inscription
Treble	∷·SAMUEL∷KNIGHT MADE∷THOS VANDERPEER∷THO^S STEPHENS CHURCH∷WARDENS M E J737
Second	S K J724 THO⌐ FEARIMAИ PETER TALL
Third	ROBERT STAINBANK, FOUNDER, FOUNDER, LONDON, 1868
Fourth	IOSEPHVS HATCH ME FECIT T ⊙ 1621 (T of "FECIT" incised)
Fifth	∞∞∞◇ GILBARD PEMBROOK CHURCH WARDEN W^M CHAPMAN OF LONDON FECIT 1781
Tenor	ROBERT STAINBANK, FOUNDER, LONDON, 1867

Dimensions of the ring:

Bell	Note	Diameter	Weight
Treble	D	2' - 6"	5½ cwt. approx.
2	C	2' - 7⅝"	6½ " "
3	B^b	2' - 10¹⁄₁₆"	7¾ " "
4	A	3' - 0¾"	9 " "
5	G	3' - 3⅞"	11¾ " "
Tenor	F	3' - 7"	13 cwt. 3qr. 12 lbs.

GEORGE KENNARD, M.A., Rector of Fordwich[1]

by

Duncan Harrington, L.H.G.

George Kennard was the son of Sampson Kennard, a joiner of St. Paul's, Canterbury. His father had stated on two separate instances that he himself was born 1557/58 within the city of Canterbury and it seems likely that his baptism would have taken place at St. Mary Magdalene within the City.[2] However, the registers of St. Mary Magdalene only start in 1559 so no entry is recorded for Sampson, but there are two entries for his sisters Johanna (1561) and Anne (1566).[3] We can obtain details of the parentage of Sampson Kennard from the City of Canterbury muniments which record that he was granted the freedom of the City in 1583 through patrimony; his father Hammond Kennard, a shoemaker of St. Mary Magdalene, Canterbury, had purchased his freedom in 1543.[4]

George Kennard was born 1592/93 and it seems very likely that he too was baptised at St. Mary Northgate although the baptismal record has not been found there. Although the parish registers no longer survive for that period, the Archdeacon's transcripts are still extant and preserved in Canterbury Cathedral Archives and Library. George's elder brother, Sampson, whom we shall mention in greater detail, was baptised at St. Mary Northgate 13 November, 1586 as Samson, son of Samson Kenwood, and George's younger brother, Augustine, on the 27 May, 1593 as Augustin son of Samson Kenete.[5]

The first mention we have of George Kennard connected with the Church is in 1600/1 when he appears in the records of the Dean and Chapter as a chorister at the Cathedral.[6] He started in the choir at the same time as his cousin Richard, who went on to become a lay clerk and was eventually buried with his first wife in the Cathedral.[7] George continued in the choir until 1605/6. He then became a King's Scholar from the 1st Term 1607/8 (Christmas 1607) until the 4th Term 1610/11 (Christmas 1611).[8]

Leaving King's School Canterbury, George Kennard matriculated a sizar from Clare College Cambridge in Michaelmas 1611. He gained his BA 1615/16 and M.A. in 1619. He was ordained deacon by the Bishop of Peterborough on the 18 September, 1618 and made a priest on the 10 March, 1619/20.[9] He was instituted Rector of Fordwich on the 10 September, 1619 and remained in that parish until his death in 1627.[10]

His Will at the Kent Archives Office reads as follows:[11]

In the name of God amen. I George Kennard sick in body yet well in sences doe make this my last will and testament as followeth First I will my soule to God who gave it, and my bodie to be decently buried and my debtes to be paid as followeth Concerning my three houses without the Northgate of Canterbury my will is that the rent thereof be equally divided betwene my mother and my wife and they to repaire the same houses Item after my mothers death I give the two great howses next to the Northgate to my wife and the other olde house to my brother John Kennard to be sould in case that there be not movables inough to pay my debtes And six powndes of the remainder of that money I give to my sister Elizabeth Robinson Now for my debts I will that my movables shalbe sould to pay them As this by name, all the joyned ware (except three cushing chayres and one long playne cheste which I give unto my wife) All my bookes my apparrell all corne which shalbe found in my house or barne or feild with wood and tymber as shalbe left at my death, one featherbedd and a coverlid for the other things I give unto my wife This is my last will and testament whereof I make my brother John Kennard my executor In witness whereof I have hereunto set my hand and seale The 11th day of March 1626. Sealed and delivered in the presence of William Dunkyn clerk and William Whitworth.

Probate of the will of George Kennard clerk of Fordwich was granted on the 27 July, 1627 to John Kennard the executor. However, this was disputed with the result that the matter was taken to the ecclesiastical court and Richard Clerk, clerk, professor of sacred theology and a surrogate in the Archdeacon's Court, gave a definitive ruling or sentence in favour of the executor on the 23 October, 1627 against Ann Kennard widow and relict of Mr. George Kennard clerk, Elizabeth Kennard widow mother, Sampson Kennard clerk and Augustine Kennard brothers, Elizabeth Robinson alias Kennard, Frances Alsopp alias Kennard and Mary Kennard sisters.[12]

George Kennard apparently died without issue. He had married on 30 January, 1622/23 Anne Furser of St. Andrew's Canterbury by licence at St. Mary Bredin.[13] The licence described her as Ann Fusser of St. Andrew's maiden, aged about 19 the daughter of John Fusser a grocer, who consents.[14]

After the death of George Kennard his wife moved to St. Andrew's, Canterbury and on 15 October, 1628 a marriage licence was issued to marry either at Hackington or Sturry, Peter Webster of 'St. Michaells royall' in the City of London, citizen and clothworker bachelor aged about 28 years.[15]

George Kennard in going to Clare was following his elder brother Sampson, who was born in 1585 and, as mentioned previously, baptised at St. Mary Northgate in 1586.[16] He started his school career at King's Canterbury from the 2nd Term 1598/99 (i.e. Lady Day 1598/99) and remained there until the 1st Term of 1602/3 (i.e. Lady Day 1602/3).[17]

From King's, Sampson Kennard went to Cambridge University, gaining a B.A. from Clare 1606/7 and an M.A. in 1610.[18] We next find Sampson being granted a licence to teach at Godmersham in 1610, then a licence to serve the cure at Eythorne on the 2 October, 1611 as Sampson Kennard M.A. clerk.[19] He apparently became vicar of St. Mary Northgate 29 September, 1612 and was buried 5 August, 1935; his successor Daniel Bollen M.A. became vicar on 2 December, 1635.[20] No will or letters of administration have yet been found for Sampson Kennard.[21]

He had married at St. Nicholas Harbledown in 1620 Susan, the widow of Richard Bix of St. Mary Northgate, fellmonger, who had died about 12 months before.[22] Apparently they had no children. The references to Sampson Kennard in the City records are quite numerous, he having attained his Freedom of the City by birth in 1614.[23] The Consistory Court papers in ecclesiastical causes also record two cases relating to tithe disputes where Sampson Kennard was the plaintiff.[24]

REFERENCES

1.   K. H. McIntosh (Ed.) *Fordwich – The Lost Port* (1975). Although not mentioned in the article by the Reverend P. J. Gausden, 'A Glance at More Predecessors', he appears in the listing on page 195.

2. CCL:PRC 39/23 f 61v 26 November, 1599 Sampson Kennard of the parish of St. Paul near and without the walls of the City of Canterbury, has lived there about 2 years. Born in the City of Canterbury, aged 41 years. Case concerns William Stafford's bastard and a defamation at 'The Falcon' in St. Mary Magdalen, Canterbury. X.11.19 f 25a 19 July, 1621, Sampson Kennard joiner of St. Pauls, Canterbury has lived there for 20 years. Born in Canterbury, aged 60 years. Sampson Kennard was buried at St. Pauls, 31 August, 1624, and letters of administration were granted 17 October, 1625 (PRC 32/32 f 99) and a probate account entered into court 13 April, 1627 (PRC 2/28 f 75) by his widow Elizabeth. (He had married Elizabeth Boucher 8 November, 1585 at St. Mary Magdalen, Canterbury). Sampson Kennard had left goods and chattels in an inventory which had totalled 80.16.9. The cost of his funeral was £5.10s. and the accounts then list the debts that his wife Elizabeth was obliged to pay and these included Mr. Furser Alderman of the City of Canterbury 10s. (father-in-law of son George's wife), Mr. Walter Bigg of Fordwich £4 and Mr. Francis Barton of the Precincts of Christchurch, Canterbury £100, which in all made a grand total of £127.12.4 leaving her £46.15.7d. out of pocket. The £100 debt to Francis Barton is intriguing and the more so since there is apparently no family connection. J. M. Cowper, *Memorials of Canterbury Cathedral* page 71 shows that Francis Barton died 4 October, 1639 aged 71 and it is possible that he may be the same Francis Barton of Christ Church, Canterbury gentleman who at about the age of 53 years was granted a marriage licence 28 August, 1623 to marry Elizabeth Fineux of Christ Church, Canterbury a widow aged about 48 years at Ickham. J. M. Cowper, *Canterbury Marriage Licences* second series, (1894).

3. J. M. Cowper, The Registers of St. Mary Magdalene, Canterbury 1559-1800, (1890).

4. J. M. Cowper, *The Roll of the Freemen of the City of Canterbury* 1392-1800, (1903).

5. CCL: The registers do not start until 1640. The Archdeacon's transcripts were contemporary returns housed at the Registry. I am grateful to Miss A. M. Oakley, M.A., F.S.A., for permission to quote from these and other records in her custody.

6. Treasurers' Account Books CCL information from Robert Ford, University of California, Berkeley.

7. Robert Hovenden, *The Registers of Canterbury Cathedral* 1564-1878. Harleian Society Register Vol. 2 (1878). He was buried 23 October, 1667. His will dated 6 August, 1667

A FORDWICH TROUT

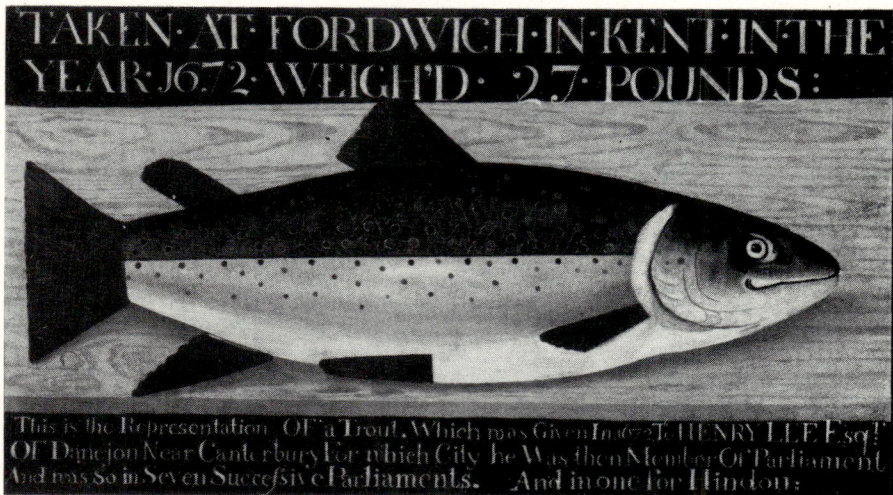

Canterbury City Museums © 1982

Oil on Canvas, English School. Presented by Mr. G. Lee Warner.
A colour postcard of this picture is available, price 6p from The Royal Museum, Canterbury.

(PRC 17/72 f 330); at that time he describes himself as of the parish of Holy Cross, Westgate, Gentleman. His first wife Mary was buried in the cloisters 19 December, 1643 and he married secondly another Mary. Robert Ford tells me that he was listed as a chorister in 1600/1 only and may possibly have then gone to the Chapel Royal. Richard Kennard appears in the Cathedral records as a substitute for a minor canon for 1635/36-1636/37 and as a lay clerk continuously from 1639/40-1641/42 (Commonwealth gap) 1660/61-1663/64.

8.   CCL: New Foundation Accounts numbers 16-19; 6-9 James I (1607/8-1610/11); information from Robert Ford. Accounts for 5 and 10 James I are extant but Kennard is not listed.

9.   J. & J. A. Venn, *Alumni Cantabrigienses from the Earliest Times to 1900* (Cambridge 1922-27).

10. Lambeth Palace Library: Archbishop's Registers 1611-1633 Volume 1 folio 316 V. from Frampton Collection CCL.

11. KAO: PRC 16/188. I should like to thank Mr. N. Yates, County Archivist, for permission to quote from this record in his custody.

12. KAO: PRC 16/188. Further material should be available in PRC 18/19 and 20.

13. J. M. Cowper, *Canterbury Marriage Licences,* 2nd series 1619-1660. A Richard Furser, probably brother to Anne, was a substitute from 3rd Term 1598/99 until 1st Term 1602/3 and a lay clerk from the 2nd Term in the same year until some time in 1623/24. A 'Furser senior' was a chorister from 1615/16 to 1617/18 (only parts of the terminal years) and 'Furser junior' 1617/18 to 1621/22 (once again only part of the terminal years). These were probably sons of Richard.

14. F. W. Tyler, Transcript of St. Mary Bredin, Canterbury parish registers 1563-1812 made in December 1943. The first two registers were severely damaged by an air raid in June 1942, and the entry is therefore taken from the transcripts.

15. Cowper, *Marriage Licences op. cit.*

16. CCL: X.11.19 f 10a 16 April, 1621. Sampson Kennard M.A. Vicar of St. Mary Northgate, Canterbury has resided there for 8 years, born there, aged 34 years. X.11.16 f.254 7 April, 1628. Sampson Kennard vicar of St. Mary Northgate has resided there 15 years and was born there, aged 40 years.

17. Robert Ford: CCL Treasurers' Books for 1598/99, 1599-1600, New Foundation Accounts No's 11 and 12; i.e. 42-43 Elizabeth I and 1 James I (1602/3).

18. Venn *op. cit.*

19. A. J. Willis, Canterbury Licences (General) 1568-1646 (1972) pp.13 & 58.

20. Edward Hasted: History of Kent, 2nd Edn. (1800) Volume 11, page 248. CALC: Burial recorded in St. Mary Northgate bishop's transcripts. Daniel Bollen or Bullen was a minor canon at Canterbury from the 4th Term (1630/31 until 1641/42 when he disappears).

21. Both the Archdeaconry and Consistory Court of Canterbury wills and administrations have been searched and also the Prerogative Court of Canterbury. It is hoped that it may be found under papers in ecclesiastical causes if it exists or possibly an administration in PRC 43/47 or 48.

22. Cowper, *Marriage Licences op. cit.* p.570. Sampson Kennard clerk vicar of St. Mary Northgate about 34; son of Sampson Kennard of 'St. Paule joynard' (? St. Paul's joiner) who consents and Susan Bix of St. Mary Northgate, widow of Richard Bix late same place fellmonger deceased about 12 months since. At St. Nicholas, Harbledown. John Lunn of St. Nicholas Hospital, Harbledown, clerk bondsman, 25 January, 1620/21. Letters of administration (PRC 3/30 f 258) were granted 9 February, 1619/20 on the estate of Richard Bix of St. Mary Northgate to Suzan Bix relict. Bound with her William Greeneleand of St. Cosmos, Blean yeoman and Richard Warrye of the city of Canterbury glover in £60.

23. Cowper, *Freemen op. cit.*

24. CCL: Against Israel Jarman or Jerman of Holy Cross, Canterbury 21 November, 1633-32 July, 1634, J/J 53/25, 54/127, 56/162 & 163. Against John Harloe of St. Mary Northgate, 19 February, 1623 J/J 33/36.

CHISLET – EVIDENCE OF LOST BRASSES

by

Leslie A. Smith

Although there are no brasses or indents within Chislet church Mr. Stephen Freeth of the Guildhall Library, London, has kindly directed my attention to an indent which can still be seen in its original position in the south west corner of the churchyard. This is in a 20 cm thick moulded slab, badly cracked and now held together by two large rusting clamps, which rests atop a chest of four course brickwork. The indent is very weathered but 9 rivets and 5 rivet holes remain and most interestingly the rivets were coated with pitch, presumably to prevent corrosion. The position of the rivets and the outline of the composition point to a foot inscription with three figures above, the outer two with scrolls. The presence of scrolls indicates that this is one of the rare pre-Reformation external brasses where physical evidence survives. Most external brasses record the erection of buildings or donations to almshouses and only two others can be said to be purely sepulchral – at Houghton Conquest, Bedfordshire, and at Bridge, Kent.[1] There are however several 16th century wills specifying burial in the churchyard with a brass on the tomb.

Another 16th century will provides us with a likely interior brass, assuming the executors carried out the instructions. William Consant,[2] in his will of 1527 requests burial 'in the chancel of our Lady and Joseph in the Church of Chistelett, from the pillar head unto the foot of the step where I used to sit commonly and a tomb to be made at my cost with a picture of my body upon it'. Although an incised stone slab cannot be ruled out this is the normal phraseology for a brass.

Reproduced by kind permission of Mr. and Mrs. N. V. Bacon

CHISLET CHURCH BY HONOR BACON

NOTES

1.   R. H. D'Elboux lists most known external brasses in Monumental Brass Society Transactions, Vol. VIII (1943-51), and also describes the Bridge indent in Archaeologia Cantiana, Vol. LXI (1948).

2.   Chislet and Westbere, Villages of the Stour Lathe (1979), p.88.

AN UNSOLVED MYSTERY
The Bells of Holy Cross Church, Hoath
by
Richard Offen

The delightful shingled spire of Holy Cross Church, Hoath, contains one of the fascinating mysteries which make bell archaeology the interesting pursuit that it is.

Two of the bells have no other indication as to their maker than some strange initials inscribed on them and the characteristics of their mouldings. These two, the tenor and treble (largest and smallest) of the ring, are simply inscribed 'IC 1696'. Who was 'IC'? A perusal of the lists of bell founders working in the home counties at the end of the seventeenth century sheds no light on the question; for it would appear that no one with the initials IC was at work in this part of Britain at that time. How then do we go about tracing the maker of this brace of bells? The answer lies in the shape of the bell and the layout of the 'moulding wires' and any decoration on the canons (supporting loops). The Reverend David Cawley, who has spent many years researching the history of Kentish bells and bell founders, suggests that the moulding techniques used to make the bells is very similar to those used on the bell at Swingfield Church, near Folkestone. This bell was also cast in 1696, but this time the maker's name appears in the inscription: John Wood.

John Wood was a peripatetic bell founder – not an unusual feature among bell founders of this period, who would travel around the country, just where ever their trade took them. In a contract for a bell cast in 1695 for Rochester Cathedral, Wood styles himself as of Chancery Lane, London, but in 1698 in a similar contract for Berwick in Sussex, his address is given as 'the parish of Bishopsgate in the Citty of London'.

Could Wood have been the founder of the two Hoath bells? Are the initials those of a Churchwarden? Or did some other, until now, unknown founder cast them? Perhaps we shall never know!

Far less of a mystery is the middle bell of the chime of three. This bell is far easier to identify, this time by a characteristic cross used as part of the inscription. This bell was probably cast at the very end of the fifteenth century and is the work of one Richard Kerner of Canterbury.

There are three bells still in existence cast by Kerner; one, sadly cracked, at Old Romney, another in the church of St. Mary Bredin in Canterbury, the last example at Hoath. The cross used in his inscriptions was obviously one that he had inherited from previous Canterbury bell founders, for it first appears on bells cast by William le Belyetere at the beginning of the fourteenth century.

Not to be outdone by its partners, the inscription on this bell is also something of a mystery: 'SAM' followed by a reversed 'C' is probably an illiterate attempt at the word 'sanctus'.

So the three bells of Hoath Parish Church remain shrouded in mystery, a mystery that will probably never be unravelled.

Details of the chime:

Bell	Diameter	Inscription	Approx. Weight
Treble	1'-11"	IC 1696	2¾ cwt.
Second	2'-1½"	+ S A M Ɔ ⛉	3 cwt.
Tenor	2'-4½"	IC 1696	4¾ cwt.

Details of the cross on Hoath
Second bell

THE HOUSES OF HOATH

by

Kenneth Gravett, M.Sc. (Eng.), F.S.A., C.Eng.

The parish of Hoath is small but has some interesting houses. Except around Rushbourne Manor, it lies entirely to the east of the Roman Road from Canterbury to Reculver, along which is the parish boundary with Herne. As at Chislet the settlement pattern is diffuse, with early houses throughout the parish. The Court Lodge stands next to the Church, the Roman road bisects the hamlet of Maypole and there is another centre at Old Tree.

Hoath Court is a complicated house, with a main block of two storeys with attics and a cross-wing of two storeys to the east. This cross-wing has two dragon beams, showing that it once had jetties on three sides. That to the north remains, with light timbering, which with the side-purlin roof points to a date no earlier than the later part of the sixteenth century. It represents a parlour wing added to a pre-existing timber-framed house on the site of the present main block, which was also originally timber-framed, one post remaining in the rear wall. It was built with two brick chimneys, a large one with two fire-places heating the cross-wing and the central living room, and a further one heating the room at the west end, clearly the kitchen from the spit-machine marks on the high lintel. The roof has side purlins and the whole block was built in the second half of the seventeenth century, and there are many re-used rafters from the medieval hall, smoke-blackened and with dovetail laps from the previous collars. The attic is of particular interest since it is fully plastered and entered from outside by a door beside the west chimney at first-floor level. As recently as fifty years ago there was a platform and outside stairs to this door and the attic was used as a sleeping loft for farm labourers. Although several other houses in the area show that they once had similar provision, nowhere else may the arrangements be seen so clearly. The red brick front, with its dog-tooth cornice and porch, dates from about 1790, while the bay windows are Victorian. There is a good brick barn with a king-post truss, built in 1833.

Almost opposite, Rotherfield is a small, timber-framed cottage of one storey and attics, built around a central chimney stack. Although completely re-roofed, the character of the timberwork, with its absence of jowls to the posts, suggests a late-seventeenth century date. It might even be as late as 1707, the date scratched on the centre of a fine, three-plank door in the kitchen/living room, beside the fireplace, with its marks for the spit-machine on the high lintel. The other side of the chimney, the parlour was enlarged, probably when the house was made into two cottages in Victorian times. Some distance to the west is the Old Post Office, a tall weather-boarded building of about 1800.

Alongside the main road at the northern edge of the parish are the scanty remains of the great brick palace of Archbishop Morton at Ford.[1] There is a great crown-post, aisled brick barn and a farmhouse which was once a gatehouse, but some half a mile to the east lies the isolated farmhouse of Shelvingford, mentioned in the thirteenth century.[2] The present house is later, the main block being three surviving bays of a four-bay continuous-jetty house built with a chimney from the beginning and with a crown-post roof, the central crown post being rebated and having four braces upwards to collar and purlin. Such construction would normally date from 1500-1530, but since Morton, with his early interest in brick, was working so close, it is just possible that the house could date from the end of the fifteenth century.[3] The original plan is not clear since in the second half of the sixteenth century the end bay was pulled down, the chimney rebuilt and a cross-wing of two bays added. This has a roof with rafters and collars only, while a dragon beam at the corner shows that it once had a jetty to the end as well as to the front. At this period the front door was in front of the chimney. The cellar with its candle niches (with shouldered heads) was excavated later (and has a brick dated 1718).

Just south of Shelvingford is the settlement of Old Tree, where there are three houses to note: Mill House, of two storeys and attics, is weather-boarded over a light timber-frame, with brick end walls and a central staircase. It must date from the end of the eighteenth century, but has Victorian alterations, including the two bay windows. The old part of Old Tree Farm is of one storey and attics and is somewhat earlier. Old Tree House is a square brick building of two storeys. The front is in elegant grey brick arranged to come forward a few inches between the windows, as if they were very wide pilasters. All the windows have very shallow elliptical heads and rubbed grey voussoirs. The door-case has an elliptical fanlight and there is a stone string-course. The back and side walls are of red brick. The slate roof is of low pitch, hipped with a central gulley towards the rear and with tuscan eaves with well spaced modillions. Structurally it has king-posts, with a continuous ridge piece and side purlins, clasped under-neath by angle struts. Towards the rear there is a single, elliptical, cast-iron skylight over the stairs. The main downstairs rooms have marble fireplaces, one with consoles and two with paterae. The main stairs have an open string and a rail of Cuban mahogany curving round the bottom post. There is a lower extension to the rear for scullery and wash-house. This house is built to a very high standard and dates from about 1820. It has many features similar to Ringwould House, known to be by Sir John Soane, and would not be unworthy of him.

Returning to the main road and proceeding towards Sturry we come to Hurst Cottage and Home Leigh (now Berry Lodge). Hurst Cottage is the older building and has brick gables originally of Dutch form, suggesting a date at the end of the seventeenth century. It was once occupied by wheelwrights, whose shop has been pulled down. About 1830 a single bay was added to the south to form Home Leigh, and both cottages were given new staircases with doric columns.

The oldest house in Maypole lies to the east of the main road. At present called Maypole Thatch, it was formerly Hoath Cottage. It is a timber-framed house of three bays, the two to the north, where there is an original top end, being the open hall. The roof is very soot-blackened, although the battens for the thatch are clear. The central truss has a crown-post with octagonal cap and shaft and there is a crenellated dais beam at the north end. The posts have the long, straight gunstock form of jowl. There must have been a combined solar and service bay to the south. All of this points to a date at the beginning of the fifteenth century or the end of the fourteenth. Some time about 1600 a chimney was inserted and the hall section floored over, making the old hall the kitchen/living room, with an ingle-nook. A bellarmine jar, used as a witch bottle, has been found near the fireplace. The solar/service bay became a parlour but must have suffered collapse in the second half of the seventeenth century since it was rebuilt in brick, with a butt-side-purlin roof.

Two eighteenth-century houses lie along Maypole Road. Orchard House has two storeys, attics and basement. The brick front is now covered with roughcast but was once elegant with windows with cambered heads and a string course. Ivy House, of two storeys and attics, was built with an integral rear outshot at a lower level than the house and, as often happens, the wall between

Photograph by courtesy of Lieut. Comm. A. W. M. Collyer, R.N.

THE MANOR HOUSE, FORD, SHOWING THE BARN

89

house and outshot is timber framed, although all the other walls are brick. The front has original sash windows with thick glazing bars and curved heads, with rubbed brick voussoirs and imitation keystones. Over the rebuilt porch is a plaque dated 1746. There is a rear extension of about 1800 to give a kitchen.

The houses on the other side of the road are strictly in Herne Parish, rather than Hoath, but it is convenient to deal with them here. Maypole House has two parallel ranges, both of brick. The first range has two storeys, with attics and basements, with a central door, up steps, two windows either side and a chimney at each end. It was built in the middle of the eighteenth century. The south room was the parlour, that to the north the kitchen/living room and the basement was used for scullery and cellar. There is a small blocked window in the north wall in front of the chimney and this was used to pay the farm hands. The block at the back was added about 1800 and the house was considerably restored about 1870. In the cellar are several chamfered joists and some old plank doors, re-used from a house of about 1600, presumably on the site not far away.

The big square brick house, The Oast House, next door to the south, was an oast attached to Maypole House when it was a farm. At the north end it incorporates two square brick kilns. Rarely the kiln floor was made of square iron bars, since incorporated in the windows, while both upper doors remain. Originally the hops were fed into the kilns from the rear over the top of former cottages, and then spread out to cool on the big stowage floor to the south.

Gyssych (or Green Oak Farm) is of red brick with front door with semi-circular fanlight and surrounding brick arch. There is a low-pitch slate roof. The front windows retain their original sashes, without horns, and internal shutters. This house dates from about 1830, with later work behind. Although the house has an intriguing Anglo-Saxon name, there is no sign of an earlier building.

At Knaves Ash, and apparently just within the parish boundary, is The Homestead. This is timber-framed, although it was not possible to see if the timbers were smoke-blackened or not. At present the front door opens into the chimney bay and the room to the south was originally the parlour. The central room was the kitchen/living room with an inglenook, while the end room to the north is reputed to have been a dairy. The brick front and probably the chimney date from 1721.

Rushbourne Manor, once a manor in Westbere, is also mentioned in the thirteenth century,[4] but nothing remains above ground before the 1659 date on the chimney stack, when the house was rebuilt by Henry Twyman. The main block is in brick with a roof of butt side-purlins not in line. There is a dutch gable at the north-east end, with another on the brick two-storey porch on the back. The parlour was at this end, the living room in the middle and the service rooms at the south-west end, where a shaped gable faces the farmyard. Behind the chimney is a high quality, closed-string staircase to the first floor, with a newel stair above to the attics, and another newel stair at the south-west end. There are additions to the rear of about 1800 for kitchen and scullery, while about 1870 there were big alterations; new windows to the front, brick modillions along the eaves and a new porch, which explains why the present front door clearly interferes with the line of mortices in the ceiling for a former wall. The barn is interesting; aisled with posts with stepped jowls indicating an eighteenth-century origin, but considerably altered in the nineteenth, when the farmyard was improved. The Victorians used diagonally splayed, keyed scarf joints, a revival of a medieval form and also seen at Chilham Watermill.

Little Rushbourne was built in the middle of the eighteenth century as a pair of cottages, with a pair of kitchens in a rear extension. The ovens have gone, but their arches are visible in the back wall. The bay on the right-hand end of the front is a recent addition.

References

1.   See paper by H. Gough, above.

2.   J. K. Wallenberg: Place Names of Kent (1934) p.512.

3.   Compare with Whitehall, Cheam, Surrey also built on one of the Archbishop's manors. See: K. Gravett: Whitehall, Cheam, in Surrey Archaeological Collections, Vol. 63 (1966), p.138.

4.   See paper by T. Tatton-Brown, above.

OLD TREE HOUSE, HOATH

EPITAPH: In Hearne church-yard, Kent

Here lies a piece of Christ, a star in dust,
A vein of gold, a China dish, that must
Be us'd in Heaven when God shall feed his just.
Approved by all, and loved so well,
Tho young, like fruit that's ripe, he fell.
(1737)

from *The Olio* by Francis Grose, 1796

91

WESTBERE HOUSE AND THE NEWMANS

by

Betty Coton

The present Westbere House, although now enlarged, was built by Dr. Francis Newman about 1730 according to available records. The Newman family had connections with the village from 1600 when Danyell Newman married Mary Best in the parish Church. Decimus Newman became rector in 1690, but only became resident, paying £24 poor rate in 1717 (and thereafter), when his son Francis is recorded as treating the sick poor. It was not until 1722 that Decimus apparently rented a further property in the village, with an additional £4 on the poor rate assessment and 6/- window tax on 16 windows. He died that June and Francis took over the £4 payment, being recorded as the tenant of Samuel Milles. Mr. Wood the new rector paid on an assessment of £34 'for his parsonage'.

In 1727 Mary, the widow of Decimus died, as did Samuel Milles. Francis Newman is recorded as Landlord on the Land Tax Return but no deed has come to light. By 1731 the number of windows taxed had increased by 3 to 19. This is the best evidence available for the rebuilt house, no plans having been found. It also ties in with the postulated age of the existing structure by Kenneth Gravett (see photograph in Chislet and Westbere). In 1734 the Churchwardens 'Paid to Mr. Francis Newman ye Money that was allowed him for ye Building of ye Churchyard Wall £3'. (Churchwarden's accounts 1733-4).

Apparently Francis had rebuilt the house for his future bride, Sarah Shrubsole, whom he married in June 1735. She lived less than a year however, and in 1738, 'F. Newman Chyrurgeon' married Ann Foche of Rochester. The Marriage Settlement in Kent County Archives at Maidstone dated 12th July 1738, states that Francis gave 'all that new built messe or tenement with the stable outhouse edifices buildings, yards garden and orchard and appurtenances to the same .... lying and being in the Parish of Westbere etc.' The following year a daughter, Elizabeth was born, but was 'burried in Woollon' four months later. A son Daniel was baptised on 31st August 1740 at All Saints.

The house drew additional tax by an increase of 3 windows in 1747, and a further window the following year, made 23 in all. Francis Newman died in 1767 aged 80, but Ann continued to live in the house and bought much property in the village, even exchanging land with Richard Milles to obtain Stockfield opposite the house. Daniel, now a barrister, also purchased in 1774 a small cottage standing adjacent to Westbere House, which eventually enabled the garden to be extended to Church Lane; the triangular piece of land at the bottom of Church Lane was also included.

Three years later Ann died, having made a deed of appointment in favour of her son, who then moved into the house with his wife, described on her marriage as 'an agreeable young lady with a handsome fortune', and daughter Anne. Daniel made a detailed plan of the village showing his property. He clearly indicated the house where Francis Newman lived, giving positive identification of the site of his 'new built house'.

THE WINDMILLS
by
B. D. Stoyel

The village of Herne is fortunate in possessing one of the few windmills in Kent which are in a complete or nearly complete condition. There are indeed a regrettably small number of windmills in the whole of England that bear comparison with it. Appropriately, it is of the type known as a smock mill, which is typical of Kent although by no means restricted to the county. Having a fine elevated position (at TR. 185665) about half a mile from the old village, it may be seen readily from the surrounding countryside and it is not surprising that it is at least the second mill to occupy such a favourable site.

Its predecessor was a wooden postmill which apparently already existed in 1510 but very little is known of its history, although it is shown on a number of old maps of the county. There is a reference to a mill at Herne in 1405 and one was advertised for sale in 'The Kentish Post' on 6 January, 1750 by miller Daniel Kingsford, but there is no certainty that either was on this site. Similar doubts arise regarding the location of miller Robert Ball who was killed by lightning in 1589.

We are however on firm ground when it comes to the history of the present mill and it is known to have been built by John Holman, then of Wingham, in 1781. It was unusual in having been operated during the whole of its working life by only two families. It was owned and worked from the start by the Lawrence family, who appear to have sold it to the Wootton family in 1879. Messrs. R. C. and E. E. Wootton were the last to use it as a windmill, until 1952, after which they continued to grind in the mill by electricity. It was sold in 1980.

The wooden smock is of three storeys, covered with black weatherboarding, and stands on a two-storeyed brick base. Prior to 1858, however, the smock came almost down to ground level, but the brick base was raised in that year so that the sweeps of the mill could better catch the wind above the surrounding trees, now replaced by a housing estate! There is a wooden stage a little below the top of the brickwork. At present there are only two sweeps, a 'boat'-shaped cap like most Kent smock mills and a six-bladed fantail to turn the sweeps into the wind automatically.

Grinding was by two pairs of French burr stones and a pair of Peak stones, driven from above on the middle floor of the smock. The gearing is partly of wood and partly of iron.

Restoration of the mill commenced in March 1971 by the Herne Society, with financial backing from several public bodies, and has continued at intervals since as funds have permitted. A major step was the fitting of two new sweeps in 1975.

Another Herne windmill of relatively modern times was the Bay Mill at Herne Bay. This was built in 1825 very close to the beach and consequently appears in more than one 19th century engraving of the sea front. It was a black octagonal smock mill of four storeys on a one-storey brick base, which was wider than the smock and had its top railed round to form a stage. It had a 'boat' cap, sweeps with shutters and a six-bladed fantail. It was built in what was then a field to the east of the pier and close to the present clock tower, at TR. 176683.

Some of the tenant-millers were Harry Thorp, Richard Beard, Thomas Winder, J., J. and E. Lawrence, William Minter, R. Springate & Co., in that order, and apparently others as well; the fact that there were probably as many as ten millers during a period of just over 50 years seems to show that the site was not a good one for a windmill – a great contrast with its neighbour, Herne Mill.

In 1878 it was sold to Mr. T. B. Gambrill, the Petham miller, as the land was required for building purposes. He dismantled the mill and made a very good profit by selling all the usable parts to other millers; even some of the timber was re-used in the construction of the houses which took its place. This little estate is now known as Sea View Square and marks the situation of the former mill.

Whilst it is not possible to say with certitude what other mills may have existed at Herne in the medieval period, references to a Mill Bank in what is now the Studhill area of Herne Bay point to a third mill site about which nothing is known. It is not to be expected that any visible trace could be found today of a windmill which presumably disappeared several centuries ago, as it is not shown on any of the well-known maps of Kent; judging purely by the contours however it is suggested that an appropriate site might have been somewhere near the present Alvis Avenue – Riley Avenue crossing, at approximately TR. 149676.

There was for many years a smock windmill at Hoath, near Old Tree Farm. The date of its erection has not been traced, and the earliest reference to it that has been found so far was in 1802, when a fire insurance policy covering the mill was issued by the 'Royal Exchange'. As it was not shown on the Kent map by Andrews, Dury and Herbert, all that can be said about its date of construction is that it was presumably some time between 1769 and 1802.

A number of millers are known to have worked the mill, as follows:

John Goldfinch (1802)
Joseph Goldfinch (1817)
Charles Holland (1834)
James Collard (1845-1847)
R. Nash (1852)
E. Collard (1855)
David Kingsland (1858)
W. Bigglestone (1862)
Jonathan Packer (1866-1882)
Thomas Taylor (1887-1899)
Alfred Judge (1903)
Edward Fuller (1905-1911)
Ebenezer Fuller (1913)

The dates quoted are mostly those of the Directories in which the names appear, presumably compiled during the preceding year.

The frequency with which the mill changed hands suggests that, according to Sir Charles Igglesden, like the Bay Mill at Herne Bay, it was not well situated, despite the strong winds that blow at Hoath. Because the Fuller family were the last to work the mill it was latterly known as Fuller's Mill. It ceased work in 1912 and collapsed on the 18 July, 1919, perhaps during one of the strong winds in question.

The mill consisted of a broad single-storey brick base, railed round the top to form a 'stage', a three-storey octagonal wooden smock probably painted black or tarred, a boat-shaped cap typical of Kent, four spring sails and a fantail. An interesting point is that the windmill was advertised for sale in 1834 for no more than £150, and the machinery etc. for a further £150. The millhouse still stands, rebuilt following a fire in 1948, and the exact site of the mill is now a sunken brick-lined garden to the west of the house (TR. 209647). A feature of the garden as a whole is that some of the paths are still paved with pieces of the old millstones. The writer is greatly indebted to Dr. and Mrs. Watkins, of The Mill House, for their courtesy in showing him the site of the mill and providing some of the information given above.

Miss McIntosh has kindly drawn the writer's attention to the fact that there is a strong local tradition concerning a second and presumably older mill at Hoath. This is said to have stood somewhere opposite the house named 'Millbank House' to the north of the village on the road from Sturry to Reculver. If there was a mill here – and certainly the name 'Millbank' appears on the current O.S. map – it is not shown on any of the old maps of Kent, nor as a place name on the 1769 map of Andrews, Dury and Herbert, which gives instead the name 'Hoathborow'. However, in a copse behind the house numbered 2, which is nearly opposite 'Millbank House', the ground rises steeply on two sides and the highest point may well represent the site of a former windmill. The situation is at TR. 203653.

So far as is known, there has never been a watermill in either Herne or Hoath parish.

HERNE MILL

Apart from where acknowledgement has been made in the text, the information in this account has been taken from the following sources:

M. I. Batten, *English Windmills,* Vol. I, 1930.

W. Coles Finch, *Watermills and Windmills,* 1933 (reprinted 1976).

Rex Wailes, *The English Windmill,* 1954.

Rex Wailes and John Russell, Windmills in Kent, in *Transactions of the Newcomen Society,* Vol. XXIX, 1953-54 and 1954-55.

John Reynolds, *Windmills and Watermills,* 1970.

Jenny West, *The Windmills of Kent,* 1973 (revised edition 1979).

Suzanne Beedell, *Windmills,* 1975.

B. J. and J. M. Turpin, *Windmills in Kent,* 1979.

Newsletters of the East Kent Mills Group (various).

H. E. S. Simmons Collection, Science Museum.

Various Kent Directories.

Herne Bay Public Library.

Personal observations and recollections of old residents, including valuable information from (indirectly) Mr. Harold Gough of Herne Bay.

HERNE AS SEEN BY...
Travellers' and Diarists' Accounts
by
Jonathan C. Clark, B.A.

The accounts left to us by travellers and diarists provide an interesting and important source to the local historian, for they yield a contemporary description of the areas through which their writers journeyed, recording what they saw and heard. The accounts show each writer's particular likes and dislikes and provide us with a personal view of a town, village, road, or coastline as it appeared to them. Travellers and diarists often only briefly passed through places while touring or when they were en route to a specific destination, remaining but a few days, hours, or moments to absorb the sights and scenery that surrounded them. It is not surprising, then, that their records often contain what appear to be merely first impressions of a town or village. Celia Fiennes (1662-1741), describing the town of Deal, wrote that it 'looks like a good thrieving place the buildings new and neate brickwork with gardens', whilst she described its neighbour, Sandwich, as 'a sad old town all timber building... its just like to drop down the whole town'. When travellers found situations which were of special interest to them they recorded them in great detail. William Cobbett (1763-1835), travelling on the road from Margate to Canterbury, noted that at 'MONCKTON they had seventeen men working on the roads, though the harvest was not quite in'. These men, who were claiming Poor Relief because of being unemployed, had been set to work on the parish's roads. This was customary, but Cobbett saw them at an unusual time of year for there to be unemployment: it was during the harvest which was normally the time of peak employment. Cobbett observes that the probable cause of the unemployment was connected with the use of 'four threshing machines' which reduced the demand for labour and created 'a shocking state of things'. Further along this road he passed through 'the village of UP-STREET, and another village called STEADY', which is more commonly known as Sturry. This shows that travellers' accounts may contain discrepancies and thus need to be used in conjunction with other histories and sources and not solely on their own – for travellers, because of the briefness of their visits, were not always able to obtain totally accurate information. Nevertheless, their descriptions are of value as a source of information because they often provide a unique insight into contemporary life. On the whole, most of the more famous travellers did not venture as far as Herne, but there are some notable exceptions.

The first of these, and the one who refers most directly to Herne, is John Leland (1503-1552) whose Itinerary was written between the years *c.* 1535 – *c.* 1543. His travels were not for pleasure but were a 'Laboriouse Journey and Serche... FOR ENGLANDES ANTIQUITEES' under a commission from King Henry VIII to diligently search through the monasteries and colleges of England to find 'monumentes of auncient writers as welle of other nations' and to bring them out into the 'lyvely lighte'. His work was an unprecedented record of contemporary England through the eyes of one of her subjects and acts as a foundation to all later topographical works. Unlike some writers, we can be sure that Leland made visits to all the places he described. There is, however, one problem with his Itinerary: it is not structured in an orderly way and thus the references to Herne appear in a number of scattered places.

Leland refers to Herne as 'Heron' and meticulously records its position relative to other places, although the distances he gives were only personal estimates and thus are often wrong. Leland gives Herne's position in relation to Canterbury, the important City and ecclesiastical centre, as four miles, and in another place writes that 'Canterbury ys v myles fro the se flat north agaynst Heron', which one must assume to be referring to the area of the coast now known as Herne Bay. He also gives Herne's position along the coastline, in relation to Whitstable, as 'iii. myles fro thens', and Reculver was noted as being ' ii . myles and more be water, and a mile dim. by land, beyownd Heron'. Of Herne, he writes that 'Yt stondeth dim. a myle fro the mayne shore'; that is, only half a mile, which even after coastal erosion since is nothing like true today. Leland also writes that 'From Heron that standith sumwhat pointing ynto the seward a sinus is to Reculver ward'. This probably refers to the point of land where Herne Bay Clock Tower now stands and the 'sinus' or bay stretching towards Reculver, as it still does.

As well as its position, Leland finds three things of note concerning Herne: The first is that 'Heron is a chapel to Reculver'. Reculver was once the site of a great Abbey, but by the time Leland visited it he found that the 'towne at this tyme is but village lyke' for the Abbey was no more. The church at Reculver was 'the mother church' of three chapels which were those of Herne, Hoath, and St. Nicholas in Thanet, although after 1310 when Herne received its own vicar instead of being served by the monks of Reculver, the link between the two churches was greatly reduced.

The second item of note is that Herne was 'wher men take good muscles cawled Stake Muscles'. Shellfish and oyster-catching were commonplace along this coast and this is shown by Lambarde in 1570, who refers to oyster-catching at Reculver and Whitstable: 'The Oisters that be dredged at Reculver are reputed as farre to passe those at Whitstaple, as those of Whitstaple doe surmount the rest of this shyre, in savorie saltnesse', whilst Camden in 1586 describes 'an open shore abounding with shell fish and oysters and plenty of oyster-pits' between Faversham and Reculver. Leland continues by stating that 'ther is good pitching of nettes for mullettes', a type of fish; the bay was a convenient and conducive site for a fishery which was significant enough in 1774 to be referred to by Jacob as 'The fishery of Hearn' in his history of Faversham. The fisherman lived near or on the coast in groups of huts, one of their settlements in the nineteenth century becoming the site of the town of Herne Bay.

Leland's third and most notable comment about Herne concerns Sir John 'Finiox chief Juge of the Kinge's Bench', who lived from *c.* 1441 – 1525, 'his principle seat being at Herne'. He was the son of William Fyneux of Swingfield, Kent, and was said 'to have begun the study of law at the age of twenty-eight, to have practised at the bar for twenty-eight years, and to have sat on the bench for the same period'. Leland writes of him: 'The Juge buildid a fairer house by Heron on purchasyd ground' and he 'builded his faire house on purchasid ground, for the commodite of preserving his helth. So that afore the phisisians concludid that it was an exceding helthfulle quarter'. Fyneux purchased the manor of Hawe in the parish of Herne and rebuilt the manor house which Buchanan in 1887 described as one of the most remarkable places of note in the parish. The manor house stood where Hawe Farm is now situated, and one can still observe the remains of the moat which surrounded it as well as fragments of the building itself. Fyneux came to Herne because of its healthy location on the advice of his doctors, as did the many people who visited, convalesced, or retired to the popular watering-place of Herne Bay in later centuries. The Fyneux family is commemorated in Herne Parish Church by a brass to Lady Fyneux who died in 1539.

The journalist and author Daniel Defoe (*c.* 1660-1731), on his tour through Kent in the early years of the eighteenth century, does not directly mention Herne but states that 'The shore from Whitstable... affords nothing remarkable but sea-marks, and small towns on the coast, till we come to Margate'. Herne was probably one of these 'small towns' which were not described further, making it seem that Defoe found nothing of note there. Alternatively, he possibly did not venture far enough inland to come across the village of Herne, or perhaps he was making a generalised statement about a stretch of the coast in which he was not particularly interested apart from its 'sea-marks'[1] whose mention reflects his maritime interest. His main interests were trade, industry, communications, naval matters, society life, and modern developments. These would obviously influence his perception of the places he visited and the ways he portrayed them. Herne, an old village with a long history, would contain very little of interest to him. Herne was off the beaten track, especially after the decline in the importance of Reculver which had already set in by the time of Leland, and thus would probably not have been featured in a traveller's itinerary. This would – and did – result in there being a dearth of travellers visiting Herne and thus of their accounts.

The hamlet of Herne Bay in the parish of Herne, which in later years became a popular watering place, was visited by L. Fussell in *c.* 1818 while on 'A SUMMER EXCURSION' around the coast of Kent. He later published a compilation of his 'ORIGINAL NOTES MADE DURING' his tour. The book was designed 'especially for the benefit of the juvenile traveller, to whom an excursion may be rendered a source of improvement as well as of pleasure and amusement'. It was meant to be an interesting and educative guidebook to the complete coast of Kent, which is why Fussell states that 'The traveller who desires completely to explore the Kentish coast, will deviate from the usual road from Canterbury to Margate, and proceed in a northern direction to Whitstaple', and thence on to Herne Bay which would otherwise have been missed. Fussell describes 'the village of that name' (Herne Bay) as being 'situated upon a point of land which juts out abruptly from the line of the coast'. This point is the one mentioned by Leland, but there were only a few cottages there at the time of Fussell's writing, whilst the main area of Herne Bay 'village' was to be found in the bay on the Reculver side centred upon the Ship Inn.

It is uncertain whether Fussell, when stating 'the village... consists only of a few cottages irregularly built round a green', is referring to the point or the area around the Ship Inn, but the rest of his description seems to apply to the latter. He writes that it had seen 'a considerable increase in buildings and improvements' and that 'An hotel was erected, which, if not elegant, was capable of affording lodging to those who could not obtain a closet or cupboard in the little habitations contiguous'. Here he is probably referring to the Ship Inn, which was not new but was at the time the only hotel in the bay and had recently been extended with the addition of an Assembly Room. Fussell also points out that 'Houses of various sizes and descriptions, and hot and cold baths, were constructed'. Other writers of around the time also point this out; one in 1822 noted 'several good houses having been of late years erected, and commodious warm and cold Baths prepared for the accommodation and recreation of the visitors', and another in 1825 that 'A few years ago, some gentlemen of Canterbury commenced building at Herne Bay:.... only a few

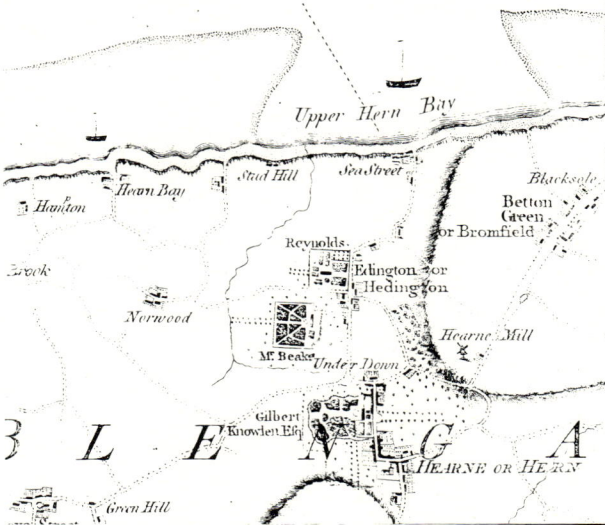

This map of 1769 shows Herne Bay's position on the coast

J. Andrews, A. Dury, W. Herbert, **A TOPOGRAPHICAL-MAP,** *of the County of Kent,* **(1769), 9.**

houses were then built, and those without any regard to taste'. The latter thus reveals the originators of the development Fussell saw as 'gentlemen of Canterbury', who recognised, as Fussell notes, that the bay was 'beginning to rise into some degree of celebrity, by having lately become the resort of company for the purpose of bathing'. Cromwell, in 1822, writes of the bay that it was 'a bathing-place to which great numbers of the inhabitants of Canterbury and its neighbourhood resort, and also many families from the metropolis and other parts of the kingdom'; and Ireland, in 1828, notes that 'As most of the fishing hamlets on our coast have, within the last thirty years, assumed the more commanding aspects of watering-places, it is not to be wondered at that Herne Bay should be resorted to by the inhabitants of Canterbury'. Fussell writes that the visitors were attracted because of the 'charms of novelty' and a 'degree of tranquility unknown to Margate in the bathing season'. Fussell visited Herne Bay at an early stage in its transformation from a fishing hamlet to the popular seaside town which was soon to dwarf its mother village of Herne.

Herne Parish Church was described in 1825 as 'one of the most striking objects we have ever noticed', and it is with this church that John Ruskin (1819-1900) is linked. Ruskin, the author, artist, social reformer, critic, traveller and diarist, is said to have commented upon the tower of St. Martin's Church, Herne, but unlike other travellers and diarists who have left us written accounts of their visits, there is no known personal record of Ruskin actually making any comment about Herne Church, or even visiting the village. Even so it is one of Herne's most often-quoted claims to fame, appearing frequently in books during the first half of this century, and passed on by word of mouth to visitors and newcomers to the present day.

To examine what Ruskin is reputed to have said, we must look to the written accounts. In 1951 R. Fitter wrote that in Herne "village there is an interesting church with good brasses and Ruskin's 'perfect tower'". The exact nature of Ruskin's supposed statement varies within the literature. The Ward, Lock Guide of 1947 stated that the tower was said by Ruskin to be 'one of the few perfect' things in the world, whilst Arthur Mee had written in 1936 that 'The architectural gem of Herne is its flint tower – one of the very few perfect things in the world, said John Ruskin'. One would think that this was a definite enough statement, but the most often-quoted is that Ruskin described the tower as 'one of the three perfect things in the world'. This appears in the books of R. Wyndham in 1940, S.P.B. Mais in 1948 and R. Jessup in 1951, as well as in various guides to the church. The earliest of these, *The Story of Herne Church,* was published some time after 1905 during the incumbency of the Rev. Giles Daubeney, who was probably the author, although in his book of 1950, *Reminiscences of a Country Parson,* he makes no reference to John Ruskin. There is no record of the quotation before 1905, but there are two earlier references to Ruskin. One was made in 1892 in an explanatory sheet to the church entitled *A few facts about Herne Church, Kent,* which describes the tower as being 'admired by Ruskin'. The earliest known reference was published in a book probably by James Buchanan, the then Vicar of Herne, in *c.* 1889, entitled *Account of Herne Church Restoration,* which stated that 'One of the most imposing features of Herne Church is its massive Tower of stone and faced flint – the oldest part now remaining – upon which Mr. Ruskin said he could gaze for hours with delight'. This is the earliest known mention of Ruskin in connection with Herne Church, and it is of importance to note that

Buchanan did not refer to Ruskin in his book *Memorials of Herne, Kent,* published in 1887, only two years previous to the restoration account. ONE must assume that he had not heard the claim when he wrote in 1887 but had by 1889; otherwise why would he have felt it worth including it in 1889 and not in 1887, when both books had the same aim of raising money for the restoration of the church? The probable reason for Buchanan including it in 1889 was to reveal what so famous a person as Ruskin had thought about the church and thereby to increase the funds raised for the restoration. But this was nothing new, for he had quoted the comments Brandon and the then Registrar General amongst others had made about Herne in his first volume.

His efforts succeeded in the raising of £6,000 for the church's repair whilst vicar. He had also succeeded in initiating the mystery surrounding the claim of John Ruskin's comment about Herne Church, by not recording a source for the quotation he gave. Either he had personally heard Ruskin make the comment or knew someone who had or who had been told about it, or he found it recorded in one of Ruskin's published or unpublished works. The quotation could otherwise have been a mistake. The first alternative is impossible to completely prove or disprove for one can never be totally sure about what has happened in the past, but there are ways in which one can determine which is the most likely. One suggestion has been that Ruskin may have come to see Dante Rossetti, who was convalescing at Hunters Forstal in 1877, and in so doing visited Herne; but there is no record by either Ruskin or Rossetti of this ever having happened. This makes the visit very unlikely, especially as Ruskin was an ardent diarist and has left an almost complete record of his travels of England and abroad in diary form. Indeed, Herne is not mentioned in his

THE CHURCH OF ST. PAUL, HERNE HILL

101

diaries, and if he had visited Herne and commented in such a way about the tower, one would expect him at the very least to write something about his visit. In Ruskin's many volumes of works, there is not one mention of Herne – let alone the church tower – and thus one has to conclude that the possibility of his having visited Herne is very unlikely. Ruskin grew up and lived for many years in the area of Herne Hill near Camberwell in South London, and there is a distinct possibility that Buchanan had heard of a comment of Ruskin's about the church at Herne Hill in which, as is recorded in his collected works, Ruskin 'was much interested', and misunderstood it to be directed to the church at Herne.

In a lecture on Venetian architecture given in 1859, Ruskin said that the rebuilt church of St. Paul, Herne Hill 'in his own immediate neighbourhood' was 'beautiful in all respects, was remarkable for a piece of colouring admirably introduced; and he doubted if it could be excelled by any of the colours in ancient art'. Thus Ruskin admired the architecture of the church at Herne Hill, and praised its architect, the famous George Street, for its design. The lecture of 1859 had been given jointly by Ruskin and Street; with Street showing pictures of Venetian architecture. One might ask if this is so, how did Buchanan learn of Ruskin's comments about Herne Hill Church so that he was able to confuse the two places? If we refer back to Buchanan's book *Memorials of Herne, Kent* 1887, we find a reference to 'the late Mr. Street' and references to one of his papers. This shows that Buchanan was acquainted with Street's work and may between 1887-9 have come across a copy of the transcript of the lecture given in 1859, which had been published by the *Builder* magazine. Thereby he would have learned of Ruskin's comments, and taking them to be about Herne Church included them in his work of 1889. Alternatively, Buchanan may have heard the comment from a third party who knew of the lecture, and had mistakenly connected what Ruskin had said with Herne and not Herne Hill. This may explain the discrepancies between Buchanan's 'quotation' and what Ruskin is recorded to have said in the transcript of the lecture, although the transcript is not, and cannot claim to be, an accurate record of exactly what was said; and thus Ruskin may actually have made the comment about Herne Hill Church without its being recorded. The modification of Buchanan's 'quotation' over the past century is probably due to its being passed on by word of mouth and thus constantly rephrased. An example of this is that I was told recently that Ruskin claimed Herne Church to be 'the eighth wonder of the world'. Therefore it seems unlikely that John Ruskin ever visited Herne, although if we accept S.P.B. Mais' description of the 'Ruskin comment' we have to look for a William Ruskin to find its author.

In this article I have discussed a few of the known travellers who have journeyed near or through the village of Herne in the past, but there must surely be many more accounts from the nineteenth and twentieth centuries, with their phenomenal growth in transport and communications, which were made by people travelling through this beautiful part of East Kent whilst on holiday. These are yet to be discovered and, in Leland's words, to be brought from darkness into the 'lyvely lighte'.

FOOTNOTE

(1) These seamarks may have been defining the boundaries of the local fisheries. The Faversham Fishery grounds, a few miles westwards along the coast, had their boundaries marked by seamarks and buoys. This is recorded by E. Jacob (1774), 87.

In Chronological Order of Writing:

Ed: L. Toulmin Smith, *The Itinerary of John Leland In or About the Years 1535-1543* (1964, I, xxxvii-xxxviii; IV, 43-4, 46, 53, 59, 69.

W. Lambarde, *A Perambulation of Kent* (1570), 234.

Ed: G. J. Copley, *Camden's Britannia Kent* (1977), 36.

Ed: C. Morris, *The Journeys of Celia Fiennes* (1947), 128-9.

D. Defoe, *A Tour through England and Wales* (1927), I, 119.

E. Jacob, *The History of the Town and Port of Faversham* (1774), 87-8.

E. Hasted, *The History and Topographical Survey of the County of Kent* (2nd Ed., 1800), IX, 92.

L. Fussell, *A Journey Round the Coast of Kent* (1818), Title page 1, 71-72.

T. K. Cromwell, *Excursions in the County of Kent* (1822), 90-1.

The Mirror of Literature, Amusement and Instruction, CLVIII, (3 September 1825), 167b-168a.

W. H. Ireland, *England's Topographer, or A New and Complete History of the County of Kent* (1828), I, 409-11.

Ed: G. Woodcock, *William Cobbett Rural Rides* (1967), 206-7.

A Picture of the New Town of Herne Bay (1835), 1-3, 16.

The Builder, 26 February and 5 March 1859.

J. Buchanan, *Memorials of Herne,* Kent (1887), 9, 27.

J. Buchanan, *Account of Herne Church Restoration* (c.1889), 1.

A Few Facts about Herne Church, Kent (1892).

The Story of Herne Church (n.d.).

Ed: E. Cook & A. Wedderburn, *The Works of John Ruskin* (1908), XVI, 462-3, XXXV, xlix.

Ed: L. Stephen & S. Lee, *The Dictionary of National Biography* (1917), VII, 782.

A. Mee, *Kent* (1936), 234.

R. Wyndham, *South-Eastern Survey* (1940), 105.

Ward, Lock, *A Pictorial and Descriptive Guide to Herne Bay.*

St. Martin's Church Herne, Kent (n.d.)

St. Martin's Church Herne, Kent (1947).

S. P. B. Mais, *London's Countryside* (2nd Ed., 1948), 56, 136.

G. Daubeney, *Reminiscences of a Country Parson* (1950).

R. Fitter, *Home Counties* (1951), 63.

Ed: R. Jessup, *South-East England* (1951), 107.

The Herne Bay Press, 31 December 1965, 12 January 1979, 26 January 1979.

H. E. Gough, *The Ancient Church of St. Martin in Herne* (n.d.)

H. E. Gough, *A Picture Book of Old Herne Bay* (1983).

WILLIAM WATMER, A Notary of Canterbury

A mss. history of William Watmer, twice Mayor in early Stuart times, has been deposited by its author, Geoffrey Whatmore, in the local history collection in the Canterbury Public Library. It fell to Watmer to negotiate the city's new Charter from James I and later to preside at a time of serious friction over Canterbury's Walloon and Flemish immigrants. He built a house at Sturry – to be known by Hasted as Whatmer's Hall – and acquired property at Westbere.

HERNE – THE HOUSES OF THE PARISH

by

Kenneth Gravett, M.Sc. (Eng.), F.S.A., C.Eng.

At first glance Herne looks different from the other neighbouring parishes, but there is still the same basic settlement pattern with older houses distributed throughout, even submerged in modern Herne Bay, but with in addition what appears to be a nucleated village, grouped around the church. As with so many places in Kent, it is really a small town, with a market founded by Archbishop Islip in 1351, and a fair.[1] It contains a number of houses of interest, mostly of small scale (and two storeys and attics).

At the north end of Herne Street, on the east side and projecting into the road, are Smugglers' Cottages, now a block of four. No.'s 1 and 2 are timber-framed, with a continuous jetty (and a likely date in the second half of the sixteenth century), while No.'s 3 and 4 have a brick front of about 1700. Around the corner in School Lane is a series of old houses on the north side. Myrtle Cottages (3 and 5) are a pair of eighteenth century red-brick cottages. No.'s 7 and 9 are later in the same century and are brown brick. No.'s 13 and 15 are very interesting in that they were apparently built as a single house, with a cellar, a brick ground floor and timber-framed and tile-hung first floor, probably in 1738, the date on several bricks in the front. The roof is wholly in pine and consists of collar and rafters, with lap dovetail joints. The main girders, floor boards and the division between the two rooms upstairs are also in pine. Later, about 1790, the first floor was rebuilt in brick with a dog-toothed cornice, and the house split into a mirror-image pair with similar front doors. The projection to the front at the east end dates from about 1890. No. 21 has an oak frame and is weather-boarded, but has many details of good quality, a front door with folded panels and an open-string staircase with round balusters, the corner ones being in the form of doric columns. It was built soon after 1800 and No. 23 was added to it about 1840.

Returning to Herne Street, there is a long group of houses on the east side of the market place and turning up a short alleyway to the east. Most are nineteenth century but the group contains some surprises. Behind their pebbledash, Colonial Cottage and Sunnyside may well be eighteenth century. Horninglow Cottage is timber-framed, but re-faced in the eighteenth century. It retains its sixteenth century front door of about 1580 and a very fine eighteenth century open cupboard. Street House was built at the very beginning of the eighteenth century, probably 1706, with two rooms on each floor on either side of a central hall. Thomas Lindredge of Beltinge, a bricklayer, probably built the buff-brick front before he sold it in 1816, and also put in the sash windows, without horns, which contain much of their original glass. He probably used the cellar as a kitchen. Forge Cottage and Street Cottage are both weather-boarded and set back-to-back. They must date from just after 1800. Chapel Cottage was built at the end of the eighteenth century with a central chimney stack, with an oven to the rear and a lobby entry in front. The roof is of coupled rafters and collars only, all pit-sawn. An extra chimney was added in the early nineteenth century and later the house was divided into two cottages.

On the other side of the street, St. Christophers (No. 22) was built about 1730 of red brick with two rooms on each floor, either side of a central staircase, and a cellar. On the ground floor, the front door originally opened into the kitchen/living room with a chimney on the north end. This has spit machine marks on the higher lintel, and a small window behind the chimney looks out on to the path outside. The staircase was originally within this room. The south room was the parlour, with a chimney stack to the rear and a fireplace with a curved back. The roof is of pine, has five bays and butt side-purlins arranged to be highest in the central bay and descending on each side. At the end of the eighteenth century, the staircase was improved with a pine rail; a corner cupboard was added to the parlour, and front door provided with a very elegant, tall doorcase with Grecian details. Late in the nineteenth century the staircase hall was divided off – hence the Victorian glass panels in the front door. There was a wheelwright's shop beyond and a repair to a partition in the cellar incorporates the shaft of a cart. The central girder is re-used, part of the wall plate of a medieval or Tudor house, showing a series of mortices for an unglazed window.

North of the church, the Post Office, Stone House and Ivy House may well be eighteenth century, while Ridley cottage incorporates some timber-framing, perhaps seventeenth century. The Windmill at Herne dates from 1781, and the Mill House (88 Mill Lane) must be similar in date.

The great palace of the Archbishops at Ford has been discussed already,[2] but at Hawe Farm are very fragmentary remains of another brick house which must have been nearly as magnificent. This was the house of Sir John Fyneux, Chief Justice of the King's Bench in the reigns of Henry VII and Henry,[3] who rebuilt the house. There is some diaper pattern in the brickwork, but the house has since been virtually rebuilt. The large, aisled barn is of eighteenth century date. It must be much later than the Fyneux house, as it is probably covering the

COLEWOOD FARMHOUSE

outer court. It appears that there was a lane between Hawe and Ford, now partially the line of a footpath. Ford Palace itself was in Hoath parish, but the road is the boundary. The house opposite the gateway to the palace is now called The Manor House, and it is interesting that its older part lies along the lane to Hawe. Also in this lane are Park Cottages, originally one house. The east end has been demolished and the walls appear eighteenth century, but the chimney is clearly earlier. To return to The Manor House, the section along the lane has through side purlins in the roof and could well date from the first half of the seventeenth century. The main block has patches of old brickwork in the front, but the roof has butt purlins arranged at alternate heights in alternate bays and was built in the second half of the seventeenth century, perhaps after the Palace was pulled down and incorporating some of the materials. The bay to the south is different in that it is higher and has a front with pilasters of rubbed brick and a cornice and windows with rubbed brick voussoirs and a keystone effect, and forms an addition of about 1700. There was a fine brick barn to the north of the house.

There are several farmhouses throughout the parish which were faced with red brick in the seventeenth or eighteenth century but are basically timber-framed. The original Colewood Farmhouse corresponded to the part of the house with the hipped roof. It had a crown-post roof and may well have had an end jetty. A piece of moulded screed beam points to a date about 1500. The roof has been much altered, but it is likely that there was an open hall, soon converted to a smoke bay, although it might have been built with a smoke bay from the beginning. Some time about 1600 a chimney was inserted. This had spit-machine marks on the lintel, a good dry cupboard and a niche showing where the oven was. At the end of the seventeenth century, the front wall was rebuilt in brick and the front doorway moved to form a lobby entrance. There are additions of about 1800 to form a dairy and a kitchen, with some good cast-iron windows. Studds Farm was probably a four-bay, timber-framed house with a central open hall, similarly encased in brick. Behind the 1920's pebbledash, Greenhill Farm has brick walls, which also hide a timber frame and a hipped roof, but this was rebuilt in the eighteenth century with butt-purlins in line. Some smoke-blackened rafters re-used in a scullery added at this time show that the original roof had crown posts and either an open hall or smoke bay. Arrangements around the present brick, seventeenth century stack make the latter more likely giving a sixteenth century date for the house. The brick stack is large and has remains of a bacon-smoking chamber. There is a good brick stable of c.1830 with a slate roof.

The finest brickwork is at Underdown House at Eddington. This contains re-used timber from a timber-framed house, but was built in brick in the second half of the seventeenth century in English bond with casement windows. It is L-shaped, with a kitchen to the rear, and a chimney with spit-machine marks. Some time about 1780 a great deal of work was done to raise the status of the house. The new brick front in Flemish bond, with moulded brick cornice, parapet and string course and rubbed brick voussoirs was added and provided with sash windows and a doorcase with fanlight and pediment, fluted doric pilasters and a frieze with triglyphs. The underside of the pediment has a greek key ornament. The opportunity was taken to excavate a cellar and re-roof the whole building in softwood. In the grounds is a fine barn of five bays. The roof has through side purlins and collars and was built for thatch. The main posts have long straight gunstocks.

Not far away in Canterbury Road, No. 203, The Priory shows that within fifty years fashion had completely changed, and the brown brick front, also with parapet, has windows with pointed heads within a square frame, giving the effect of Gothic. It has recently been re-named, The Baskerville.

Broomfield still retains the air of a detached hamlet. The Huntsman and Horn public house dates from after 1800, while Pond Cottages date from the end of the eighteenth century. The original section of Parsonage Farm was built as a prosperous farmhouse about 1650, as a square block of two storeys with attics built around a chimney with four flues. The roof has butt side-purlins, arranged at alternate levels in alternate bays. A fine original door is re-used in the attic. In the early eighteenth century a new kitchen was added and there was a large new wing of the 1880's. There is a large aisled barn of eight bays (and two end bays) and two midstreys. The roof has queen struts and butt purlins, similar to those in the house, and it must be the barn built with the house about 1650. Goldfinch Farm is built of brick and is of two storeys and attics, with a single-storey-and-attic kitchen extension to the rear, this attic being used for farm hands to sleep in. The same dentil course at the top of the walls of both sections, shows that they were built together at the end of the eighteenth century, perhaps in 1787, one of the dates scratched on bricks by the front door, where there is also a fine reconstructed nineteenth century pump.

In Thornden Wood Road, The Share and Coulter public house must date from about 1800. Tinker's Thatch is very interesting in that it contains fragments of an earlier house, including two fine doors of c.1600, with tongued-and-grooved vertical panelling. The present house is also timber-framed. The type of bracing and the principal uprights without jowls point to a date in the second half of the seventeenth century and perhaps later. It was apparently thatched

THE HUNTSMAN AND HORN, BROOMFIELD

from the beginning. The front door opened directly into the kitchen/living room, with a brick chimney (but perhaps a plaster chimney originally) and an unheated parlour. At Hicks Forstal Farm is a thatched barn, aisled and with side purlins, and, clearly built for thatch, it dates from the seventeenth century.

Within the built-up area of Herne Bay, No. 125 Grand Drive is a brick house with a main block of two storeys and two hipped-roof sections towards the road. It was clearly there long before Grand Drive was built, and the present front to the road was the original back. The main block has two rooms on each floor and a chimney at each end. The roof has butt side-purlins in alternate heights in alternate bays and the two hipped sections have a single principal rafter put in each side. They are clearly contemporary with the main roof and date from the second half of the seventeenth century. The house was restored about 1925, and at this time a number of extra timbers were introduced, notably some clearly redundant queen strutts in the roof.

An interesting fragment is the one-bay bakehouse with a large chimney and bake oven built into No. 37 Margate Road. This is part of an out-building and all that remains of the house of Dante Gabriel Rossetti; it dates from about 1800.

With so many isolated houses in the parish and so much that is submerged in modern housing, I am very conscious that there may be many houses in this parish which I might well have missed.

NOTES
1.   E. Hasted, *History of the County of Kent,* Second Edition (1800), Vol. 9, p.86.
2.   See paper by H. Gough above.
3.   Hasted *ibid,* p.87.

THE BLEAN BASTILLE: BLEAN POOR LAW UNION 1835-1846
The Work of a University of Kent Adult Class
under the guidance of
Dr. H. C. F. Lansberry M.A.

In 1617, Sir William Sedley in his will instructed his executors to purchase an annuity of £3.6s.8d. for the use of the poor of Herne; instead of carrying out these wishes to the letter, one of the executors, Sir John Sedley, joined in a conveyance for the purchase of land for the use of the poor. He contributed £55, and Robert Knowler and other parishioners put up another £9, from another charitable bequest, to acquire from John Welby nearly ten acres of land in the adjacent part of Chislet parish, the profits of which were to be bestowed on the poor of the parish of Herne by the trustees. By 1791 this land was let at £10 a year.

An Act of 1722-23 gave parish overseers power to rent premises for workhouses, and to lodge, maintain and employ the poor. The Window Tax returns of the 1730's show that a house in the Borough of Hampton belonging to Richard Fuller, taxed on 9 windows, was occupied as the Poor House, or Workhouse. The Borough occupied most of the area of the present Town Centre of Herne Bay, and it is not possible to identify the site of this early poorhouse more closely. Later references to this or other poorhouses have not been found.

108

Gilbert's Act of 1781-82 allowed parishes to combine themselves into Unions for the purpose of building a Workhouse to contain their poor, and in 1791 the Vicar of Herne and certain parishioners purchased for £20 a small piece of land beside the road leading out of the village towards Canterbury, to build a house for the poor, out of a lump sum of £240 obtained from Thomas Reynolds for a 102-year lease of the land in Chislet at £2.2s.0d. per annum. It seems that the income from this land had been paid hitherto into the Churchwardens' or the Overseers' accounts, and not devoted to the use of the poor, and the latter had thus been deprived of the benefit of Sedley's will – a fact which seems to have escaped the Vicar, as did the fact that the commutation of the annual rent for a lump sum had now removed the source of that income.

When the new poorhouse was built at a cost of £772.1s.7½d. and in use, the parish officers advertised in April 1794: 'A house having been lately built for the reception of the Poor of the parish of Herne, which is found by experience to be very useful and convenient for the intended purpose, and can take in any number of poor from twenty to forty more than their own, any parish not having a convenient house for their poor may have them taken in by applying to the churchwardens or overseers of the Parish'. Thus, while not actually creating a Gilbert Act Union, Herne was bowing towards the spirit of that Act by offering hospitality to the poor of other parishes.

In this case the site of the poorhouse is known, just on the Canterbury side of the village of Herne; nothing is known about its appearance or the accommodation it offered.

Following the Napoleonic War, and consequent on the rapid growth of 19th century population, a Commission of Inquiry into the Poor Law led to an Act of Parliament in 1834, formally setting up Unions of parishes and Boards of Guardians representing those parishes, under the central control of Poor Law Commissioners. Fifteen parishes joined to form the Blean Union, by an Instrument dated 19 October, 1835.

The new Guardians decided to build a workhouse at a cost not to exceed £5,000 with a capability to house 500 people. The site chosen was on Herne Common, well south of the village, and the Archbishop of Canterbury, as Lord of the Manor, granted permission for the use of the required four acres, subject to a bond of indemnity in case actions involving rights of common were brought against him.

Sir Francis Bond Head, the Assistant Poor Law Commissioner for Kent, imposed on the Guardians his strict views on the design of a Workhouse. 'Build poor men's houses, but instead of having one long street, bend it into a quadrangle, which forms also a prison'. The Architect concerned tried to introduce improvements to the proposed plans approved by Head, to provide some shelter for exposed areas, for example, but the Commissioner over-ruled him.

Tenders for the building ranged from £4,949 to £6,000 offered by seven builders; the lowest tenderer, a local man, later withdrew. The next offer, of £5,300 by Sherwood of Lambeth, was accepted only on condition that it was pruned to reduce it to the magic figure of £5,000.

One economy promptly insisted upon was the omission of outside drains – truly a false economy, since water soon attacked the foundations, which had to be underpinned with concrete and the walls rendered; the drains had to be restored belatedly to the plans, with a consequent inflation of the costs.

Sir Francis continued to cast his shadow over the work. He decided that as each men's dormitory was to hold eight beds, these must be two-tier bunks, or hammocks, to his own design, slung from iron rings in the ceiling in each corner of the room.

At the end of October 1835 the Workhouse was insured for £2,300, and bedding was ordered – 100 bedsteads, 100 pairs of blankets, 100 rugs for bed-covers, as well as sheeting and palliasses.

The appointed Master took possession on 1 November, although the building was not yet ready for occupation. Within a month the officious Sir Francis Head announced his own appointment – as Lieutenant Governor of Upper Canada – in an admonitory farewell letter to the Guardians.

'I earnestly advise you above all things most strictly to enforce all the orders of the Poor Law Commissioners and especially to adhere to the dietary which after a tedious trial you have at last unanimously agreed on. I strongly recommend you . . . to retain in your service no one whose character is not in every way irreproachable . . . . . a band of resolute sensible well-educated men faithfully devoted to your service.'

'I consider you now sufficiently armed to protect the Poor Rates of your County, to repel every species of attack upon them, to detect every case of imposition, to crush every attempt of intimidation, and force as soon as you shall deem it necessary all those who would indolently hang on to their Parishes for support to seek it by immigration into those Districts which are at this moment offering them but in vain high wages and constant employment. The sooner you resolutely stop all Outdoor Relief the sooner you will establish between the Pauper and Independent labourer a distinction which will eventually prove of considerable advantage to both.'

Head's inauspicious term as guiding hand over the Blean Union House was followed by a disastrous period of clumsy administration in his transatlantic Province.

Within a few weeks of the arrival of the first paupers in January 1836, the Union House and its controllers began to betray their stern weaknesses. The jerry-built wall dividing the men from the women blew down in a gale, just a week after the first admissions.

Thomas Spratt was committed to St. Augustine's Gaol for indulging in riotous conduct in the Workhouse, while a 9-year old girl was punished for a minor offence by being shut up all night in the mortuary with a corpse. A subsequent enquiry resulted in the dismissal of the Master and Matron. In 1837 Thomas Webb hanged himself from a ventilator after a brush with authority.

Another case of apparently unsympathetic treatment was that of John Moys, formerly a Fordwich bricklayer, who died in January 1841. He had become violent, cutting his hand on a broken window glass and smearing blood on the walls; he tore his clothes and kicked the walls. He was tied down, and dumped in an unheated room with another inmate to watch him, because he was noisy and violent. Here he died; the cause of death was recorded as 'spontaneous mortification'.

One of the economies incorporated in the design of the building was the omission of any windows in the external walls, as a security measure. In September 1841 the workhouse was described by a traveller from abroad as the 'windowless Herne Bastille . . . a receptacle for the outworn poor'. Only in July 1843 was a concession made, when one window was inserted in the outside walls of the old men's and women's dining halls.

Over the years – freed from Head's stern gaze – various improvements were introduced – water closets in the infirmaries, the conversion of the stables into additional wards, and the erection of fresh stables and a carriage house. In 1845 existing privies were replaced by water-closets, and a Fever Ward was added – above the stables. Water for the house was obtained from wells within the building complex; an additional deep well was sunk in 1860.

Later, with improving social attitudes towards the poor, facilities for nursing the sick were increased by the building of four general wards and two isolation wards in 1874, while trained nurses replaced the older system of leaving the sick to the care of other inmates.

The food provided for the inmates was at first of a spartan nature. The Commissioners had devised a range of six standard diets – the Guardians' choice was to be governed by the principle that the one selected was not to be as good as, or better than 'the ordinary mode of subsistence of the labouring classes of the neighbourhood'. Sir Francis Head had advised the Blean Guardians to adopt diet number 6.

It is by no means unknown for the sea at Herne Bay to freeze during a severe winter. The last occasion was in 1963 when the ice extended some three miles out from the shore. Some idea of the spectacle may be obtained from this photograph in which a boy with a long pole is supported by the ice several yards 'out to sea'. Herne Bay pier can be seen stretching across the horizon.

Photograph by P. Ransome-Wallis

A Dickensian glimpse is afforded by his suggestion of 'the substitution of gruel for the children's breakfast and suppers where it may be found inconvenient to provide milk'. Suet puddings and vegetables, or bread and cheese seem to have formed the greater part of the adults' main meals, with water to drink; the older paupers were allowed tea with milk for breakfast and supper. An average allowance for food was 2s.5d. per week, and seems to have provided about 1,000 calories for an able-bodied man.

Again, conditions, though still depressing, improved gradually over the years, and the Guardians seem to have become a reasonably enlightened body, apprenticing children, and ordering the lives of their parents in a responsible manner. The diet improved beyond the Poor Law Commissioners' strict limits, and the Union House gained the reputation of being 'as humane as possible in the circumstances'.

When workhouses and Boards of Guardians were abolished in 1930, the building was taken over by Kent County Council as a home for women, described as 'difficult', mainly epileptic or mentally retarded, with a few old men left to look after the gardens. By 1939 the place was almost self-supporting in vegetables and fruit, and pigs and rabbits were kept – the rabbit skins were sold for glove-making.

Throughout its history, the Union House had not been restricted to long-term inmates – tramps and travelling homeless had been admitted as 'casuals' for a night's lodging in return for a few hours work. There remained a 'casual ward' available down to 1948.

The coming of the National Health Service in 1948 turned the old building and its later additions into 'Herne Hospital' housing the chronically sick, and the whole place was modernised and upgraded with additional facilities for both patients and staff.

This is not the place to discuss the present state of the Hospital in detail, or to consider its future in the framework of the Health Service, except to contrast the present use of the basic building with its original grim function and stern philosophy.

FURTHER NOTES ON STURRY AND FORDWICH HOUSES
by
Kenneth Gravett, M.Sc. (Eng.), F.S.A., C.Eng.

When this series of books was commenced, only timber-framed houses were studied and it was only with Fordwich and Chislet and Westbere that later houses were included. This short note is a belated attempt to repair this omission and also to admit that some timber-framed houses were also missed.

The most important of these was The Swan Inn, Sturry. This is a timber-framed building, behind its present Victorian frontage. It was once a very fine house with a continuous jetty along the front and also a jetty at the south end, with a dragon beam across the corner. There was also a contemporary cross-wing at the north end. In the bar are remains of what must have been a very fine plaster ceiling with applied motifs which had been cast in moulds, and of these a fleur-de-lys, a Tudor rose and a lion-mask remain.

The main roof has side purlins, collars and queen strutts in two trusses, with the principal rafters reducing above the purlins to common rafters. There is no sign of smoke blackening, so there must have been a chimney, but this has since gone. All of this work points to a late Elizabethan date, perhaps about 1580. It was not necessarily built as an inn, but is more likely to have been the home of a prosperous farmer, or even a bailiff for the big house.

The Royal Oak is more of a puzzle, as it appears to contain a dragon beam and thus the present ceiling may well remain from a timber-framed house. However, the joists are not visible, the walls have clearly been rebuilt and they and the present roof, with its central valley, clearly date from after 1800.

The Old Vicarage is also timber-framed and of two storeys, but the central gable shows that it was once attached to a large wing in the west, probably demolished when it ceased to be the Vicarage in 1852. The timbers are all pit-sawn and the absence of jowls suggests a date in the middle to second half of the seventeenth century. The large chimney and oven at the south end are contemporary. The part remaining represents the kitchen and service rooms. The more important rooms were all demolished and the gap in the west wall filled with Victorian bricks.

Of similar or perhaps a little later date is the Cottage of St. John in Fordwich Road, but this is remarkably complete. It is of two bays with a kitchen/living room to the north and an unheated parlour. The original stairs remain in the corner by the stack. Upstairs there were two bedrooms. Later a small wing was added to the rear at the north end to form a scullery, bakehouse and kitchen when cooking was taken out of the living room. This is a most interesting survival of a basic cottage plan.

THE SWAN,
STURRY

Sturry also has a very good example of the very end of timber-framing, in numbers 5 & 6 Chapel Lane. These are a back-to-back weather-boarded pair, of two storeys and attics, with a chimney in the party wall, casement windows and doors with flat hoods or brackets. They probably date from the second quarter of the nineteenth century.

Hoades Court was a brick house, built around a central chimney, with a lobby by the front door and a kitchen/living room on one side and parlour on the other. It dates from the second half of the seventeenth century, but unfortunately it was bombed and the old brickwork in English bond, with a plinth, is only visible at the east end.

Oaklands Cottage was once a pair of cottages, each with a similar plan to the Cottage of St. John, but with an integral outshot and a brick front wall, although the rear wall, under the outshot, is timber-framed. The south-west cottage has a date stone of 1705, and by the stairs beside the chimney is a recess in the wall for a candle. The north-east cottage is probably slightly older: both are only 1½ storeys and have a tie beam interrupted for the doorway between the two upstairs rooms.

There are several good brick eighteenth century houses in the High Street and Mill Road. Both Bridge House and Mill House must date from about 1800, the former in red brick and the latter with a white brick front and two curved bay windows. Only a little later is the fine red brick farmhouse at Buckwell, with a wooden cornice along the front and brick cornice at the sides and south windows. Just over the parish boundary in Westbere, St. Anne's Convent was a house commenced in 1812 and the section nearest the road is of this date. The main block has a softwood roof with a ridge-piece and five rooms with reeded doorcases, with squares in the upper corners, each with a flower motif; and upstairs a marble fireplace with paterae. All this points to a date of 1830-1840.

Since writing on Fordwich houses it has been possible to study three of them further. It was possible to look in the roof at Oak Cottage. Behind the eighteenth-century front this was timber-framed, but the roof was clear with side purlins and collars only. The inglenook had been opened up and a lintel found with a four-cornered arch and hollow spandrils (and also showing the marks of a spit machine). All of this points to a date at the end of the sixteenth or beginning of the seventeenth century.

It has also been possible to see into the roof at Spring Cottage. Although I had thought that it might be a diminutive hall, the roof turned out to be completely clear and with side-purlins, collars and wind-braces, so it must have had two storeys from the beginning. The chimney was in nineteenth century brick, so I suspect that the original stack was in the centre of the back. It was probably built in the first half of the seventeenth century, with two rooms on each floor, but by about 1700 it was given a new front in brick. The bricking of the back was more piece-meal and it was greatly altered at the end of last century.

The most interesting discovery occurred at the Old Rectory. From the outside this looked like an eighteenth-century brick house with outshot at the back. The western bay contains a dragon beam, showing that the floor was once jettied to front and end, and that this was once the fire parlour wing of a timber-framed house of before 1500. The timber-framing is not visible in the centre section, which certainly occupies the site of the hall, but the service rooms have clearly been lost before the eighteenth century brickwork. There is a good, inserted chimney of c.1600.

VOTE FOR DERING?

by

David S. Cousins, B.A., D.M.A., A.L.A.

In the mid-19th Century Herne (including Herne Bay) and Hoath were included in the East Kent constituency which returned 2 members to the House of Commons. In February 1852 a by-election resulted in William Deedes (of Sandling Park, Hythe) being joined in Parliament by Sir Brook William Bridges, Bart. (of Goodnestone Park, Wingham). The defeated candidate was Sir Edward Cholmeley Dering, Bart. (of Surrenden Dering). Bridges only kept his seat until July, however, when Dering and Deedes were returned at a general election.

At the next general election in 1857 the two baronets were returned and Deedes lost the seat he had held since 1845. A local newspaper commented:

'The East Kent election has terminated in a manner little expected. There were three candidates from which to choose. They were all essentially of the same principles – Conservative; though there existed slight shades of difference among them. The old members were regarded as good conservatives, though of the two Sir Edward Dering was a little more inclining to Liberalism; but on the other hand Mr. Deedes claimed perfect independence, and generally gave his vote according to the convictions of the moment. Sir Brook Bridges is more of the ultra school. He is for no compromise of any kind.'[1]

The election result was declared at Barham Downs, but Herne voters only had to travel to Canterbury Cattle Market to vote. The voting was public and afterwards poll books were published showing how each elector had voted. These poll books still exist[2] and have been used by Michael Drake to investigate electoral behaviour at Ashford, which was also in the East Kent constituency.[3] Drake found that Deedes and the two baronets each received about the same proportions of the total Ashford vote in the general elections of 1852 and 1857. The pages of the poll books for Herne, however, tell a different story:

Candidates	Ashford 1852 votes	%	Ashford 1857 votes	%	Herne 1852 votes	%	Herne 1857 votes	%
Dering	70	48	80	50	48	36	8	11
Deedes	56	38	56	35	37	27	20	26
Bridges	20	14	24	15	50	37	48	63
Total	146	100	160	100	135	100	76	100

Although the 3 candidates received about the same percentage of the total Ashford vote in both elections Drake discovered that 'many of the electors who took part in both changed their voting pattern'. Indeed 'of the fifty voters who voted in one way or another for Dering in 1852, only twenty-eight voted for him in identically the same way in 1857'.[4]

Five of the eight 'Herne' electors who voted for Dering in 1857 had voted for him in July 1852. Three voted the same way in both elections: William Fryer, John Swinford and Jehu Taylor voted for Dering and Deedes. Alfred Trow, however, gave his other vote to Bridges in 1852, but to Deedes in 1857. William Watson voted for Dering alone in 1852 but also for Bridges in 1857.

Some of the 'Herne' electors lived miles away, but of the local residents whose names appear in both poll books 28 voted for Dering in 1852. Their votes went as follows:

1852	1857					
	DB	d	B	Bd	Dd	Ab
D 9	1	2	3	1		2
Dd 10			4		3	3
DB 9			2	4	1	2
28	1	2	9	5	4	7

D = Dering, d = Deedes, B = Bridges, Ab = Abstained

Dering himself was miles away during the 1857 election – he had gone abroad to recover his health. Before the end of the year he resigned his seat and Deedes was returned unopposed. Ten years later, however, Deedes was dead and the members for East Kent were again Bridges and Dering.[5]

FOOTNOTES

1. *'Kentish Gazette'* 7 April 1857, page 4.
2. Poll books for the East Kent general elections of 1852 and 1857 can be consulted in the local collection at Canterbury Public Library. See also Bergess, W. F. & Riddell, B. R. M. *Kent directories located'* Kent County Library, 1978 2nd. ed.
3. Drake, M. *'The Mid-Victorian voter'*, *'Journal of Interdisciplinary History'*. Vol. 1, No. 3 Spring 1971, pages 473-490.
4. *Op. cit.* page 486.
5. For further information about the candidates see *'Who's Who of British Members of Parliament'* Vol. 1, Harvester Press, 1976.

NINE CARD DON

by

Jack A. Baker

This card game, which I have played in Broad Oak since 1913, does not appear in the standard reference books of games. It is played with the usual pack of 52 playing cards by 4 people in partnerships of two. It is scored on a five-bedded peg board of 60 holes plus the winning hole.

A cut is made for deal, the highest card winning (Ace high). One of the opponents deals nine cards to each player. The winner of the deal declares trumps and leads this suit (usually the highest card). An Ace counts 4 points, a King 3, a Queen 2 and a Jack 1; in addition, the nine of trumps counts 9 points, the five of trumps 10 points and the fives of other suits 5 points. As a trick is made in the normal way the winners of the trick count all the points therein and mark the score on the peg board; the lead passes to the winner of the immediately previous trick.

At the end of each game the points in the tricks are counted (including tens which each count 10) and the pair of players holding the higher score is awarded 8 extra points. Play lasts until the first pair has played three times round the peg board and into the winning hole, i.e. has scored 181 points.

A photograph of a tournament of Nine Card Don, which is vaguely related to partner whist, appeared in 'The Kentish Observer' in 1967.

MORE DISSENTERS

by

Ian. B. Moat

According to the historian Trevelyan, Cromwell's England had left to the restored Kings an island of 'a hundred religions'. Another historian, A. G. Dickens, commenting on the Anabaptists says they 'may be placed among the pioneers of the liberalising process in western history' and of the Baptists, Quakers and other dissenters he says they might be regarded as a second English Reformation. Whatever view may be taken concerning the contribution of non-conformists since the seventeenth century, it must be recognised that they have made a considerable impact in the villages of this part of the world.

HERNE

If Bishop Ridley can be considered to be the first Herne man to display the spirit of religious non-conformity then there were many others willing to follow him – albeit without such severe suffering and also outside the established church. Despite the Conventicle Act of 1664 which allowed only *small* private meetings of non-conformists, on pain of heavy fines, imprisonment and even transportation, the 'excommunicate' Anabaptist George Houson held meetings in his house. During the year 1669 we are told that '40 or 50 from severall places: meane people' met together to hear 'Itinerant Teachers'. This compares with 80 or 100 Anabaptists who met at John Russell's home in Chislet. Whether these meetings included the same people is not known but the Anabaptists seem to have been numerically strong in the area. Further reference is made to them in the Compton Census returns in 1676 where George Houson and his wife are listed, together with three other Anabaptists, Jonas Epsly and his wife and Widow Singleton. Three Quakers, John Kempe and his wife and John Hutt, Senior, complete the list of dissenters. These Quakers could well have met up with the meetings started in Canterbury in 1661. Thomas Robinson and John Huntley were noted as 'neglectful'.

Whilst the Toleration Act of 1689 gave dissenters the right not to attend Church of England services and greater toleration was manifested, we still find that over one hundred years later, in fact until 1852, Dissenters' places of worship had to be certified and registered in the Bishops' Registry. Thus on 16 December 1791 a Meeting House certificate records the erection of a building to be used by Baptists, adjoining the house of Joseph Baldock. This house, owned by John Stupple, was in an area now called Blenheim Close, off Lower Herne Road. The wording of the certificate suggests a purpose-built structure. It was signed by six people, including Elizabeth Porter, (a number of dissenting movements allowed women in Church government and even to preach) and Copper Chapman, the Canterbury draper who signed a Sturry certificate three years before.

Another Baptist certificate was signed on 1 June 1811 at a meeting this time at the home of Sarah Greenstead. In 1811 she owned two properties in Herne, one was the shop part of the Smugglers Cottages and Rose Cottage, now demolished but standing at the junction of Herne Street and Albion Lane. The seven signatures include Thomas Spratt and James Andrews.

Just three years later, on 18 January, 1814 James Andrews' house was certified as a meeting place, but signed by a Methodist, Jonathan Bundock. He was a Stay and Corset maker and one of the original Trustees of St. Peter's Methodist Church, Canterbury. Jonathan Bundock signed another certificate dated 10 April, 1818 relating to a meeting in William King's house in Herne.

Thomas Spratt, like James Andrews, appears to have changed his affiliations, because his house in Herne is mentioned as an intended place of worship by Methodists, the Meeting House certificate being signed by the Canterbury Methodist minister John Newton, on 5 May, 1821. By this date many people were espousing the Methodist cause and all remaining certificates and chapel buildings in Herne reflect this.

A certificate dated 5 October, 1822 applies to Thomas Tappenden of Herne, a lime and brick maker who possibly lived in the Streetfield Estate area. It is signed by Thomas Hobday, who was a Trustee of St. Peter's Methodist Church, Canterbury, a local preacher and also a coal merchant and Deputy Registrar of the city of Canterbury. An 1807 Methodist Class register shows him in the Preachers' class and he was possibly related by marriage to James Parnell, the Independent minister and his Methodist wife Ann (nee Bissaker).

The aforementioned Jonathan Bundock signed the certificate dated 24 March, 1823 referring to 'a newly erected Chapel'. The chapel and building which can still be seen (somewhat altered) at the end of Chapel Row on the right was built on ground purchased from William and Sarah Greenstead with Thomas Tappenden as one of the principals of the indenture dated 9 May, 1822.

It was at this time that an open letter to the inhabitants of Herne was circulated. Dated 22 February, 1823 and signed 'A Churchman', the pseudonym of George May Esq. of Strode Park, it was an indignant response to a small book entitled 'An account of the Introduction of the Gospel at Herne Bay, in Kent'. In it the author describes how the Gospel was *first* introduced at Herne by *himself* in the Summer of 1822! (my italics) and that before this the village and surrounding area had been 'destitute of the Gospel'. George May complains that not only are they being invited to the Meeting House to hear the Gospel but that their preachers each week are of a different religious persuasion from the last. Their only common goal was in attacking the 'established religion' which George May goes on to defend rigorously, boasting that 'not one Dissenter . . . . is to be found amongst us'. Scriptural references back up his argument. Just as 45 years later in Sturry (see Chislet and Sturry p.111) it can hardly be said that love or tact prevailed on either side. The Methodists, however, had seceded from the Anglican Church in 1795 and to many clergymen nonconformity in general and Methodism in particular continued to represent an unwelcome threat to their hitherto monopoly in religion.

An 1866 Indenture concerning Trustees of the Methodist chapel mentions Jonathan Packer of Chislet, Miller; William Spratt of Herne, cainer; George Turle of Herne, grocer; John Hogbin of Herne Bay, cabinet maker and James Neeve of Hoath, farmer. This building, however, was obviously not big enough and a nearby site adjacent to the main road was utilised to build the present chapel. The Quarterly Circuit Meeting stipulated that the cost should not exceed £500. The foundation stone was laid on 30 May, 1887. A traditional chapel building with high frontage and tall finials, it is fronted by heavy but intricate iron railings. Inside the simple rectangular sanctuary are rows of plain wooden pews and a communion table dominates the front.

The same year the chapel opened. The old chapel and its land, pews, seats and pulpit were sold to George Sayer, a carpenter, for £38, a provision being that the land and premises should not be associated with the liquor trade in any way. Five months later Sayer let the chapel to the Salvation Army for £6.10s.0d per annum. General Booth personally signed the agreement. My family has passed on a tradition that my grandfather Josiah Moat personally drove the General when he visited the district. One wonders if he drove him to Herne to sign this agreement?

Primitive Methodists were active in the village and looked to the Canterbury (Borough) Primitive Methodist Church for leadership. Igglesden informs us that there was a Plymouth Brethren meeting in a room next to the Baker's shop around 1900.

HOATH AND MAYPOLE

It would be easy to miss the Compton Report for Hoath because it was written out by Henry Hughes, Vicar of St. Dunstan's, Canterbury and Reculver and Hoath. For all this he was unable to report any Recusants or Dissenters amongst the 75 inhabants of Hoath.

A Meeting House certificate dated 11 August 1815 records that a house occupied by Henry King in the parish of Hoath was being used for worship. The denomination of the signatory Robert Benjamin Rogers, Coach-maker of Canterbury is not known but a Sister Rogers and Sarah Rogers are amongst the Canterbury Methodist class of 1807. Also mentioned in an 1807 class – that of Brother Bundock – is William Crippen. On 1 January 1851 a householder, William Frederick Crippen of Guildhall Street, Canterbury, signed a certificate for a house occupied by Mr. Richard Larkin of Maypole, the property of Mrs. Elizabeth Staines of 25 St. Peter's Street, Canterbury (near the Methodist Church). Richard Larkin was the Maypole black and white smith who was a key witness at the inquest in the Hoath murder case recorded elsewhere in this book. His forge at that date was at the present Forge House, south of Millbank, so this was probably the building registered for worship in 1851.

Maypole Wesleyan Chapel dates from 1860 as the plaque on the frontage still indicates. Brief extracts from the Wesleyan circuit minutes state that in June 1884 Mr. Larkin was asked to take charge at Maypole and recommence the Sunday School. In October 1902 it was suggested that the Maypole Chapel be closed but in 1909 they state the chapel was redecorated at a cost of £10.9s.0d. It was again renovated and re-opened on 3 September, 1939 – the day World War II started. Mr. A. E. Cole who preached on the original circuit plan recalls that in the early thirties there was a thriving Sunday School but it decreased to about 30 in 1939. Membership also dropped and the final service in the Plan commenced at 2.30 p.m. on 27 December, 1959 – 99 years after its opening. He mentions that the interior of the chapel had box pews, each with its own door, as did the pulpit. After use by other denominations for a short while, then as a furniture store, it has now been converted into a private dwelling.

BROOMFIELD

The earliest reference to a meeting in Broomfield is in a Meeting House Certificate dated 24 July, 1840 referring to a 'room in the occupation of George and Charlotte Brice'. George Brice, a tenant of William Harnett, lived in a cottage on the west side of Bogsole Lane (formerly Chapel Lane). The certificate was signed by Josiah Viney of Herne who was the Herne Bay Congregational Church minister between 1840-43.

In 1863 cottage meetings began at Hunters Forstal 'in the last of four houses on the right hand side of the road going from Herne Bay'. These meetings continued intermittently for about ten years. However, the need for a chapel in Broomfield itself was always paramount and in January 1869 a Herne farmer, Mr. William Brown, sold ground for this purpose opposite George Brice's cottage for the sum of £5. Pastor Acomb, who was instrumental in founding Broad Oak Chapel two years previously, wrote in his journal, 'The good folks of this village (Broomfield) are delighted at the prospect of a chapel in the centre of it'. It must have been good news for those at Hunters Forstal also.

The chapel was built at a cost of about £150, including 'fitting up' and was opened on 20 July, 1869. The preachers that day were Mr. Viney and the minister of Watling Street Congregational Church, Canterbury, Mr. Valentine Ward. Encouraging and well attended meetings marked the beginnings of this venture. It is worth noting the Trustees of the Chapel. They were headed by the Rev. Thomas Blandford who had succeeded Josiah Viney, also Rowland Taylor, Draper; Jonathan Clarkson, Gentleman; John Bunce Turner, Schoolmaster; Thomas Haward, Butcher; Thomas Christian, Gardener; all of Herne Bay: Joseph Gore the Elder of Herne Parsonage Farm, Farmer; and from Canterbury, Henry Ovenden, Ironmonger; Edward Beasley, Dyer; Frederick William Fairbrass, Coal Merchant and Thomas James White Flint, Gentleman.

In 1894 an American organ was given to the little chapel but we read that the cause suffered from the erection, in 1903, of the Baptist Church in Beltinge. Attendance must have rallied, however, because the little chapel was superseded by the larger building in Margate Road, now the United Reformed Church. This church was opened on 14 June, 1932. At the Dedication a tribute was given to Mr. H. B. Worrell, who had given the site and 'contributed largely to the funds' and also to Miss Beatrice Robinson. It was she who bought the old chapel, which was used mainly for youth work; but she sold it in 1947, when it became a bakery.

Mr. W. Lawrence of Tankerton became 'Honorary Missioner' whilst Mr. R. J. Gore became Church Secretary. Sunday and week-night services thrived as did the Sunday School with a roll of 52 in September 1932. In November, however, an outbreak of fire, probably arson, nearly destroyed the building; but it was discovered in time and extinguished. The premises were further enlarged and the work has continued to the present day.

BELTINGE

James Parnell, the Canterbury Independent minister, signed a Meeting House certificate on 18 June, 1825 relating to a 'house occupied by John Bird'. From a map of 1837 showing the proposed Turnpike Road, this house is shown on a plot of ground at the junction of the present Grange Road and Rose Gardens. The house, pulled down to make way for this development, was Beltinge House, a photograph of which is opposite. It is open to question whether these windows were mere Victorian Gothic or did they have a more ecclesiastical connection?

120

Another house 'Situate on Beltinge Green' was certified for worship by Protestants on 13 January, 1836. It was occupied by Edward Maxted which the map already referred to shows as living on Reculver Road, opposite the Baptist Chapel. The denominational affiliations of the signatory Martha Bennett are unknown, although Bennett is quite a common Beltinge name.

The site opposite the 'Rising Sun', adjacent to the parish boundary, was the probable site of a meeting room in the occupation of Thomas and Mary Pitcher. Their certificate was signed on the same day and by the same person as the first Broomfield certificate of 1840.

Herne Bay Baptists opened a mission station, in fact, cottage meetings, in Beltinge in 1887 but it was not until 1903 that a chapel was built and opened. The work grew steadily and on 3 February, 1925 the chapel celebrated its independence. Beltinge Baptist Church has expanded its building and has had five full-time ministers, the last one being the Rev. Mark Musk.

(There are references to Quakers and Anabaptists who lived in Beltinge but these are under Herne).

BIBLIOGRAPHY

Compton Census (1676), Canterbury Diocese. Cathedral Library.
Meeting House Certificates. 1789-1852. Cathedral Library.
Land Conveyance. (Broomfield Chapel). (1869).
Herne Bay Congregational Church Magazines.
History of the Congregational Church, Herne Bay. J. Watkinson (1910).
The Journal of W. J. Acomb, 1866-1923. Baptist Church House, W.C.1.
Plan and Book of Reference of proposed Turnpike Road from Faversham to Birchington (1837). Kent Archives Office.
Wesleyan (Methodist) Circuit Minutes.
Canterbury Methodist Church, Class Lists (1807), etc.
We've been here for 100 years. Herne Bay Baptist Church. 1879-1979. W. Stant.
The Society of Friends in Kent. Karl Showler (1970).
Original Records of Early Nonconformity. Prof. G. Lyon Turner, M.A. (1911).
Saunters through Kent. Charles Igglesden.
Stapleton's Directory (1838).

Photograph by courtesy of Ian B. Moat

BELTINGE HOUSE, C.1905

HERNE AS PORTRAYED IN COMMERCIAL
DIRECTORIES OF 1847 AND 1907

by

John Whyman, B.Sc. (Econ.) (London), Ph.D. (Kent), AIPM

The nineteenth century is well served by local historical sources, which present no problems of access or interpretation. This statement is true for commerical directories of the nineteenth and early twentieth centuries.[1] They are immensely useful for local historians of villages or parishes. For Professor W. G. Hoskins they 'give us a good start for reconstructing the kind of community which existed over a period of about a hundred years from the 1830's to the 1930's'.[2]

Victorian and Edwardian trade directories are judged by the information which they provide under two main sections, as illustrated on page 349 of the 1851 *Post Office Directory of the Six Home Counties. (See opposite page)*.

1. An introductory 'sketch' touching on some aspects of the size and site of a place, its history, local government, economy, places of worship, schools, charities or poor law provision, followed by

2. Lists of principal residents, tradesmen and craftsmen.[3]

Herne from the 1820's did not follow the predictions of earlier writers. In 1776 Charles Seymour saw the village as 'an agreeable recess in the summer season, on account of its vicinity to the sea'.[4] In 1818 L. Fussell noted how 'Herne Bay and the village of that name, which consists only of a few cottages, . . are beginning to rise into some degree of celebrity, by having lately become the resort of company for the purpose of bathing'.[5] A somewhat different picture emerges from commercial directories of 1847[6] and 1907.[7]

Herne in 1847 was introduced as 'a considerable village, situated in a sheltered situation nearly in the centre of the parish', the latter containing 4,828 acres of land, mostly a strong fertile clay intermixed with gravel in some parts. The population of the parish, including the hamlets of Eddington and Broomfield, but excluding Herne Bay, stood at 1,469 in 1841, occupying 280 houses.

The gentry or private residents of 1847 numbered fourteen comprising the vicar, the curate, two 'gents', four 'Esq.' one Captain, one R.N. Lieut., one plain Mr., two Mrs. and a single Miss. There were thirteen principal landowners, six of whom were farmers: John Collard of Prospect House, Eddington, at Broomfield, Thomas Wacher, John Swinford, Charles Hilder at Westbrook, Joseph Goodwin at Studds and George Denne at Beltinge. Three of the remaining seven landowners were also resident locally: Edward Collard at Eddington, John Palmer, 'gent', at Herne Common and the corn millers, Job, John and Edward Lawrence. Four were non-resident: Edward Torney, George Dering, Gilbert Pembrook and Capt. Shakespeare.

122

Commercially fifteen trades and fifty-one names were listed, as follows:

Bakers	4	Farmers	19
Beerhouses	4	Grocers and Tea Dealers	4
Blacksmith	1	Inns and Taverns	4
Boarding School	1	Saddler and Harness Maker	1
Boot and Shoemakers	5	Surgeon	1
Bricklayer	1	Tailor	1
Carpenters, etc.	3	Tile Maker	1
Corn Miller	1		

Almost every community in the mid-nineteenth century possessed a surprising number of shoemakers. Although industry was represented by milling and tile-making, the economy of Herne was primarily agrarian, with farmers comprising well over one third of the persons listed commercially, yet also approximately 15% functioned as beerhouses, inns or taverns. Herne's inhabitants were serviced by one blacksmith, one saddle and harness maker and one surgeon and had access to four bakers, five boot and shoemakers and four grocers and tea dealers, compared to six, seven and five respectively in Herne Bay. In total 66 names were listed privately or commercially in 1847, including the Governor of the Union Workhouse.

The principal edifices of the parish were St. Martin's church and the workhouse of the Blean Poor Law Union. The church was described as forming 'a large handsome structure, consisting of three aisles and three chancels, with a noble tower at the north-west corner, in which are six bells'. The Blean Poor

CONVEYANCES :—

Omnibus arrives from Tenterden to meet the 7 a.m. up train to London, & leaves for Tenterden after the arrival of the last down train

Elijah Couchman's van for passengers & luggage, leaves the 'King's Arms,' Headcorn, ¼ past 8 mon. tues. thurs. & sat. passing through Sutton & Langley to Castle inn,

for the up & down trains to London and Dover. On thurs. the van will leave Maidstone one hour later

James Holland's luggage van leaves the Headcorn station for Tenterden immediately after the arrival of the first down train ; returns from Tenterden about 4 aft. in time for the last up train

HERNE is a parish situated to the north of Sturry, in a wild lonely country, the soil of which is a stiff clay. Herne Street or Town stands about the centre of the parish. This district is in the lathe of St. Augustine, Hundred of Bleangate, and Union of Blean, 7 miles distant from Canterbury. The church, dedicated to St. Martin, is a handsome building, consisting of three ailes and three chancels, with a square tower. It is partly in the early English and partly in the perpendicular style. The church is 113 feet long and 59 broad, with many tombs and brasses. Archbishop Islip, in the 25th of Edward III., obtained a grant of a weekly market, now disused ; and a fair on the feast of St. Martin and the day following. The workhouse of Blean Union, containing 67 persons, is on Herne Common. The population of Herne is 1,469, of the whole parish, 3,049. The area of the parish is 4,560 acres. The assessment to the Property Tax of the whole parish was, in 1842, £17,670.

Belsey Miss
Carey David, esq. Herne street
Dakin Dr. John Horsley [curate]
Goddard Lieut. Geo. R.N.Huntersfostall
Hilton Mrs. Herne street
May Rev. James Sex, M.A. [vicar]
Micleburgh John,esq.Sharper's hall hill
Palmer John, esq. Herne common
Warder Mrs
Whiddett Mrs

TRADERS.

Baskevelles Eddington,boarding school
Bean Henry, veterinary surgeon

Best William, grocer, baker & butcher
Brown John, beer retailer
Brown John Grant, carpenter
Downs George, ' Prince Albert '
Downs John, builder
Evans William, surgeon
Goodwin Joseph, farmer, Colewood
Groombridge James, builder, Herne st
Grinded Mrs. Sarah, grocer
Harnet James, Upper ' Red Lion,' & post office
Harris George, sexton
Harrison George, shoemaker

Hilder Charles, farmer, West brook
Jones Alfred,master of the Union house
Lawrence Job, John & Edward, millers
Mann Edward, grocer
Port Henry, blacksmith
Sayer William, builder
Swinford John, farmer, Stroud farm
Thorpe Edward, parish clerk & baker
Wacher William, farmer, Underdown
Whiddett Joseph, farmer, Northwood
Wilson Mrs. Sarah, grocer
Winch Richard, schoolmaster
Wood John Francis, baker

POST OFFICE.—James Harnet, postmaster. London letters arrive from Canterbury by mail cart at ½ past 6 a.m.; dispatched ½ past 7 p.m

Union House, Alfred Jones, master
For Conveyance, see Herne Bay

HERNE BAY is a watering place of very modern origin, having sprung into existence within a few years. It is frequented in the summer season for the purpose of bathing, and for the enjoyment of the healthy same time as an excellent land-mark for mariners. A market-house has also been built. Here is a chapel of ease, capable of affording accommodation for upwards of 800 persons, inclusive of 300 free sittings, and National

Law Union workhouse served an area of 27,034 acres and a population of 14,387, spread over sixteen parishes including Chislet, Herne, Hoath, Sturry and Westbere. Administered by nineteen guardians it had been erected in 1836 about half a mile from the church on Herne Common, at a cost of £6,300. It could accommodate 420 inmates in 'a spacious brick building, forming a quadrangle'. Apart from registrars of births, marriages and deaths, who served the Union, the guardians at their Thursday weekly meetings in the Board Room supervised the work of three surgeons, including William Evans of Herne, two relieving officers, and one clerk, chaplain, governor, matron, schoolmaster and schoolmistress.

Whether or not Herne in 1847 possessed the post office which is mentioned in 1851, the sixty years separating 1847 and 1907 saw several changes, which confirm Professor Hoskins' observation that from commercial directories,

'one not only gets a static picture of a place
in certain years, but it is also possible to
draw some preliminary conclusions about the way
the place has changed, . . . whether its population
has declined or risen, . . . [or] whether
certain old trades and crafts have died out'.[8]

By 1901 a modest growth had lifted Herne's population to 1,716 including seventeen officers and 146 inmates in the Blean Union workhouse, which in 1875 had seen the construction of a hospital with beds for 60 patients and a smaller hospital for infectious cases. One mile northwards lay Herne Bay station on the Margate and Ramsgate branch of the South Eastern and Chatham railway, which provided access to a wider world outside Herne or Herne Bay. The predominantly flint church of St. Martin's afforded 1,000 sittings, all of which were free in 1907.

Other notable changes can be plotted chronologically:

1. A mixed public elementary school was erected in 1866 and enlarged in 1889 for 208 children, having an average attendance of 170 in 1907.
2. A cemetery was opened in 1880, occupying three acres, and having one mortuary chapel under the control of a burial board of nine members.
3. A Wesleyan chapel was erected in 1887, in addition to a Congregational chapel at Broomfield.
4. In 1894 under the provisions of a Local Government Act Herne and Herne Bay were separated for civil purposes, leaving Herne with a Parish Council consisting of nine members.
5. At Beltinge a Baptist school chapel was erected for £579 on freehold land in 1902 from designs by Mr. F. W. J. Palmer, C.E. The chapel built of red brick seated 120 persons, adjoining which was a vestry and classroom.

Postal services by 1907 had expanded to include a post office in Herne Street and at Eddington, with a pillar box on Herne Common and a wall letter box at Broomfield. Some aspects of local life in 1907 remained unchanged compared to 1847, namely the annual fair which was held on the feast of St. Martin and the day following, while the vicar from 1905 onwards, the Rev. Arthur Giles Daubeney, M.A. of Magdalen College, Oxford, still presided over a living with a net yearly value of £326 with a residence.

There were fewer principal landowners in 1907. Among a total of six were Earl Sondes and Charles William Prescott-Westcar, J.P., B.A., who resided among 223 acres at Strode Park. The remaining landowners were descended from names which had been familiar in 1847: G.C.A. Dering, J. K. Pembrook and William and J. J. Wacher.

For 1907 the listings of private and commercial names were divided as between Herne and Eddington. Including the vicar and the curate the numbers of private residents had increased enormously to 39 for Herne and to 35 for Eddington, these totals being broken down as follows:

Category	Herne	Eddington	Total
Vicar	1		1
Curate		1	1
J.P.'s	3		3
Mr. or Esq.	22	19	41
Mrs.	10	12	22
Miss	3	3	6
Total	39	35	74

Commercially Herne had 55 persons in 30 trades in 1907 compared to eleven persons in nine trades in Eddington.

Photograph by courtesy of Dr. J. Whyman

Trade	Herne	Eddington	Total
Apartments	2	1	3
Bakers	4		4
Beer Retailers	3		3
Blacksmith	1		1
Bootmakers	2		2
Builders	1	1	2
Butcher	1		1
Canine Specialist		1	1
Cemetery	1		1
Coal Agent	1		1
Convalescent Home	1		1
Dairyman	1		1
Draper	1		1
Farm Bailiffs	2		2
Farmers	12	3	15
Golf Club		1	1
Grazier	1		1
Grocers	4		4
Herne Bay Water Works Co. Pumping Station	1		1
Insurance Agent	1		1
Landowner	1		1
Laundryman	1		1
Laundry Training Home	1		1
Maltster		1	1
Miller (Wind & Steam)	1		1
National Telephone Co. Public Telephone Office	1		1
Nursery		1	1
Physician and Surgeon	1		1
Post Office		1	1
Poultry Farmer	1		1
Preparatory School	1		1
Private Gardener	1		1
Private School		1	1
Public Houses	4		4
Shopkeeper	1		1
Surveyor	1		1
Total	55	11	66

Herne's bakers, grocers and public houses had maintained their numerical strength at four apiece, with three of the public houses preserving their 1847 names, viz: the Huntsman and Horn at Broomfield and the Prince Albert and the Red Lion in Herne Street. An Edwardian postcard confirms the 1907 entries for Frederick George Gray, Lower Red Lion Public House, Herne

Street, and John Edmund Martin, Upper Red Lion Public House, Herne Street. Recreation outside the public house was provided by the Herne, Herne Bay and Neighbourhood Gardeners' Society and by the Herne Bay Golf Club in Eddington.

Over the sixty years 1847 to 1907 both beer retailers and farmers had slipped more or less proportionately, respectively from four to three and from nineteen to fifteen, and yet in 1907 there was greater agrarian diversity when measured by two farm bailiffs, a dairyman, a grazier, the Eddington Nurseries and a poultry farmer. The chief crops of Edwardian Herne were wheat and barley, with some land given over to pasture. One mill and one blacksmith operated at both dates. In 1907, however, the miller, Thomas Wootton, used both wind and steam power at Herne Mill, and the agricultural community was served by a female blacksmith, Mrs. James Port. Mrs. Arnold of Broomfield Hall employed Samuel Pearce as a private gardener. Dog lovers could call on the services of a canine specialist in Eddington, D'arcy Barnes.

Occupational elimination affected the boarding school, three boot and shoemakers, the bricklayer, the three carpenters, the saddle and harness maker, the tailor, and the tile-maker, as listed for 1847. Among the completely new and interesting occupations of 1907 were a convalescent home, a golf club, a laundry training home and the public services of water supply and telephone.

Although considerably more detail could have been included within a longer contribution to this volume, it is clearly the case that population and residential expansion, and physical and occupational change, emerges from commercial directory entries for Herne as between 1847 and 1907. It was, however, Edwardian Herne rather than Victorian Herne which began to reflect

Edwardian Postcard, Valentine Series

pre-Victorian predictions of attracting people for purposes of sea bathing or sea air. By 1907 apartments for visitors were being offered by William Hammant at Ridley House, Herne; by William Holman in Herne village, and by Mrs. Caroline L. Gammon in Eddington village, added to which there were two convalescent homes in Beltinge. The first to be erected in 1898 was the Beltinge Convalescent Home, standing in 7½ acres of ground, constructed of fine red brick, with freestone dressings, for '50 patients from friendly societies, in connection with the Passmore Edwards fund'. A Convalescent Home for Railwaymen opened its doors in 1901 for up to 150 patients who were housed in a Queen Anne style building, erected mainly at the expense of Mr. Passmore Edwards, at a cost of about £13,000, and standing in about four acres of ground.

FOOTNOTES

1.   Most local libraries contain sets of commercial directories. For Kentish directories known to exist and where they can be located, see Ed: W. F. Bergess and B. R. M. Riddell, *Kent Directories Located* (2nd Ed., K.C.C., 1978).

2.   W. G. Hoskins, *Local History in England* (2nd Ed., 1972), 30.

3.   In recent years there have been many assessments of the historical value of commercial directories, including Hoskins, *op.cit.*, 29-30; D. Page, 'Commercial Directories and Market Towns', *The Local Historian,* Volume 11, Number 2 (1974), 85-8; or G. Shaw, 'The Content and Reliability of Nineteenth Century Trade Directories', *The Local Historian,* Volume 13, Number 4 (1978), 205-9.

4.   C. Seymour, *A New Topographical, Historical and Commercial Survey of the Cities, Towns and Villages of the County of Kent* (1776), 457.

5.   L. Fussell, *A Journey round the Coast of Kent* (1818), 72.

6.   S. Bagshaw, *History, Gazetteer and Directory of the County of Kent,* Volume 2 (Sheffield, 1847), 216-8, 220-1.

7.   *Kelly's Directory of Kent* (1907), 363-4.

8.   Hoskins, *op.cit.,* 29-30.

HERNE NATIONAL SCHOOL
"In the beginning...."
by
Robert and Tricia Spain

'Herne is a parish, situated to the north of Sturry, in a wild lonely country.' At least that is how it was in 1866 when the Rev. James Robert Buchanan was appointed to the parish of St. Martin of Tours. However, the 1861 Census had noted the presence of 1,644 people in the district of Herne and it seems that the new vicar's immediate concern was to be for the education of the youngest members of his parish.

On 14th March, 1866, James Buchanan completed a form of Application for Aid and dispatched it to the National Society for the Education of the Poor in the Principles of the Established Church. Plans were, by this date, already well advanced for the erection of a school to accommodate 195 boys and girls. The total estimated cost of the school and teacher's residence was £1,080 and a sum of £931 had been raised or promised leaving just £149 to find.

The National Society had been founded in 1811 at which time it acquired a number of existing schools from the S.P.C.K. (the Society for the Propagation

128

of Christian Knowledge). When the Government made its first grant of £20,000 in 1833 towards the provision of schools the money was channelled through the National Society and the British and Foreign Schools Society thus contributing to the education of both Church of England and Dissenting families. Not until 1870 did the Government take a more direct initiative for the provision of schools for all children. The 1870 Education Act encouraged the establishment of School Boards in areas where the voluntary societies had failed to provide schools of their own. The decade leading up to this Act, however, had seen a growing acceptance of the importance of education and Herne School was one of the many National Schools for which the need had already been acknowledged.

SCHOLARS AT HERNE SCHOOL, 1919

Back Row:
Peter Buckley; Albert Sayer; William Keen; Cyril Cullen; Ralph Steed; William Pressley; Harold Page; Leslie Scott; Jack Johnson.

Third Row:
Charlie Finch; Dick Ruck; George Ewell; Lily Hudson; Headmaster 'Jimmy' Worth; Dorothy Stebbings; Alfred Hewett; Charlie Whitehead; Charlie Sinden.

Second Row:
May Strand; Molly Keen; Marion Glenny; Elsie Jessop; Hilda Bubb; Elsie Parkinson; Dorothy Jones; Elsie Pritchard.

Front Row:
Joyce Goldfinch; Florrie Hopkins; Lily Addley; Daisy Ruck; Emily Parnell; Florrie Oliver; Millie Ball.

Photograph in possession of Ralph Steed.
Identifications by Florrie and Stanley Oliver.

In the letter accompanying his application for aid the Rev. Buchanan stated why he thought support from the National Society ought to be forthcoming. Herne, he pointed out, was the largest parish in the Diocese without a school. In fact, there was a school of sorts, a 'Dame School', but this would only have provided a limited education for a few children. The people of the parish were chiefly engaged in agriculture he said and 'the children of the poor' were 'neglected and ignorant'. His continuing support for the Society was pledged and he drew attention to the cash collection he had made for them in the previous September.

The population of the area was given as 3,147 but this included Herne Bay where Christ Church School was already established. A Sunday School which 158 children attended was being held in the Church at this time and it was presumably expected that these children might also attend the new school.

Building work commenced according to the plans drawn up by the London architect, William Powell, and adhered to the designs and standards common to many National Schools of the period. There was to be one large room, seventy-three feet long by eighteen feet wide, divided by a partition, and a small room eighteen feet long by fourteen feet wide. In addition the teachers' residence was to comprise a parlour, kitchen, scullery and three bedrooms.

By December the school was completed but the costs, inevitably, had risen and the Vicar was impelled to request an additional grant. The total bill had risen to £1,344-12s-4d. Despite an increase in the Government's grant a debt of £83-12s-7d remained. The undoubted strain of the efforts to finance the school showed in the admission that 'we have exhausted all our resources'.

His troubles were not yet over. In March, the National Society received a further letter. Like so many of his fellow clergymen, James Buchanan had invested money of his own into the project to ensure its survival and eventual success. Still more was needed. In his letter dated March, 1867 he says:-

'I am now in this position. The schools are quite ready for opening – but we have neither books nor school apparatus of any kind except Children's Desks and Forms ...'

Having built and furnished the school, maintenance was to become the next continuing problem. It had been proposed to levy a 2d fee a week per child and further income was to be derived from subscriptions by parishioners, collections in Church and the Government's grants, but a year after the school opened the National Society received a further request for assistance which was duly given, and received with thanks.

However, six years passed before the National Society was approached again and this time it was for a grant towards a supply of books, materials and apparatus, perhaps a major re-stocking exercise. The Balance Sheet for 1874 was enclosed showing that expenditure had exceeded income by £7 for the year. Subscriptions and donations totalling £53 still formed the largest source of income. The Government's capitation grant brought in £50-2s-0d while the 'school pence' paid by the children amounted to £34-18s-0d. An amount of £3 from other sources completed the income. Teachers' salaries accounted for £124 of this sum, books and apparatus just £3-10s-0d and other unlisted expenses amounted to £20-10s-0d. The school was fighting hard for its existence.

That the School survived is not in doubt since it remains with us today. Its connections with the founding Church have also been maintained. The Herne National School of the nineteenth century has developed into a Church of England School of the twentieth century. The Rev. James Robert Buchanan can never have envisaged the transformation in the lives and learning of the children of Herne for which he provided a beginning.

Sources – National Society – Records – School No. 174.

HERNE (HERNE BAY) KENT.

Kelly's Kent Directory, 1867.

THE HOUSES OF CHISLET — PART 2

by

Kenneth Gravett, M.Sc. (Eng.), F.S.A., C.Eng.

Since the first part of this article there have been further discoveries on Marshside. The most interesting has been Shersby's Cottage, which is timber-framed of one and a half storeys. It contains three re-used smoke-blackened rafters, each with a notch for a dovetail halving, presumably from an earlier house on the site. They are clearly not *in situ,* since they were designed for a roof of steeper pitch. The north end of the house had a jetty and this bay could be sixteenth century, but the rest of the building and the whole roof were rebuilt in the second half of the seventeenth century, with re-used timber. The chimney is of the same date and the house was probably originally thatched throughout – the old ties for the thatch remain. About 1800 a copper and oven were installed beside the chimney and probably the weather boarding added. (Tarring would be possible after a local gasworks started). About 1890 a short extension was made to the south. The barn next door has two aisles with a roof with side purlins and collars at the principal trusses only and clearly intended for thatch. However, the posts have long, stepped jowls with face-pegs, while the scarf joints have a division in the vertical plane (face-halved and bladed), and these features make a date earlier than the eighteenth century unlikely. The Blandings is a brick, central-chimney house, with an outshot to the rear and a thatched roof. It is clearly all of one build, dating from the very end of the seventeenth century or the beginning of the eighteenth, while numbers 1 and 2, Under-the-Wood, form a pair of early eighteenth century cottages.

At Chislet, Manor Cottage and Church Cottage are an eighteenth century pair in red brick with grey headers. Interestingly, they have no windows overlooking the graveyard.

Highstead forms an interesting settlement. Highstead Farm contains on its west side a two-storey wing of two bays with a crown-post. This was clearly a cross wing, probably added to an earlier house at the end of the fifteenth century. The main section of the house was rebuilt with a large brick chimney, some time in the middle of the seventeenth century. Except for the north end of the crossing, the house is now encased in brick, with a front in grey brick dating from the very end of the eighteenth century. The cellar, scullery, some fireplaces and the south windows at the west end of the main front date from about 1850.

Walnut Tree Farm is of brick of the second quarter of the eighteenth century, but again with considerable additions of about 1850, including a new kitchen block. A little way to the south-west is Bay Tree Cottage, which is a timber-framed, central-chimney house, of the seventeenth century. It may have been thatched and until about 1960 was clad with tarred weatherboarding. Thatched Cottage dates from about 1800, but one of the adjoining cottages may be a little earlier.

THE FORD PUMPING STATION

by

Jack H. Roberts

The first borehole for water in the area was sunk in the 1870's at Mickleburgh Hill and by 1879 my grandfather – the first J. H. Roberts – was laying water mains up the High Street and along St. George's Terrace. There was however no greensand in the ground below Mickleburgh Hill and the supply of water soon dried out.

It was then that the borehole at Ford was sunk and the first pumphouse built. Since 1883 the water from Ford – some half a million gallons a day – has been pumped to Herne Bay. The hole goes down 170 feet into chalk. Leading off from near the bottom there are five headings (or addits) into the chalk layer. These total 2,865 feet – having been greatly extended in the 1930's and again in 1951, though Ford is now only what is called a make-up station.

The name of the first engine has been lost to memory – it was perhaps a Hindley. Its successor was made by James Warner of Cripplegate and was in service until 1928. Quite soon a second steam pumping engine was needed and one by James Simpson of Cricklewood was installed. The Warner was replaced in 1928 by a 2-stroke diesel by Marshall of Gainsborough – which in its turn

The Alexandra steam engine removed from the Ford Pumping Station in 1966. The actual pump rod is visible in the centre forefront of the picture. This engine was capable of pumping one million gallons of water per day the two and a half miles from Ford to Mickleburgh Hill, Herne Bay – which is some one hundred feet higher.

worked until 1950. The Simpson was replaced in 1931 by a diesel made by Mirlees Bickerton and Day of Stockport.

There was – not surprisingly – an increasing demand for water by the growing town of Herne Bay and in 1901 an addition was built on the Pump House and the magnificent Alexandra Steam Pump installed in it. This engine, featured in the accompanying photographs, worked until 1966 when it was removed.

Present day pumping equipment consists of a 100 h.p. 5-cylinder Ruston and Hornsby Diesel driving a Worthington Simpson pump and a 100 h.p. electrically driven pump by the same maker, both with a capacity of around 50,000 g.p.h. at 270 feet head. These engines pump the water from Ford to the two reservoirs at the top of Mickleburgh Hill which have a capacity of 750,000 and 350,000 gallons, while the water tower itself holds 100,000 gallons.

My grandfather stayed with the Water Company for 56 years, dying in 1935. He also had a long association with the Herne Bay Fire Brigade in the not unexpected role of turncock. My father – another J. Roberts – became manager in 1921 and also served over fifty years. In fact long service was the order of the day with the old Company. An uncle, E. A. Roberts (Ted) who was concerned mainly with the distribution side, was also with the Company all his working life. Harry Newport, who joined the Company in 1926, is now the only surviving member of the station staff. I did a stint of 42 years – which in the words of the old song 'didn't seem a day too long'.

Photographs by courtesy of the Mid-Kent Water Company

Another view of the Alexandra steam engine showing the low-pressure cylinder and the rather unusual CORLISS valve gear. This engine was installed in 1901, having been delivered by horse-drawn flat trolley from Herne Bay Station.

HERNE BAY WATER.

ARRANGEMENT OF MAINS
AT FORD PUMPING STATION.

Scale : ⅛ Inch to a Foot.

Note:
Spindles turn in the direction of the arrows for closing valves.

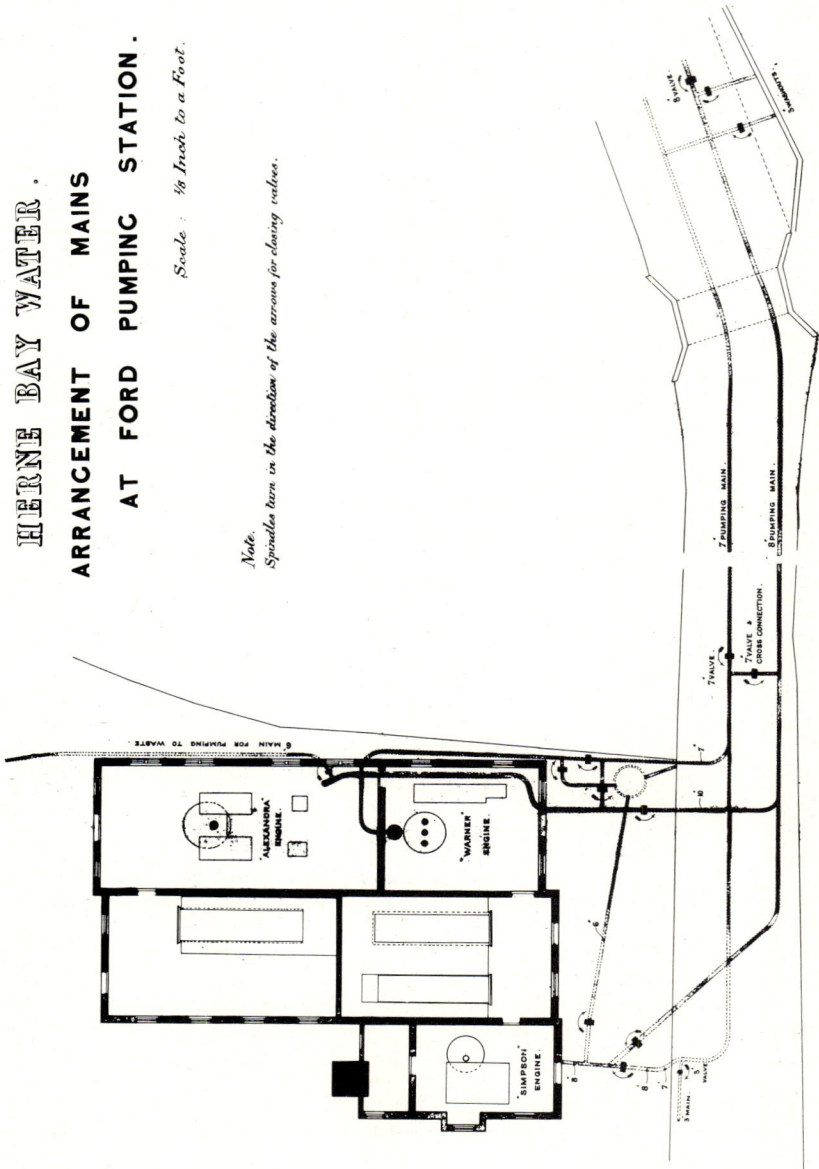

8" VALVE.

8" PUMPING MAIN.

3" BRANCH.

7" PUMPING MAIN.

8" PUMPING MAIN.

7" VALVE.

7" VALVE &
CROSS CONNECTION.

6" MAIN FOR PUMPING TO WASTE.

'ALEXANDRA'
ENGINE.

'WARNER'
ENGINE.

'SIMPSON'
ENGINE.

6" VALVE

5" VALVE

3" MAIN

THE SHAFT AT FORD PUMPING STATION
Mr. G. R. Brown of 16 William Street, Herne Bay, built this 85 foot chimney, laying every brick himself in 3 months using 50,000 bricks.

THE MARIST BROTHERS OF GROVE FERRY

by

Rob Williams

The effect of the French Revolution on the Church in France was disastrous. There was an urgent need to bring Christian teaching back to the schools. For this purpose the Institute of the Marist Brothers Teaching Order was founded by Marchellin Champagnet in the country village of La Villa in the Archdiocese of Lyons, in the year 1817.

Father Champagnet, as Superior and Founder, started with two young men from the village. He trained them as catechists. They were soon joined by others as the order spread rapidly throughout the Archdiocese of Lyons, the Brothers teaching in small country schools with admirable results.

The order soon spread throughout France and houses were formed in other countries. The Brothers first came to England in December 1852 to St. Anne's Parish, Spitalfields – one of the neediest quarters in the East End of London.

It was a Dickensian London at that time with all the horrors of poverty and poor living conditions. The Brothers, brought up among the wheatfields and warm plains of Northern France, stood up bravely to their heroic task and by the end of the century had formed six further schools in London: St. Patrick's, Soho; St. Aloysius, Clarendon Square; St. Francis, Peckham; Corpus Christi, Drury Lane; St. John's, Islington; and Notre Dame, Leicester Square. By this time they had also formed schools in Dundee, Dumfries, Glasgow, Sligo and Athlone.

In 1903 all Religious Orders were expelled from France and at that time the Marist Brothers' College at Beauchamps, near Lille, catered for a large number of English boys. The Beauchamps College had to close down, and it was natural that the French Brothers should seek asylum in Britain. They sought to transfer the College and its pupils to the South of England and after looking at property near Brighton eventually purchased a suitable site near Grove Ferry in the village of Upstreet, in the parish of Chislet near Canterbury. There they formed the Marist Brothers' College, Grove Ferry – a daughter house of the College at Beauchamps – to continue their task of providing 'a thoroughly Catholic education to enable pupils to pursue honourably and successfully the profession they may adopt . . . in a word, to form good Catholics and worthy members of society'.

The property at Upstreet had been part of the estates of the many branches of the Denne family, one of the major land-owning families in the parish of Chislet during the 18th century. In 1769 Thomas and Frances Denne built what was then called Grovehill House and is now known as Grove Court. They had three children; Elizabeth, Thomas and Ann. The son Thomas married Frances Slater of Margate and they had three children; Thomas, John and Alfred, none of whom married. Frances Slater's sister Mary also married a Thomas Denne of the Sarre branch of the family.

By the time of the 1842 Tithe Map the sisters were both widows without any direct family, and they are named as the owners of adjacent properties – Frances Denne owned Grovehill House, and Mary Denne owned Shrublands, a similar mansion and estate to the east of Grovehill House.

Frances Denne died in 1846, aged 76, and Mary Denne died in 1853, aged 86. Mary Denne's benefaction remains today as part of the Chislet Charities having left £200 three per cent stock 'the interest arising therefrom to be distributed by the Churchwardens of Chislett in Bread and Coals yearly on Christmas Eve among the most deserving and necessitous Poor residents of Upstreet'.

After the death of Mary Denne, Shrublands was owned by one Haëkins and tenanted by Mr. J. J. Morse, who by 1889 had named the mansion 'The White House' although the name of Shrublands remained for the whole estate. In 1899 it was owned by Florence and Ethel Stewart who sold it to George Downing, a Professor of Chemistry at Cambridge; Edward Liveing, a Physician of London; and the Reverend Delavel Ingram of Essex, for the sum of £1200. The urgent need of the Marist Brothers in 1903 resulted in these three gentlemen being able to sell the property for £2050 to the representatives of the Marist Brothers in James Blake of St. Genis, Luval, France; Richard Mooney of Islington; Edward Decoopman of Glasgow; and Henry Currie of Ireland.

The estate they purchased comprised the mansion, stabling, outbuildings, park and pasture land, a double cottage with garden and orchard (Greengorgon on the banks of the River Stour), four semi-detached villa residences (fronting the main Thanet road), and lakes known as The Fishponds (formed when the railway was constructed across the route of the meandering River Stour), totalling just over 7 acres. The rest of the estate comprising the sloping orchard known as Ferry Bank and the land alongside Grove Ferry Hill was rented from the Archbishop of Canterbury.

Thirty six Brothers and 110 boarders came across the Channel to open the College in October 1902. The Brothers and boarders were mostly French; they

The Chapel

137

were under the jurisdiction of the French Province of Nord, but their doors were open to English boarders as the doors of the Beauchamps College had always been. It was a predominantly French College with French language, customs, food and games; and they became known locally as The Frenchmen.

The White House became the residence of the Director and Headmaster, the Library, the Laboratory and the Refectory. The Villas fronting the main road became the classrooms and dormitories. A Chapel was constructed in the grounds and in due course a recreation building was constructed, with the whole complex connected with a timber framed corridor, known affectionately by the boys as 'The Tube'.

The College prospered and gradually over the years it became more anglicised; English became the official language, games such as cricket and soccer were introduced, and English boarders became the majority. In February, 1914, the College completed their investment by purchasing the land hitherto rented, the conveyance being between the then Archbishop of Canterbury, Randall Thomas Davidson, and the four College Trustees, the original James Blake and Edward Decoopman, and two new members, John O'Connell of St. Joseph's College, Dumfries and Edward Joseph McMullen of Mount St. Michael's, Dumfries.

At the outbreak of the First World War many of the staff and boarders returned to France and there were thoughts of closing the College. However, the English Province came to the rescue with additional staff and by the end of the war there were over sixty pupils.

The College had just returned to the routine of more peaceful days when, in 1919, tragedy struck with the disastrous fire which burnt down The White House. It has been suggested that the fire started as a result of the sun shining through a magnifying glass but whatever the cause the main part of the building was a total loss with only the single storey eastern wing remaining. Many of the boys joined in the manual pumping of water from the river but to little avail. It was a heavy blow but the College survived even with the depleted accommodation. The remains of the White House became the Refectory with the Kitchen and Staff quarters in the outbuildings.

Cricket became very popular during the early 1920's with matches against St. Nicholas College, Margate College and Eddington College; but although the English influence was increasing, the daily programme for the boarders was still very French and spartan. The boys got up at 6.30 a.m. All attended Mass in the College Chapel at 7.00 a.m., celebrated by one of the Benedictine Monks from the Abbey at Ramsgate. After Mass, breakfast in the Refectory – bowls of coffee, bread and chocolate, and perhaps cheese; Brothers and boarders dining together. Dinner and Supper were typically French with fruit, vegetables and wine. Even the youngest, French or otherwise, could quaff off their flagon of vin rouge which came in barrels from Beauchamps regularly. There was no afternoon tea, but at 4.00 p.m. when classes finished, the boys had Gouter which consisted of a chunk of dry bread which they ate as best they could while playing tennis or cricket. Then two hours of homework before Supper at 8.00 p.m. and more vin rouge.

In 1930, at the end of the first phase of the College's history, there were about forty boarders, including boys from France, Spain, Yugoslavia and Greece, and several day boys from the local area. The Brother Director and

Headmaster was still the original Frenchman, Brother Chumald, a man who spent his devoted life between Beauchamps and Grove Ferry. He was assisted by another stalwart from Beauchamps, Brother André, a French gentleman, exquisitely polite and profoundly humble. These two excellent Brothers set the whole tone and high standard of the College.

Brothers Chumald and André were assisted by two Brothers from the English Province, Brother Urban from London and Brother Athanasius from Dumfries; with Brother Paul, a German, Brother Alberto from Spain, and Brother Jarlath O'Rourke, a young apprentice. The boys were presented for the College of Preceptors Local Examinations; senior, junior and lower forms.

In 1931 there were major changes in the running of the College. Brother Chumald, who had been Director and Headmaster of the College since it started in 1903, was relieved of his responsibility. The English Province now incorporated Grove Ferry and made it a wholly English College. Brother Urban, a Scot, became the new Director and Headmaster. English food and customs were introduced; the 4.00 p.m. Gouter was out and afternoon tea took its place. The Oxford and Cambridge Local Examinations were introduced; and the name of the College was changed to St. Mary's College, Grove Ferry.

The staff also changed with the new set-up. With Brother Urban were Brother Athanasius as Bursar and Sub-Director; Brother Paul teaching Modern Languages, and Brothers Lewis, André and Bennet teaching various other subjects. Brother André, one of the founder staff, retired to Beauchamps for a well earned rest, but his founding colleague, Brother Chumald, now in his late seventies but relieved of his Headmaster's duties, remained at his post to teach English Language and Literature – a Frenchman teaching English; but after

The Refectory

over 28 years of teaching this subject he was a past master and could not be surpassed.

Under the new regime there was also a greater emphasis on Sport. Apart from cricket played in the College grounds, soccer was now played in a field at Port Farm, Upstreet.

Under the canonical rules of the English Province the Superior could only remain in office for six years and so when Brother Urban's term expired in 1937, Brother Leo was appointed Director and Headmaster. Brother Leo was a born Londoner. He was very popular with the boys and the College continued happily under his gentle rule.

Sport continued to prosper and there was a new emphasis on Physical Training under the ex-military instructor, Mr. Furnace, known by the boys as 'Physical Nip'. The Annual Sports Day, including a Physical Training Display became a major event in the College calendar.

By 1938 the College began to widen the scope of its activities. Apart from the Sports Day, the P.T. Display was also included in a Garden Fête held in aid of the parish church, with a Dance in the evening. The boys also participated in the fête at St. Anne's Convent at Westbere. In addition to the annual Corpus Christi procession in the College grounds, the boys also joined in the procession of the Blessed Sacrament in Canterbury and the procession of the Relics of St. Mildred of Minster in Minster Abbey. There were additional cricket fixtures against Chislet Colliery Welfare and Chislet Park Farmers' teams. There were outings to Dymchurch, with tea on the return journey at the Dutch Tea Rooms in Canterbury, and at the end of the summer term there was a Summer Camp at Great Chart, near Ashford.

In 1939, with the war clouds already gathering, the kind and gentle Brother Leo, held in such great affection by the boys, gave way to Brother Joseph Benedict, who was much sterner. However, his time as Director and Headmaster was short lived. As the College was close to the war zone, the responsibility of a boarding school was felt to be too heavy. The Superiors, therefore, decided to evacuate the pupils to Dumfries and close the College.

It was hoped that the College would open again after the war and Brother Edward James was sent down from Dumfries to look after the property. In no time the military moved in; first the RASC and then the Hampshire Regiment. Brother Edward James remained in residence and relations with the military were very cordial. The story goes that Brother Edward and the Commanding Officer enjoyed their glasses of punch and cigars every night of the duration.

After the war, however, the College did not re-open and the property and land were sold in separate lots – the Villas to the local council for £2350 for much needed post-war accommodation, the Trustees selling the College being the remaining Edward Joseph MacMullin of Mount St. Michael, Dumfries and Thomas Ward of Glasgow.

Although the span of the Grove Ferry College was relatively short, the Marist Brothers Teaching Order continued to grow in Europe and the other Continents and has today some seven to eight thousand members teaching in hundreds of schools in nearly all the countries of the world. In Britain, the Brothers have also faced the modern challenge of mixed comprehensive education with large comprehensive schools in Dundee, two in Glasgow and one in Wolverhampton; and St. Joseph's College, Dumfries, traditionally a boarding school for over a hundred years, is changing to a fully comprehensive mixed school for Catholics and Protestants.

In this context, therefore, the College at Grove Ferry from 1903 to 1940 was a small capsule in itself. The youthful foreign tongues and smart blue and yellow uniforms were part of the village scene; the Brothers, exemplary in their kindness, gentleness and humility, extolled to their pupils the true meaning of the College motto – Honora Deum et Benefac – Honour God and Do Good; and the Shrublands estate was the perfect setting for their way of life. It is not surprising, therefore, how much the closure affected the Brothers, as was expressed by Brother Clare:

'It was a grievous loss for the London Brothers because the College was a charming place for Retreats and holidays in the richest part of England's green and pleasant land. . . Before the visitor in summertime unrolled the rich green of the marshes sweeping down to the sparkling white of the chalk cliff and the deep blue of the sea, the shimmering bronze of wheat and the scarlet flare of the poppies between, the pale gold of barley, the white ribbons of roads that looped the undulating fields, the silted loam and sombre green of the hop gardens, clusters of red apples and black cherries peeping over orchards where comical sheep, smothered from nose to trotters in wool, wandered in full-bellied ease, the mellow rust of ancient farm walls, the deep copses, and over all, a flood of yellow sunlight. . . . It was the one patch of paradisal earth that we owned in all the Province.'

Acknowledgements:
Brother Jarlath O'Rourke
Old Boys Barry Bridgland and Norman Unicome.

✂✂✂✂✂✂✂✂✂✂✂✂✂✂✂✂✂✂✂✂✂✂✂✂

FRIENDSHIP, FELLOWSHIP & HARMONY

'Upper Red Lion' Inn,
Herne.

Sir,

I have the honour to inform you that a FAT PIG SUPPER with other joints for other tastes will be held at the Upper Red Lion Inn, Herne, on Thursday Evening November 23, 1876 at Seven o'clock when we hope to add another pleasant evening to those already enjoyed on former occasions.

Previous Fat Pig Suppers at Herne have been of the most harmonious and agreeable description – thanks being due to the harmonious and agreeable company which honours these occasions – not forgetting the first class specimens of tender youngsters of the pork persuasion, and I have much pleasure in inviting you to join our Herne and Herne Bay friends in another such evening for the purpose of testing some new articles of the same brand as mentioned above, and doing honour to our copyright motto:

Friendship, Fellowship & Harmony,
I am Sir,
Yours obediently,

J. B. Harnett.

141

WESTBERE VILLAGE HISTORY

by
Allan Butler

I found the following notes in the Parish Records:

'Appointment of Parish Historian – The Rev. Theodore J. Parks of Trinity College, Dublin, Assistant Curate of Westbere and Parish Councillor. 1st December 1897.'

'By a resolution of the Parish Council of Westbere dated December 1st 1897 it was decided to purchase a book in which should be written from time to time a history of such matters of general interest to the inhabitants of Westbere as the Council in the exercise of its discretion should consider worthy of placing on record.'

The first article of the Rev. T. J. Parks was a description of the events in Westbere to commemorate the Diamond Jubilee of Queen Victoria on 22 June, 1897. The contribution on the Parish Pump dated August 1897 reproduced below was followed by further entries, but the history soon lapsed – presumably upon the departure of the 'parish historian'. The book is with the parish records deposited with the Cathedral Archivist.

THE PARISH PUMP

EXTRACT FROM WESTBERE VILLAGE HISTORY

It was felt that with a well open to all comers, human and animal, when the door was by mischance left open, there was at least the possibility of contamination.

To correct this possible evil, the parish council resolved to close the well by padlock and key and to conduct the water from the inconveniently low level at which it was then obtainable, to the higher and more convenient level of the village street, and further, to erect a pump, by the manipulation of the handle of which a pure and ready supply of water might be obtained.

A committee of the Whole Council was appointed and we doubt not that the meetings of this body of capable administrators were characterized by keen debate and searching insight, and, as a practical result there stands the Pump. Long may it stand to fulfil its useful function, until, in the halcyon days of the future it shall be replaced by, perhaps, a more ornate but we are confident, a not more useful erection.

Rev. Theodore J. Parks,
Assistant Curate of Westbere.
August, 1897.

142

NOTES ON SOME MOSSES FOUND IN THE DISTRICT

by

A. E. Side, F.L.S.

Because of their medicinal use flowering plants have been studied and described for more than two thousand years. By the eighteenth century they were being studied in Europe, and systematically classified, for their scientific interest irrespective of their use in medicine. Bryophytes, mosses and liverworts, have been studied much more recently and it was not until the eighteenth century that any work on them was published. Since then their beauty and interest have been realised and their importance in the study of ecology and pollution recognised. The distribution of every known British species is being mapped. I have been occupied in mapping the Kentish bryophytes for twelve years and have records for many districts in Kent and maps for many species. Work on the bryophytes of churches and churchyards has been a special feature of this study.

The bryophyte flora of the Herne-Hoath district is not particularly rich. A visit to Hoath church produced only eight different species, while in some more sheltered, damper areas, lists of twenty-five species or more have been made. One wonders what was the position before pollution was an ecological problem. It seems important that present results of studies should be published for comparison with future works.

East Blean Wood was of particular interest, for in my notes of the visit I find the word 'abundant' against three of the species found there. One of these three would certainly not have appeared on a list from the last century for it was not seen in Britain at all until 1920. Somehow it had found its way into Cheshire

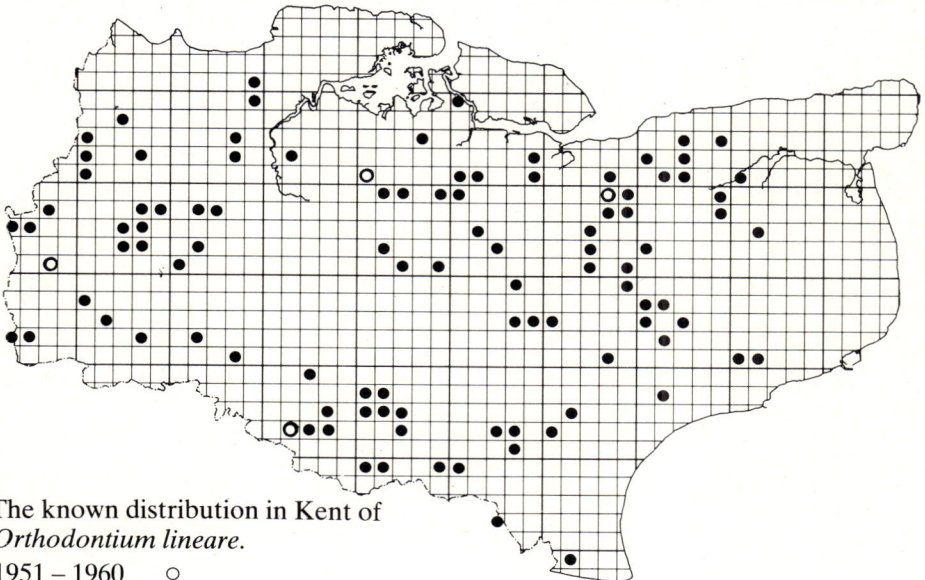

The known distribution in Kent of
Orthodontium lineare.

1951 – 1960   ○
1971 onwards   ●

143

from the southern hemisphere, perhaps New Zealand, bringing its name, *Orthodontium lineare,* with it. It lives on rotting tree stumps and will produce a great number of capsules from which the dust-like spores can be blown by the wind in all directions and spread the species to other localities. It was first recorded for Kent in 1949 by Francis Rose at Petts Wood. Since that locality is now in the Greater London area it does not appear on the Kent map but the first record for East Kent does. T. Laflin found it near Detling in 1951. By early 1960 it was known from four places, marked by the hollow circles on the map. The solid circles mark the places where I, myself, have seen it from 1971 onwards and they show how successfully it has made itself at home in an alien land. Its habitat is limited so its abundance is not likely to oust our native species and it should be admired for its vitality.

Both of the other two mosses abundant in the wood are native to Britain and both are noted for the fact that they very rarely produce capsules in this country. They reproduce vegetatively by means of propagules which are easily detachable and are dispersed by rain, wind or other agency. *Aulacomnium androgynum* grows on bark, usually of branches, or on peaty soil in woodland. It is of a bright green colour with a tiny drum-stick-like growth at the summit of each stem. The tinier propagules grow on the ends of the drum- sticks. It is a rare plant in the north and west of Britain but frequent in the drier parts, which perhaps accounts for its abundance in East Blean Wood.

The third mentioned species is *Isopterygium elegans* which forms mats on the woodland floor, looking for all the world as if it had been flattened by running water and washed bright and clean by the same. On its surface tiny branchlets can usually be found produced in the leaf axils, by which it is propagated. It is frequent and widely distributed in non-calcareous woodland. There are numerous other species of moss in the wood but the three described would probably be the most interesting to a bryologist.

HERNE WESLEYAN SUNDAY SCHOOL 23/6/1915 — at Boarded House Farm

KEY

1. Mrs. Till.	18. Doris Allen.	37. Fred Hudson.
2.	19. Nellie Whitehead.	38. Annie Parnell.
3. Mrs. Lisle Gates.	20. Walter Holness.	39. Janet File.
4. Mrs. Bubb.	21. Mrs. J. Holness.	40. Alice Sayer.
5.	22. Mrs. G. Richardson.	41. Edie Bubb.
6.	23. Mrs. C. Whitehead.	42.
7. Mr. L. Till.	24.	43.
8. Emily Pooley.	25. Mrs. F. Parnell.	44. Emily Parnell.
9. Lily Bubb.	26. Miss Hudson.	45. Doris Pritchard.
10. Mrs. Clark.	27. Frank Gates.	46. Olive File.
11. Doris Clark.	28. Jack Holness.	47. Lily Hudson.
12. Rachel Savage.	29. Joe Blackaby.	48. Flo Gates.
13. Ted Stone, Sunday School Superintendent.	30. Charlie Whitehead.	49.
	31. Fred Parnell.	50. Harry Holness.
14. Annie File, Sunday School Teacher.	32. Reg Bubb.	51. George Parnell.
	33. Albert Sayer.	52. Ethel Parnell.
15. Mr. Allen.	34. Harry Wells.	53. Elsie Hudson.
16. Rev. H. Phelps.	35. Ralph Steed.	54. Ivy Bubb.
17. Mr. File, Farmer.	36. Lennie Till.	55. Beattie Pritchard.

56. Lily Holness.	60. Emily Sayer.	64. Millie Pritchard.
57. Alice Parnell.	61. Hilda Bubb.	65. Ernie Parnell.
58.	62. Ivy Whitehead.	66. Frank File.
59. Dorothy File.	63. Cicely Till.	

Photograph and identification provided by Mrs. H. Nicholls (Ivy Whitehead).

SERGEANT HARRY WELLS, V.C.

by

Gregory Blaxland.

There are sixty-six names of men killed in the Great or First World War on the base of the war memorial in the centre of Herne, listed in alphabetical order without rank. Among them is that of Harry Wells, and against it, no larger than any other capitals, are the letters VC. This marks him as the recipient of the highest award within the Sovereign's gift, of which the crimson ribbon takes precedence even over the blue of the Most Noble Order of the Garter. Sadly, Wells never wore it, having been killed in the act of winning it.

Investigations carried out by Mr. Harold Gough, honorary curator of the Herne Bay Records Society, established that Wells was born on September 19, 1888, at Hole Cottage, Millbank, a building subsequently demolished that stood on the boundary of the two parishes, just inside that of Herne. However, he went to school at Hoath and left at the age of 12. He took a job as a farm labourer at Ridgeway, Herne, and lost two fingers, chopped off by a hay slicer. He then worked for Mrs. Wootton at Herne Mill.

He enlisted at the age of 16, and maybe because he thought it would be easier to conceal his true age far from home, he did not join The Buffs at Canterbury, but The Royal Sussex Regiment, of which the Depot was at Chichester. He was a well-built lad, 6 feet tall, and apparently a loner. In research carried out fifty years after his death Mr. Gough could find no evidence that he had any close friends in Herne or Hoath.

A soldier's standard engagement was for seven years with the colours and five on the reserve. Wells joined the police at Ashford on finishing his colour service in 1911. It is to be assumed that he was recalled in August 1914 and was posted to the 2nd Battalion The Royal Sussex Regiment at Aldershot, for every home battalion was in need of a huge draft. During the year that followed the 2nd Royal Sussex took part in some hectic fighting, from which they gained the accolade of 'Iron Regiment' conferred by their enemies, and were to be awarded nine battle honours. It would have been almost impossible for Wells to have survived this year without being wounded at least once.

Evidence came to light that Wells was fond of a girl in Ashford and that he went there on leave shortly before his death. He is said to have expressed a premonition that it would be the last leave he would have. He returned to France as a platoon sergeant in the 2nd Royal Sussex, who as part of the 2nd Brigade of the 1st Division belonged to one of six divisions ordered to make the opening assault at Loos in September 1915.

It was the first joint offensive launched by French and British, and the British troops were not to know of the gloom with which their commanders – most of all Haig, of the British First Army – viewed the prospect. However, they knew that a gas cloud was to be put down in front of them, and although the Germans had been the first to use gas, it was presented as the secret weapon by which decisive results would be achieved. In the event, it merely increased the number of British dead. Most battalions of the 1st Division had a horrific encounter and met complete repulse. The part played by Sergeant Wells is described in his citation as follows:

For most conspicuous bravery near Le Rutoire on 25th September, 1915. When his platoon officer had been killed, he took command and led his men forward to within 15 yards of the German wire. Nearly half the platoon were killed or wounded and the remainder were much shaken, but with the utmost coolness and bravery Sergeant Wells rallied them and led them forward. Finally, when very few were left, he stood up and urged them forward once more, but while doing so he was himself killed. He gave a magnificent display of courage and determination.

Seldom if ever can such valour have been devoted to so forlorn a cause. Part of the inspiration may perhaps have come from the officer who signed the citation, Lieut E. A. McNair. Five months later he himself won the V.C., for driving off a German attack preceded by the eruption of a mine. He lived to receive it.

A replica of Wells's Victoria Cross and an oil painting of his heroism, a lone resolute figure amid chaos and collapse, can be seen in the Royal Sussex part of Chichester Museum. In Herne, he appears to have no memento, other than as a member of the flock who died in the cause of freedom. His grave in France is similarly aligned with those of comrades in death by violence, in a cemetery that could have been named from the high command, Dud Corner.

Reproduced with kind permission, 'The Royal Sussex Regiment' (1701-1966)

Sergeant Harry Wells, 2nd Battalion, winning his Victoria Cross at the Battle of Loos, 1915. An oil painting by Ernest Ibbetson.

147

THE BROOMFIELD LANDING GROUND

by

R. N. E. Blake, F.R.G.S.

Throughout its long history Broomfield has stood in the path of regional communications. Just a few hundred yards east of the village lies the course of a Roman road which connected Canterbury with the coastal fort at Reculver and until about fifty years ago the principal highway between Herne Bay and the Isle of Thanet wound its way past the village post office and pond. In the middle of the nineteenth century the Ramsgate branch of the London, Chatham and Dover Railway cut across fields a little north of the village and in 1935 the newly-constructed Thanet Way impinged more closely still on the local farms and cottages. But what few people appreciate is that earlier this century Broomfield played host to a quite novel kind of transport – the aeroplane. For a few years the community had a 'landing ground' on its doorstep, which played a small, but useful, role in the aerial defence of the nation. Although now obscure, this rudimentary airfield is not totally forgotten and several older residents have clear memories of it during its heyday.

The existence of such an establishment came unexpectedly to light during a recent visit by the author to the Public Record Office, Kew, in connection with another aspect of aeronautical research. The name 'Broomfield (Herne Bay)' crops up on a number of listings of military landing grounds compiled during the First World War and on one particular file a sketch map distinctly earmarks the boundary of the site.[1] The airfield in question stood on land belonging to Parsonage Farm, between Margate Road and the future line of the Thanet Way, and extended from the farmhouse almost as far as Heart in Hand Road. Figure 1 depicts the local setting but, for the reader who likes to keep an Ordnance Survey map handy,[2] the centre of the field can be pinpointed at grid reference TR. 204 668. If there had to be an aeroplane facility in the Herne Bay area, this surely was the most suitable place for it; but otherwise today's passing motorist is given few clues, other than the flattish and exposed environment, that flying ever took place there.

According to official documents,[3] Broomfield was selected by the War Office in late 1916 for use by No. 50 (Home Defence) Squadron, Royal Flying Corps. This unit, with headquarters at Stede Court, Harrietsham, near Lenham, had flights detached to three East Kent aerodromes – Dover, Bekesbourne and Throwley.[4] The initial task of Home Defence was to intercept Zeppelins over British soil but by the spring of 1917 a far more serious threat was posed by the 'Gotha' bomber aeroplane which, from bases in Flanders, did considerable damage to coastal towns in south-east England.[5] Because fighters had very short operating ranges, auxiliary landing grounds were required at close intervals and Broomfield was probably planned as a touch-down point on the patrol line between Sheppey and Thanet. Figure 2 shows the disposition of all known First World War airfields in East Kent.

However, residents who witnessed aircraft at the field tell a slightly different story from that implied by documents of the period. Interception of enemy aircraft did not, in their recollection, play any significant part in Broomfield's duties; indeed the only hostile action locally is reputed to have been an aerial torpedo aimed at Broomfield Hall where other military personnel were housed.[6] The main use to which the Parsonage Farm landing ground was put involved flying training units from the Royal Naval Air Service aerodrome at Eastchurch, on the Isle of Sheppey.[7] Airmen used to fly across the Swale to Broomfield where they regularly carried out gunnery practice over the field, frequently parking their aeroplanes at the farm for an overnight stay. Up to a dozen airmen were at the airfield on some occasions. The only clue to inter-Service arrangements is contained in a notification dated 1917 that certain RFC landing grounds were now available for use by the Manston Naval Air Station,[8] but a comparable use by Eastchurch is not mentioned. No operational records can be found which specifically describe gunnery taking place at Broomfield, although the main types of aeroplane and some of the individual airmen who frequented the farm have now been identified, thanks to oral evidence supplied by eye witnesses.

To deal first with the aircraft, a fair variety of makes are recalled by locals. Mr. R. N. Marshall, who now lives at Bridge, remembers BE2C's being the most common visitors but he recounts that RE8's appeared increasingly in the later stages of the war and on one occasion a Nieuport Scout landed with engine trouble, ending up in a ditch at the northern end of the field. Mr. Marshall further remembers Sopwith Pups from the Isle of Sheppey which used to fly 'in a line ahead along Herne Bay seafront', one of which got into a spin and crashed in the sea off the Ship Hotel.[9] Whether these Pups were bound for Broomfield is not known but their presence near the town is worth noting.

Miss May Seager, who was born at Parsonage Farm and lived there throughout the First World War, recalls a Henri Farman 'with all its wires' and a Sopwith Camel which 'came in from France with playing-card jacks painted on the side'. Miss Seager confirms the predominance of Sheppey-based visitors

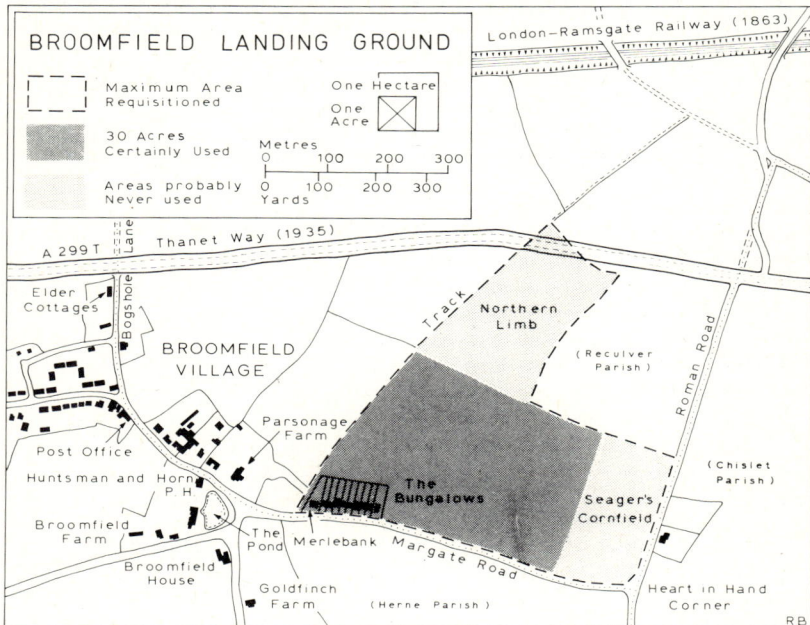

Fig. 1

but also referred in a recent interview to the occasional plane from Bekesbourne and Throwley, suggesting that there may have been some limited Home Defence use after all. Mr. Ted Wise, who still lives at Elder Cottages, Bogshole Lane, was greatly impressed with the Avro 504's, which were fitted with front skids to prevent tipping up on rough ground, while Mr. Sidney Finch, a contemporary of Ted's, remembers most vividly the Sopwith Triplanes which used the field. What these various aeroplanes looked like can be found in several standard references on the period.[10]

May Seager explains that before the airfield was commandeered there was a detachment of the Royal Horse Artillery billetted at Parsonage Farm, though whether this had any bearing on its eventual choice as a flying ground is unclear. Once the airfield had been established, four soldiers made up the permanent staff, including a Herne Bay man called Rolfe and a Corporal Morphy who married Lil Ingleton from the Huntsman and Horn P. H. where the airmen (and presumably also the guards) used to have a drink. The soldiers occupied one downstairs room of Parsonage Farm as an office, the telephone being the only such device in the village for some years to come, and two upstairs bedrooms. Their task was to take telephone calls relating to arrivals of aircraft and to go out at night, if necessary, to lay a flare path (L-shaped, as May Seager recalls). The overnight arrivals were accommodated, then given breakfast by the Seagers before departure. Mr. Marshall remembers that aircraft were guarded by 'an old man from the farm who was in the equivalent of the Second World War Home Guard', presumably one of the four soldiers described above.[11]

Mr. E. Harvey, who today lives in Beltinge, was about nine years old when the landing ground was established. His parents ran The Plough P. H. at Hunters Forstall, and he took a lively interest in events at Broomfield. According to Mr. Harvey, the target for firing practice was a circular pit in the middle of the landing area, filled with chalk. He believes that a wall by Parsonage Farm still bears bullet marks but this particular piece of industrial archaeology has yet to be authenticated. May Seager lends credence to stories of misdirected fire by relating that her father got very upset when sheep were accidentally shot at the back of the house.

Of special interest to the aviation historian is the recollection of Mr. Harvey's that practices were carried out at Broomfield with machine guns synchronised to fire through the propeller arc, a technique first introduced by the Germans in 1915 with alarming results on the Western Front. Sopwith Pups and Sopwith Triplanes each had front-mounted machine guns and are the most likely types to have been involved in this activity. Ted Wise, about ten years old in 1916, remembers aeroplanes flying low across the field and aiming their fire at the roundel on a scrapped wing anchored into the central pit. When gunnery practice was over, he and other local boys would run onto the field and pick up spent bullets and cartridges. One of the tasks which the sentries therefore had to perform, other than fixing tarpaulins, swinging propellers and removing chocks, was to evict excited children from the field when flying was in progress. Sidney Finch, who today lives in one of the bungalows later built on part of the airfield, retained some old cartridge cases but sadly he parted with these many years ago to Joe Barling, the Canterbury rag and bone merchant. Boys and girls were not necessarily unpopular, however. They would run errands for the airmen and soldiers (there were two shops in the village at that time) and in exchange for cigarettes and home-made cakes they would sometimes get a free ride up.

150

A more romantic story, which May Seager tells, involved one of her sisters. One day some airmen from Eastchurch came over to Herne Bay for a 'bit of a spree' and when they landed, the Seager girls ran out onto the field to meet them. The oldest girl, Muriel, caught the eye of Flight Lieutenant René de St. Leger and when the other airmen had left the field he remained behind. Later he used to fly over, circle the farm three times, waggle the wings – to farmer Seager's annoyance – then throw down a letter attached to a brick which the girls would have to go and search for. Muriel and René were married at Herne Bay Catholic Church on a snowy 2 March, 1918, the best man flying across from Eastchurch to Broomfield and then back again.[12] St. Leger concluded his air force career as a Group Captain and went on to become official host at Rolls Royce, Derby, using his facility in numerous languages to entertain foreign visitors. After the First World War he had served in the Middle East and India and on one mission in the North West Frontier he was shot down by tribesmen and held to a ransom of 10,000 rupees. May Seager explains with pride that her late brother-in-law was able to negotiate his own release in fluent Hindustani and was presented with a knife belonging to the headman of the tribe.

St. Leger certainly made an impression on Broomfield, in more ways than one. Mr. Harvey remembers the flier overshooting the landing strip and skidding into a ditch, where the propeller broke up. One of the Harveys retrieved a fragment of that propeller and our informant believes that either he or his brother still has it somewhere among the family heirlooms. The boss of the propeller was also preserved and made into a traditional clock which St. Leger gave to his (St. Leger's) parents.

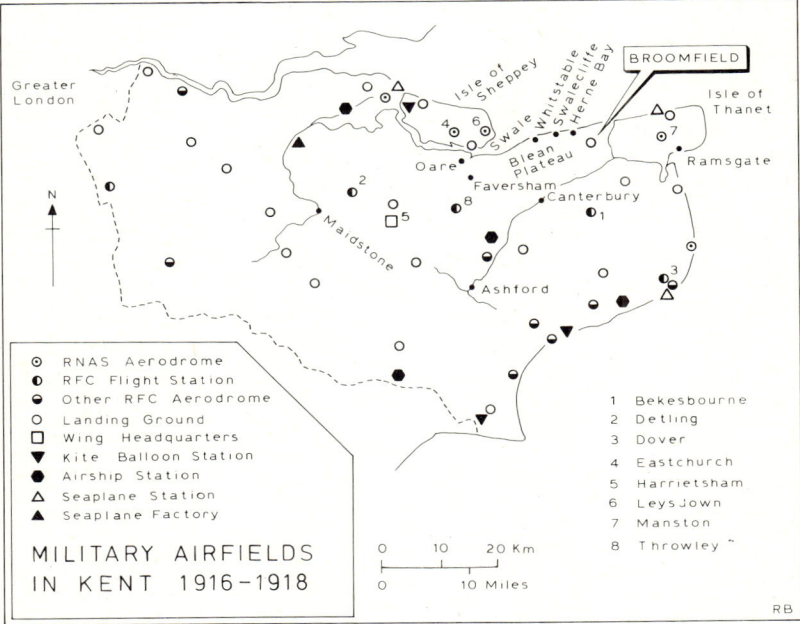

MILITARY AIRFIELDS IN KENT 1916–1918

⊙ RNAS Aerodrome
◐ RFC Flight Station
◒ Other RFC Aerodrome
○ Landing Ground
☐ Wing Headquarters
▼ Kite Balloon Station
● Airship Station
△ Seaplane Station
▲ Seaplane Factory

1 Bekesbourne
2 Detling
3 Dover
4 Eastchurch
5 Harrietsham
6 Leysdown
7 Manston
8 Throwley

0 10   20 Km
0   10 Miles

Fig. 2

But what of the airfield itself? Its size and shape are of much interest to the archaeologist and historical geographer and therefore need to be accurately described here. Figure 1 shows the *maximum* thought to have been acquired by the War Office, delineated by the pecked line. A retrospective measurement of the site yields an area of some 48 acres (20 hectares) which is identical to the figure that May Seager recalled (unprompted) as the acreage requisitioned from the farm. However, May is quite certain that the eastern extremity continued to be cultivated by her father; indeed she remembers a DH4 which overshot and made 'a half-moon track through the standing corn'. As Figure 1 shows, the full requisitioned area was, like many landing grounds of that vintage, L-shaped although there is some conflict of evidence as to whether the northern limb was ever used. A file dating from the closing months of the war,[13] which disappointingly contains no plans of landing grounds, states that the Broomfield site by then covered only 30 acres and thereby suggests that neither the northern limb (12 acres) nor Seager's vulnerable cornfield (say 6 acres) were meant to be used. The main rectangular block nearest to the farm (mapped in dark stipple) coincides closely with a parcel known as 'Great Kitchen Field' at the time of the 1838 Reculver Tithe Map and was probably in pasture when War Office Surveyors first considered it as a potential flying ground.

Strangely, whereas the effective landing ground seems to have been *reduced* in acreage as the war progressed, the linear dimensions quoted in official files appear to have actually *increased*. In 1916 the field was described as measuring only 400 yards x 300 yards,[8] which could be comfortably fitted into 48 acres, but by 1918 the available strips were noted as being 550 yards x 350 yards.[13] It is difficult to fit the longer of these strips into the assumed 30-acre site and one is left with the impression that the field was always rather constricted. This conclusion is backed up by the fact that Broomfield never achieved higher status than a '3rd Class' landing ground (the lowest category), despite its excellent natural drainage and generally favourable terrain. From the very outset pilots were warned about the obstacle of 'houses on the south-western approach'.[8] Initially the field was 'unlit' (by flares) but from Christmas 1916 onwards it was classed as 'lit'. There were no buildings on the site but a pole with a wind-sock ('like a pair of trousers') is said to have stood in the south-west corner where 'Merlebank' house was later built. Tents were also erected from time to time in the same area, according to Sidney Finch.

When the war ended in November 1918, Broomfield's landing ground became surplus to requirements and was quickly given up by the Air Ministry.[14] There is no evidence of subsequent military use but its days as an airfield were by no means over. Weekly notices in *The Aeroplane* and *Flight* magazines indicate that at various times from 1919 until the early twenties Broomfield was, like many other defunct wartime fields, designated by the Air Ministry as a 'civil landing ground'. Mrs. Freda Brand Lawrence (née Cottew), who lived at Parsonage Farm during the years immediately following the Armistice, remembers two ex-RAF pilots – Captain Stack[15] and Captain Stallard – who gave joy rides in a surplus aeroplane which they had bought.

As a girl, Freda went up several times with Captain Stack and on the odd occasion she took the Captain's ten-month old son, Jimmy, on her lap. When Jimmy Stack grew up he passed out of Cranwell as the best cadet of his year and progressed to the rank of Air Chief Marshal[16]. Mr. F. W. Cottew (Freda's father) rented grazing land at the top of Mickleburgh Hill (Grid Reference

TR. 188 678) and from those fields the two captains also gave joy rides. When Freda was going into Herne Bay they would sometimes fly her from Broomfield to a point near St. Bartholemew's Church (a distance of about a mile) whereafter she would walk the rest of the way. At that time St. Bart's was little more than a wooden hut and on one occasion the two fliers asked Mr. Cottew, with no irreverence intended, if they could park 'the old bus' inside. Both captains later re-joined the RAF and left the plane near St. Bart's as it was worn out. The local mechanic took it and got it flying, but later it crashed, killing the mechanic and his passenger.

Another civil flying use which Freda remembers was the occasion in about 1918 when the surgeon from the Kent and Canterbury Hospital, Mr. Whitehead Reid, came over to the Queen Victoria Hospital, Cavendish Road, Herne Bay, to perform an operation.[17] He flew from Canterbury (field unknown) and landed at Broomfield where a chauffeur-driven car was waiting. After the operation he picked up his plane for the return journey. The element of formal organisation in this anecdote suggests that Broomfield was then regarded as the proper place to land when visiting Herne Bay by air.

By the late twenties the field seemed more or less abandoned for flying purposes but in 1932 a new venture in British aviation brought it temporarily back to life. This was Sir Alan Cobham's legendary 'Flying Circus' which he founded both to entertain the public and to educate local councils in the merits of setting up proper aerodromes. The *Herne Bay Press* dated 23 July, 1932 carried the following advertisement: 'Friday (i.e. 29 July), 11.30, Visit of Sir Alan Cobham's Aviation Display, Parsonage Farm, Broomfield'. This event is also recorded in Cobham's recent autobiography[18] which usefully carried a schedule of all the many towns (though not the precise fields) where he gave

TWO GENERATIONS OF A GREAT FLYING FAMILY
Captain T. N. Stack (1896-1949) with his young son, Jimmy (later Sir Neville) Stack in a DH6 at Broomfield in September 1920.

153

displays. May Seager was among those who flew in a Cobham aeroplane (at five shillings a go) and remembers how tiny Broomfield and its pond looked from the air. She recalls a pilot named Captain Parkinson, who gave her a signed picture postcard, and another called Captain Illingworth who took a photograph of her sister standing beside the Avro aeroplane. In the *Herne Bay Press* dated 6 August, 1932 there is a report of the Broomfield display, mentioning the various aircraft,[19] the cost of the flights ('from four shillings') and a civic luncheon which was held for local notables with an informal 'National Aviation Day' talk by Cobham. A particular memory of Sidney Finch's from this era is the man who walked on the wings of an aeroplane while in flight. This was almost certainly Martin Hearn, but the type of aeroplane he used at Broomfield is not recalled.

It is worth mentioning in passing that the *Herne Bay Press* of 23 July also carried a rival advertisement for: 'Flying Daily at Swalecliffe Aerodrome, 10 a.m. till dusk, flights from 5/- . . . The Gordon Aviation Transport Company . . .' Swalecliffe was in many ways a much better location for attracting spectators, being equidistant from Herne Bay and Whitstable and near a new Southern Railway halt (which Broomfield never got).[20] Significantly, when Cobham toured the country again in the summer of 1933 he ignored Broomfield and instead used Swalecliffe, apparently having ousted the Gordon Aviation Transport Company. The exact configuration of the Swalecliffe Aerodrome is uncertain, nor is it strictly relevant here, but its very existence must have had some bearing on the demise of Broomfield as a flying venue.[21]

Thus 1932 would seem to have been the last year that organised flying took place at Broomfield. During the Second World War many old landing grounds were notified to the RAF for emergency use but there are no memories of forced landings at Broomfield even during the Battle of Britain.

Between the wars a certain amount of other recreational use seems to have been made of the landing ground, however. In 1929 the Broomfield Football Club rented part of the site from the Brands for as little as one shilling for the season, as Sidney Finch recalls. Ted Wise has recollections of another sporting connection – racing cars. He is not absolutely clear which models were exhibited on the field, or when, but he believes that either Sir Henry Segrave's 'Golden Arrow' or Kaye Don's 'Silver Bullet' came to Broomfield.[22]

Freda Lawrence recalls that not long after the Cobham era her then husband, Ronald Brand, had divided up the old landing area into smaller fields with electric fences. The Land Utilisation Survey of Britain, carried out in 1934 by Professor L. Dudley Stamp of the London School of Economics, shows the whole site under arable cultivation except for some very new housing in the south-west corner.[23] A year later the Thanet Way (or 'Coastal Road') stole about an acre from the northern limb but since then there has mercifully been no further urbanisation of the site. The Second Land Use Survey, carried out by Alice Coleman of King's College, London, in 1958 recorded roughly equal proportions of grass and cereal crops.[24] Today the site is again wholly arable, with crops of corn and potatoes in recent years, and is classed by the Ministry of Agriculture as 'Grade 2' land, being among the most fertile in Britain.[25] The sub-soil is Head Brickearth lying on the basement of London Clay which outcrops in the cliffs at Beltinge and the surface of field stands at about 115 feet above sea level.[26]

The history of Parsonage Farm itself falls outside the present study but a few words about its changing ownership since 1916 may be of some value to local historians in the future. The 450-year old farm was owned by Lord Sondes throughout the First World War and let to a tenant farmer, Mr. William Seager, whose father had come to Broomfield from Oare in about 1891. Bill Seager had eight children (three boys and five girls) of whom one boy and two girls (including Miss May Seager) survive at the time of writing.[27] In 1919 the estate of Lord Sondes was sold up and, with the coincidental death of Bill Seager (at the age of 54), Parsonage Farm was bought by another Herne Bay farmer, Mr. F. W. Cottew. In 1921 Mr. Cottew sold the farm to Mr. F. W. Brand in order that the latter's son, Ronald, could begin a career in farming. In 1925 Ronald Brand and Freda Cottew were married and they went to live in a new house called 'Merlebank' built specially for them on the farm. When Mrs. Brand senior died in 1938, Ronald and Freda moved back into Parsonage Farm with their young family and the couple farmed it until Ronald died in 1968. Freda continued farming for a few years until 1972 when she married the Reverend H. Jesse Lawrence, TD, and moved to Beltinge where they currently live. Parsonage Farm is today occupied by Freda's son, Mr. Gordon Brand, and is operated in conjunction with his own farm, Hawe, making an excellent overall unit.

All this said, many crucial questions about the landing ground remain unanswered. Who selected the site, and why?[28] Was it located, one wonders, near the intersection of a Roman road and a railway line for ease of recognition

BROOMFIELD'S MOST REMEMBERED SERVICE AVIATOR
René John Max de St. Leger (1895-1958) standing next to a DH9A aeroplane, probably at Eastchurch.
DH9A's were not introduced until late 1918, so this photograph was almost certainly taken after the
Armistice. Although his rank is concealed by his leather flying coat, St. Leger was by then definitely a
Captain in the fledgling Royal Air Force but he is seen here still wearing a Naval airman's cap (as was
permitted for a period after the amalgamation).

from the air? Do the deeds of Lord Sondes's estate provide any clues to the process of land acquisition and the terms of its release? Where exactly was the firing pit, of which there seems no trace today? Were any airmen killed or badly injured while engaged in practices at Broomfield? Who, indeed, were St. Leger's fellow pilots and gunners, and are any of them still alive to tell us more of what went on?[29] Did Cobham have a manual of old wartime landing grounds at his disposal when he planned his tour in 1932? How many spectators actually attended the 1932 Display and what precisely were the types of aeroplane which landed and took off from Parsonage Farm? There is clearly no end to an investigation of this kind and many relevant questions have not even been posed.

Finally, it needs to be emphasised that Broomfield's landing ground was by no means unique. There were over 500 airfields of one sort or another in Britain during the First World War and nearly fifty lay in Kent beyond the present Greater London area. At least a dozen Home Defence landing grounds lay east of the Medway, plus several aerodromes of a more substantial character (Figure 2). What gives Broomfield some local distinction is that it was the only *official* airfield to have existed at any time within the former Herne Bay Urban District. It is, moreover, with Bekesbourne, one of only two military airfields to have been located within the present Canterbury District, an area consisting mainly of well-wooded clay hills which the aviator has for the most part shunned for good practical reasons. Further information on Broomfield and other flying venues in the locality will be gratefully received by the author.[30]

NOTES AND REFERENCES

1. PUBLIC RECORD OFFICE/AIR 2/10/87/8247 and 8248, *Home Defence Stations and Night Landing Grounds: Arrangements to take up land for,* (Autumn 1916).

2. ORDNANCE SURVEY OF GREAT BRITAIN.
   1 : 63 360 (One Inch) 7th Series, Sheet 173 *East Kent.*
   1 : 50 000, Sheet 179 *Canterbury and East Kent.*
   1 : 25,000, Sheet TR 26.
   1 : 10 000 (formerly Six Inch scale), Sheet TR 26 NW.
   1 : 2 500, Sheets TR 2066 and 2067.
   Strictly speaking, Parsonage Farm stands in Reculver Parish, the boundary between Herne and Reculver running along Margate Road and therefore through the middle of Broomfield village (see Fig. 1).

3. PUBLIC RECORD OFFICE/AIR/1/823/204/5/44, *Re-naming of Royal Flying Corps Home Stations,* War Office (29 December, 1916).

4. LEWIS, P. M. L., *Squadron Histories : RFC, RNAS, RAF since 1912.* Putnam (1959). Later in the war, all three Flights of No. 50 Squadron were concentrated at Bekesbourne as new squadrons were formed at the other aerodromes. Harrietsham was then up-graded to a Wing H.Q. with control over several squadrons.

5. FREDETTE, R. H. *The First Battle of Britain 1917-1918,* Cassell (1966).

6. The walls of Broomfield Hall were badly cracked by this explosion. The Hall was eventually demolished and the site is now occupied by modern housing (Grid Reference TR 194 666).

7. Until the formation of the Royal Air Force on 1 April, 1918, the aerial defence of Britain was split between the Royal Naval Air Service, which carried out off-shore duties, and the Royal Flying Corps, which dealt with all engagements over British soil and on the Western Front. Eastchurch was the home of British naval flying (which started there as early as 1910) and towards the end of the First World War a special gunnery practice aerodrome was established at Leysdown, also on the Isle of Sheppey.

8. PUBLIC RECORD OFFICE/AIR 1/215, *Royal Flying Corps Home Defence Flight Stations and Night Landing Grounds within a 45-mile radius of Manston Air Station,* Commander-in-Chief, The Nore (20 July, 1917).

9. The pilot concerned was Captain Stuart Pratt – he survived the crash and was treated by Dr. Grogono, a Herne Bay G.P.

10. ANGELUCCI, C. and MATRICARDI, P., *World Aircraft: Origins to World War I,* Sampson Low (1977).
    BRUCE, J. M., *British Aircraft 1914-1918,* Putnam (1969).
    DAVIES, G. C., *World War I Aeroplanes,* Ward Lock Super Source Books (1974).
    MUNSON, K. G. *Aircraft of World War I,* Ian Allan (1968).

11. The personnel who looked after landing grounds were provided by the Royal Defence Corps and were mostly old soldiers no longer fit for active service.

12. The marriage was conducted by the Rev. Fr. Bonaventure Fitzherbert, C. P., with Geoffrey Robinson (probably the best man) and Constantine Seager as witnesses. The couple went to live on the Isle of Sheppey, their first house having no piped water which was not uncommon in rural areas at that time.

13. PUBLIC RECORD OFFICE/AIR 1/453/15/312/26, *Quarterly Schedule of Stations of the Royal Air Force – Part IV: Home Defence,* (September 1918).

14. The Air Ministry was created in 1918 to administer the newly integrated Royal Air Force, taking over relevant responsibilities from the Admiralty and War Office who had administered the two constituent air arms. Throughout the inter-war period the Air Ministry was also responsible for civil aviation in Great Britain.

15. Captain T. Neville Stack (1896-1949) was to become one of the most celebrated aviators of the inter-war period. In 1926 he and Bernard Leet made the first flight in a light aeroplane

Crown Copyright Reserved

BROOMFIELD'S MOST DISTINGUISHED LIVING AIRMAN
Air Chief Marshal Sir (Thomas) Neville Stack, KCB, CVO, CBE, AFC (born 1919) photographed
shortly before his retirement from the Royal Air Force in 1978.

to India, for which they won the Air Force Cross (rarely awarded to civilians). In 1931 Captain Stack made record times to Istanbul, Warsaw and Copenhagen. Apart from these memorable individual flights, he held many key positions in civil aviation, including first paid instructor to the Lancashire Aero Club, chief pilot of National Flying Services (based at Feltham, Middlesex), air superintendent with Hillman's Airways Ltd. (based in Essex) and sales pilot for Smiths Aircraft Instruments. In 1939, while test flying a Fairey Battle, he crash landed on a railway embankment near Birmingham after engine failure and was very seriously injured. He was eventually able to resume a flying career and was embarking on a new venture after the Second World War when he died of a heart attack.

The activities of Captain Stack in a wider historical context can be found in two excellent books on aviation of the period:

PENROSE, H., *British Aviation: Widening Horizons 1930-1934,* Royal Air Force Museum/ H.M.S.O. (1979).

BOUGHTON, T. B. A., *The Story of the British Light Aeroplane,* John Murray (1963).

16.   Jimmy Stack (so named to avoid confusion with his father) was born in 1919 and is today Sir (Thomas) Neville Stack, KCB, CB. In 1939 he passed out of the RAF College, Cranwell, as the best all-round cadet of the year and saw wartime service on Coastal Command flying boats. His post-war career in the RAF has included appointments as Commandmant of Cranwell and Air Officer Commanding-in-Chief, Training Command. Since his retirement from the RAF in 1978, Sir Neville has been Gentleman Usher to Her Majesty The Queen. Further details of Broomfield's most notable living air passenger can be found in *Who's Who.*

17.   Dr. E. D. Whitehead Reid (1883-1930) had learnt to fly while serving during the First World War. On leaving the Service he bought an SE5 and later an Avro and a DH6, all of which he based at the former military aerodrome at Bekesbourne. He had already been Consulting Surgeon to Herne Bay Hospital before the war and gained a reputation in the twenties for flying to visit patients. On 20 October, 1930, while flying from Shoreham to Canterbury (presumably making for Bekesbourne aerodrome), he ran into bad weather and tried to land on the disused wartime aerodrome at Detling, near Maidstone. He hit a tree, which tore off the wing, and both he and his passenger, the daughter of a friend, were killed.

18   COBHAM, Sir Alan, *A Time to Fly,* Shepheard-Walwyn (1978).

19.   The *Herne Bay Press* report mentions 'Two three-engined airliners carrying ten passengers, smaller craft and special machines, including an autogiro'. The three-engined types were probably the custom-built Youth of Britain II and III (mentioned in Cobham's above-cited autobiography). 'Smaller craft' probably included various D. H. Moths, a Desoutter I, a Comper Swift and one or more Avro 504Ks. The autogiro was the Cierva C.19.

20.   Chestfield Halt was opened on 6 July, 1930.

21.   After the Second World War joy rides were also given from a field at Kite Farm, Swalecliffe, which was subsequently engulfed by Arthur Fitt's Caravan Site. It is believed, however, that the pre-war 'Swalecliffe Aerodrome' was located *south* of the old Herne Bay to Whitstable road, between the railway and the The Plough P.H. New light has been shed on flying at Swalecliffe in a recent booklet:

BLAKE, Tony, (1982), *Stop Me and Fly One: An Account of Pleasure Flights and Flying Circuses in North Kent,* published by the author, Tudor Lodge, Chestfield, Kent.

22.   These two racing cars were exact contemporaries and were topical in 1929 when Segrave took the world land speed record (231 m.p.h.) in 'Golden Arrow'. Kaye Don's 'Silver Bullet' reached only 190 m.p.h. Since Segrave was killed in 1930 while attempting a speedboat record on Lake Windermere, it seems likely that any visit to Broomfield of racing cars took place in 1929.

HARDING, A., *The Guiness Book of Car Facts and Feats,* Guiness Superlatives Ltd. (1971).

23.   LAND UTILISATION SURVEY OF BRITAIN, *One-Inch Sheet 117 East Kent* (Surveyed 1931-34; edited by L. D. Stamp 1935).

24.   SECOND LAND USE SURVEY OF BRITAIN, *1 : 25 000 Land Use Sheet 192, The Isle of Thanet* (Surveyed 1958).

25. MINISTRY OF AGRICULTURE, FISHERIES AND FOOD, Land Classification of England and Wales, *1 : 63 360 (One-Inch) Sheet 173 East Kent,* (Surveyed 1968).
Grade 2 land is defined as that which has only minor limitations (for example, exposure) on cultivation. A wide range of agricultural and horticultural crops can be grown and it is usually the variable soil depth which prevents a Grade 1 classification. Only 18 per cent of all soils in England and Wales are classed as Grade 2 or better, therefore Broomfield is by national standards a very fertile locality.

26. GEOLOGICAL SURVEY OF GREAT BRITAIN (ENGLAND AND WALES)
1 : 63 360 (One-Inch) Sheet 273 Faversham (1953).
1 : 50 000 Sheet 273 Faversham (1974).

27. Sadly, Muriel Seager (widow of René de St. Leger) died on 14 January, 1982, in Sussex. She had requested donations to be made to the RAF Benevolent Fund.

28. It is possible that Lord Sondes actually suggested Broomfield to the War Office, although no positive evidence on this point is yet to hand. The logic of this hypothesis is the fact that Throwley Aerodrome (TQ 990 535) had come into existence earlier in 1916 on land which either belonged, or stood close, to the Sondes's family home at Lees Court, Sheldwich (TR 020 560). If Lord Sondes was sympathetic to airfields being developed on his lands, then it may not be too fanciful to postulate that he recommended Parsonage Farm.

29. May Seager and her sisters took the trouble to collect the autographs of the airmen who visited Parsonage Farm, but with the passage of time this valuable archive has unfortunately been mislaid.

30. It is disappointing that no photograph has come to light which unmistakably shows aeroplanes standing on the field near Parsonage Farm. Shots of such before 1919, or during the Cobham Display of 1932, would be a priceless acquisition.

Acknowledgements

The author wishes to thank all those respondents named in the text for freely conveying their reminiscences about flying at Broomfield. He is also

BROOMFIELD LANDING GROUND AS IT IS TODAY

This photograph, taken by the author after the 1981 harvest, shows the row of inter-war bungalows which occupy part of the former landing ground adjacent to Margate Road (see Fig. 1). Merlebank House is just visible but Parsonage Farm is hidden by the crown of mature trees.

especially grateful to Harold Gough, Honorary Curator of the Herne Bay Records Society, for researching local archives and providing company during field work. Background information on First World War aviation was kindly supplied by Mr. J. M. Bruce, Keeper of the Royal Air Force Museum, Hendon, and by Mr. Brian Martin, of Solihull. Details about the life and times of Captain T. N. Stack came from his son, Sir Neville Stack. Finally, thanks are due to Rolls-Royce, Derby, for supplying information on the career of René de St. Leger.

A HOATH CHILDHOOD

by

Millicent Culshaw

I lived in Hoath as a child during the years between the wars. We were very isolated although I doubt if we realized it at the time – we'd never known anything different. It is only now, looking back fifty years, that our solitary position can be appreciated.

There was no public transport until the late 1920's so unless you had a bicycle you walked. A day at the sea was a walk of four miles to Reculver, and even more to the point, another four weary miles home. A shopping trip meant walking two miles to Sturry for the train. I can vividly recall my mother coming in with a basket on each arm, having walked from Sturry with the Christmas shopping. Even for such a minor item as a postal order you walked to Chislet. If you couldn't walk and you had to travel you hired a cab!

But we were a very close community. The Church and the school were the dominant factors of village life. The old school, now the village hall, was a church school, and the Vicar came in now and again to hear us recite the Catechism or Creed. Sometimes a party of schoolchildren went to church for a specific service on Empire or Ascension Day or perhaps for a Remembrance Day service, this last was an emotive issue for practically every family, as the village mourned its young men who hadn't returned.

The old school had a house attached at the back, where the Head Teacher lived. Miss Anstey (later Mrs. R. B. Stephens) is the first I can remember. One day she had a burst pipe in her kitchen and she came into the schoolroom to ask who knew of a plumber. I told her Mr. Setterfield was a plumber – he was the landlord of The Admiral Rodney then! Somewhat doubtful, she asked how I knew Mr. Setterfield was a plumber and with all the confidence of six years I told her 'Because he sells plums!'

We often put on a pageant for Empire Day, we were very proud of our Empire in those days, every child would be included and we dressed up as the various peoples who made up the Empire family. Several times school concerts were produced. In one I took the part of a fisher girl, Tilly, while my brother Conn (Harold Snoad) had become infatuated by a mermaid who tried to pull him off the rocks by flinging a long rope of pearls round his neck. I was to pull him back and was supposed to hold the necklace at the join and let go at the appropriate time, but I didn't and in the scuffle it broke and the pearls went everywhere! It took us all next day to round them up from between the planks of the staging, and re-thread them for the second night's performance! Hope Brice was the mermaid, she sang like an angel.

Every year there was a party at Christmas, one of the highlights of our year, with a present for every child from the tree – someone had worked hard for our sakes. One memorable year a party of Hoath children was invited to the King's Hall at Herne Bay, to join in the large party given every year by the Cheerful Sparrows. Three of us went and had the time of our young lives. When it ended we found the Hoath children had left hours before and there we were stranded! A lady who knew us walked us to Broomfield, where she lived, my brother Reg was protesting loudly – he was only about seven. There a Mr. Bish, the coalman, got his car out, bless him, at ten thirty at night and took us the rest of the way home. My mother was just setting out for the policeman's house, the other village children having been home several hours.

A group of girls of those years was taught dancing by Mrs. Swinford at Shelving Farm. The older girls performed National dances, we younger ones did Nursery Rhymes, all dressed in flower-petal dresses made of crêpe paper. On the great day there was a performance on the lawn at Shelving, and tea afterwards in the farm kitchen.

A repeat performance was given at the Summer Fete; that was another red-letter day in our lives – the village fete. We were entirely unaware of its chief aim – fund raising for the Church. To us it was a great day out with races, ice creams, coconuts; it was a day of fun for the whole village. One year we won the pig, but having nowhere to keep it, my mother insisted we sold it again, and so reluctantly we had to part with it for 5/–.

Another event that enlivened our summers for us was the annual 'invasion' of hundreds of Londoners to the summer camp at Old Tree. It was

THE DANCING CLASS AT HOATH, 1936
Winifred Curtis, Mabel Miles, Milly Miles, Mary Morgan, Ethel Dale, Vera Curtis, Elsie Morgan, Winifred Sladden, Joyce Amos, Flossie Pilcher, Vera Bryant, Adelaide Sage, Florence Amos, Jean Bounds and Hilda Gisby.

Photograph by courtesy of Mrs W. Wells

run by Father Bartlett for his parishioners at Poplar. Whole families came, having contributed their sixpences all the year, for a week's holiday in the country. The men and boys camped in tents, the women and younger children were housed in a wooden building over the stable block. We often heard them making their way back to camp at night after an evening out at the Prince of Wales. As they came down Maypole Lane they were sometimes laughing and happy or maybe there would be harsh words and fighting, depending I suppose on how their evening had gone.

We very rarely saw a Doctor – ours was Dr. Tom Bowes from Herne Bay. He always wore a top hat and was one of the first people we knew to use a motor car. There was great excitement in 1926 when my brother Reg caught Diphtheria. He was whipped off to an isolation hospital near the Share and Coulter and we, after having our swabs taken, settled down to wait for the ambulance to come for us. All that week we hung over the gate, confidently expecting it, but none of the rest of us developed it and we were bitterly disappointed. A great many children did though, in that year. Some schools were closed because of the epidemic.

In those days of course, there was no such thing as school dinners; the majority of children went home at mid-day. If we were lucky we met Mr. Beadle the milkman on his way home at the end of his round, and we would race after him, jump up on the step at the back of the milk float and have a ride home. Milk was delivered in huge shining churns by the farmer who had actually produced it. There was a tap on the bottom of the churns from which Mr. Beadle filled his smaller can. This was brought to your door, and the milk 'dipped' out in a pint measure and into your milk jug, however many pints you needed that day.

Archie Chapman, on Right. Talleyman, Mr. East

Mr. Harrison and his brother with hops

Photographs by courtesy of Miss A. Chapman

162

The different tradesmen came out to us, the opposite of today. Quite a number of grocers from Herne Bay and Sturry, and butchers and bakers too. Our baker was Mr. Wyborn from Marshside. He made the most wonderful bread; it was baked in an old fashioned oven where a whole faggot was burned on the floor of the oven, the ashes raked out and then the bread put in to bake on the hot stones. Bread never seems to taste like that now!

Clothing shops also sent roundsmen out who would order what we needed, so although we were off the beaten track our various needs were catered for quite adequately.

One trader you would never see today was the oilman as we called him, Goodman's of Canterbury. There were shelves along each side of the van for soap and candles and hardware of every sort, and at the back was a large tank of paraffin oil, with the copper measuring jug dangling from a hook. Every household needed paraffin for lamps – Hoath did not have electricity till 1938.

It was a daily ritual during the Autumn and Winter months, cleaning and filling the lamps. A newspaper was spread on the kitchen table and all the lamps collected. Then, after refilling, the glasses were cleaned and the wicks trimmed and woe betide you if you left one uneven. Your incompetence was revealed when the lamp was lit that night: a flaring point trailed up the glass and could even crack it if it wasn't attended to at once.

Before the days of universal radio or television it was sometimes a problem to be sure of the correct time. We went by the 'hooters' – there was one for the Gas Works at Herne Bay which blew four or five times a day, or if the wind was from the other direction it was the Colliery hooter from Chislet – they were both utterly reliable.

Transporting coal for the oast house from Herne Bay Station. Mr. Bish's house at the junction of Bogshole Lane and Broomfield Road, with Mr. A. Chapman leading the horses.

Photograph by courtesy of Miss A. Chapman

My Grandfather was the builder in the village, the builder's yard being Millbank on the top of Ford Hill. I often went there for shavings, which we used to kindle the fire in the mornings – the quicker you got the fire going the sooner you had a cup of tea and your breakfast.

There was a great square hole in the ground round at the yard, the saw pit, where my grandfather stood at the bottom and one of the uncles at the top, and with a huge cross-cut saw they cut the whole trees up into planks or whatever they needed. It was stacked in great piles to mature, for five or six years there was all the time in the world in those days. He also mixed his own paint. He was a wheelwright, too. I have watched him making a cart wheel. With the hub and the spokes already fitted together, he would fix them to the centre of a circle of stones in the yard. Then having carefully cut the felloes to shape he would hammer one on to each pair of spokes and keep turning it round and hammering until it exactly matched the circle of the stones. Last of all the iron band was fitted, smoking hot from the forge, and water poured on quickly so that the wood did not catch fire. It was a fascinating business to watch.

He sometimes repaired the old Kent wagons for the local farmers, religiously fitting the correct type of wood for each part, oak for the body, ash for the undercarriage and elm for the wheel hubs and axle trees. How smart they looked when freshly painted.

An equally complex bit of joinery Grandfather did every year was the tally sticks for the hop garden at Ford. The tallyman wore a necklace of these sticks, one for each row or basket of hops. They were all numbered and part of each stick had been split off and numbered to match. These smaller parts were given to each family on the first morning of hop picking; they were drawn out of a sack actually, because no-one wanted the outside rows, where the hops were always small and therefore unprofitable. When you had picked five bushels of hops –

KEYWORTH'S MIDSEASON   *PROGRESS*   *WYE NORTHDOWN*   *WYE TARGET*

WYE CHALLENGER   *FUGGLE*   *YEOMAN*   *BRAMLING CROSS*

that is a tally – your number was found on the string of sticks, the small piece fitted into the parent piece, and with a file the tallyman made a mark across the two. So you had a record and so did the farmer. At the end of hop picking the marks were counted up and you were paid accordingly. It was no way to get rich. I can remember the reward was sometimes 10d or 1/–, for picking five bushels of hops.

There were two large hop gardens at Ford, these were always picked first, the hops soft and fluffy. And there was another smaller hop garden of Fuggles, some little distance away, across the stream. These Fuggles were a different hop altogether, tight and hard, and of a darker green and a longer shape, presumably they gave a different flavour to the beer. We only knew they were much easier to pick, the baskets were filled sooner, and, it being the last garden, it meant the end of hop picking was in sight. We were tired of it by then!

Mrs. Frank Spanton used to come round in her car at election times to take the women to vote. She would insist on them all voting, saying 'those women have fought a long battle on our behalf, now the least we can do is vote'. The polling station was at Chislet, which was very much the administrative capital of the district; unemployment insurance cards were issued there, the telephone exchange was there, even the school was staffed by a Headmaster, as befitted the principal village. My father and all his brothers had to attend Chislet school – grandfather thought a woman teacher was unable to maintain the discipline necessary for boys.

Yes! we were a close community in Hoath, all those years ago, we all belonged. The days all seem to have been long and sunny and happy. One tends not to remember – or at least to mention – the cold wet and miserable days. It was a Good Life.

An outing from 'The Prince of Wales' in 1927 with Mr. and Mrs. D. Payne in front. The vehicle was a Morris one ton chassis, fourteen seats charabanc body bought by the East Kent Road Car Company in April 1927. It was sold by the Company in 1933 and converted into a lorry: and scrapped in 1937.

Photograph by courtesy of Miss A. Chapman

MURDER NEAR MAYPOLE

by

Harold Gough

A small gravestone, overgrown with bushes, in the churchyard at Hoath is the silent and neglected reminder of a grim tragedy of more than a hundred years ago.

The brief inscription reads: "Our beloved father Richard Steed died 3 May 1863 aged 55. Give him eternal rest O Lord and let perpetual light shine upon him".

There is nothing in these words to show that the man buried here died violently after a quarrel on a lonely footpath near Maypole one Saturday evening – struck down, and his face battered beyond recognition by a railway navvy's boots.

A man arrested the next morning was charged with his murder, tried at Kent Summer Assizes, sentenced to death, and publicly hanged in front of Maidstone Gaol in the presence of about six thousand spectators.

Richard Steed was a carrier and general dealer living at Hoath; while the railway line from Herne Bay to Margate was being laid, he supplemented his income by running a little shop in a shed by the cutting at Bogs Hole, between Broomfield and Hillborough. Here he sold bread, and coffee and other beverages to the workmen. One of these "navvies", Alfred Eldridge, had lived at Hoath with his wife and child for four months; in fact he had lodged for a time with the Steed family. Eldridge, aged 32, had been discharged from the army "without a character" after serving in the Crimea and the Indian Mutiny. He was tall and strongly built. The first description after his arrest, printed in the Kentish Gazette, said: "his features are somewhat sharp and there is something sinister in his appearance though the cast of his countenance is not repulsive". He had recently spent three months in Canterbury Gaol for stealing timber.

Early in 1863 Steed had lent Eldridge some money, and when it was not repaid, he took out a summons in the County Court. Next day, Eldridge tried to pay a shilling off the debt, which Steed said he could not accept as the matter was in the hands of the Court. Eldridge was forcibly put out of the house, threatening to "do for" Steed before many weeks.

On the fatal Saturday, about 3 p.m., Steed had nine shillings and nine pence in his pockets, silver in one and copper in the other; his 11-year old son Albert set off home with the cart, and we next hear of his father when he left the railway pay-office about 6.20, and arrived at the "Prince Albert" Inn (now the "Smugglers Inn") at Herne Street soon after 7 p.m., when he entered and saw Eldridge. Both men appeared quite sober, and greeted each other in friendly fashion. Steed said "Are you going home? We will go home together". Soon afterwards they were seen in that part of Broomfield Road now called School Lane, "going along very friendly together", and they turned on to a footpath leading towards the Ridgeway. They passed the back garden of Isaac Pooley's cottage in Albion Lane about 7.30 p.m. Pooley knew Steed and called out a greeting, but did not recognise his companion. He noted the latter's brown coat with a patch on the back of the neck, as they passed by.

At the top of the hill, by Ridgeway Farm, there was a choice of tracks leading towards Maypole and Hoath. One fairly broad track, now classified as a bridleway, continued the Ridgeway past Hawe Farm, and by a rather lengthy route reached the main road by two possible exits at Millbank, between Ford and Maypole; the other, a mere field path, led more directly across country to a stile by the road almost opposite the "Prince of Wales" public house at Maypole. The latter was the more logical way for anyone going home after a day's work, though less well defined than the other.

In the same way, it was the logical route, across the fields on a spring evening, for George Turk of Maypole to walk his lady friend, a widow named Naomi Connor, back towards her home at Herne Bay. They set out soon after 8 p.m. About a quarter of a mile along the path, as they passed a copse called Moat Wood, they heard groans, and found a man lying in a ditch, terribly battered about the face and unrecognisable. Mrs. Connor became upset, and . Turk took her back out of sight of the man, and then returned to him. He knew Steed by his clothing, and lifted him out of the ditch; then he took Mrs. Connor back to Maypole, found a neighbour, William Petts, to go and guard the victim, and went on himself to tell Steed's family.

Young Albert took his mother and George Turk in the cart to bring his father home, where he died before Dr. W. Jameson of Sturry arrived soon after 10 o'clock. The doctor found extensive fractures of the front part of the face and forehead; the right eye was out of its socket. He decided that the injuries could have been caused by stamping with heavy boots, and found marks on the skin probably made by the nails of such boots. In Steed's pockets were found but sixpence in silver and fourteen pence in copper.

Meanwhile, Alfred Eldridge emerged from the other footpath just before 9 p.m., opposite Richard Larkin's forge near Millbank, where the smith's son, and neighbour Elizabeth Cullen saw him. He strolled along the road to

Mrs. Saunders' bakery, and unconcernedly bought a loaf of bread; he paid off two shillings of a three-shilling debt, but had the loaf added to his bill. Mrs. Saunders chatted to him for some minutes, and noticed nothing unusual in his manner. He then went home to his cottage near Hoath Church.

Early on Sunday morning, Superintendent Walker and Sergeant W. H. Gower of the Kent County Constabulary arrived with a constable to examine the body and visit the scene of the crime. In the ditch was a mess of blood and brains, lying in a depression "as if a man's head had been pummelled into the ground". There was also the mark of a boot heel in the ground, but no other signs of a struggle there; the soil was dry, and not even the prints of those who had removed the body could be seen. By the "bush-telegraph" of a rural area they learned of Pooley's sight of the two men passing his garden, and also identified Eldridge as the probable second man. By 10 o'clock they were at his cottage back at Hoath demanding to see the clothes and boots he had been wearing the day before. Eldridge was then wearing shoes, and clean socks; he eventually produced the boots from a cupboard, but was evasive about the socks. The coat which he produced was patched in the way Pooley described it.

The boots had apparently been washed and dried, but still bore brownish stains, and traces of mud with hairs embedded in it. His trousers were marked with reddish spots. When invited to describe his movements on the previous evening, he said he had walked with Steed to the junction of the paths, and had then taken the left-hand, longer way, while Steed set off across the fields by the track where he was later found. The Superintendent got Eldridge to take them back along the route he had described; they were led along an even more circuitous way than they expected towards Herne, and did not pass Pooley's garden at all. Perhaps it is significant that he took them across fields where no track existed, which suggests that he was not averse to the sort of short cut which might have taken him from where Steed was found, across to the other track.

Eldridge displayed no physical signs of a struggle or fight; he said he had heard from a neighbour when he got home that Steed had had an accident, and had told his informant where they had parted. Sergeant Gower asked about his relationship with the dead man, and he said they had not been on good terms for the last four months; Steed had once served him a dirty trick. Supt. Walker then charged him with the wilful murder of Richard Steed, and took him into custody.

On Monday morning the accused appeared before the Canterbury Magistrates, when a host of witnesses assembled to tell their stories of the events of Saturday. During the hearing a letter from Larkin, the blacksmith, to the Police was read, and the Court adjourned until 4 o'clock so that Larkin could appear in person. When he arrived he produced a ploughshare which he had found near the place where the body had lain, and drew attention to marks on it which Dr. Jameson agreed were blood; the doctor agreed, too, that this share could have caused the original injuries before, as he put it, "the boot went to work".

Eldridge made a statement denying the charge, but was committed by the magistrates for trial at the Summer Assizes. On the same day an inquest opened at the "Admiral Rodney" at Hoath, but as all the material witnesses were then appearing in Canterbury, it was adjourned for a week after evidence of identification, to permit the body to be buried. When it was resumed, the witnesses repeated their stories in substantially the same words, and the jury, "which was a very respectable one" according to the Kentish Gazette, returned a verdict of wilful murder against Alfred Eldridge.

When the case was heard at Maidstone, on July 30, Dr. Jameson announced that he had now examined the supposed bloodstains with a microscope, which confirmed his earlier opinion. He had also compared the hairs found in the mud on the boots with clippings from the dead man's hair and beard, and they matched.

Two other medical expert witnesses, Doctors Taylor and Pavy, were called, and explained at length their methods of forensic examination of the trousers, boots and hairs, as well as of fibre samples in the mud, which matched the cotton threads in a red "comforter" or scarf worn by the victim. They concluded that the boots had been washed, which had altered the consistency of the blood, but not thoroughly enough to remove all the blood, or the mud and hair adhering to them. Dr. Pavy said he had been occupied with the trousers alone from June 4 to 20. The crude simple methods then available could distinguish blood from vegetable staining by dripping ammonia on the spots, but would only allow of the assumption that it was human rather than animal, and thus the inference that it was Steed's blood. The identity of the hair and cotton samples was thus crucial to the case against the owner of the boots.

What must have been the sensation of the trial, however, was the evidence arising from the rail journey from Canterbury to Maidstone, when the prisoners were being brought up for the Assizes. Two warders who were in a compartment with Eldridge reported conversations overheard between him and other prisoners, when he appeared to admit to the murder, that he had kicked Steed's brains out because of an old grudge, that he had been drunk at the time, that he had only been a minute about it, but that he did not know Steed had died until the next day.

Alan Steed at Murder Site, pointing along footpath to where the body was found.

Eldridge had pleaded Not Guilty, but had not retained a defence counsel; the Court appointed a Mr. Barrow to defend him. Mr. Barrow found he had very little to base a defence on, and had to content himself mainly with trying to discredit the expert witnesses and the Police, but without convincing success. In his closing address, however, he drew attention to the lack of definite motive or intention at the time of the murder, whatever might have happened on the evening in question, and pleaded that the various uncertainties made it unsafe to condemn the accused on the evidence. As for the alleged remarks in the train, Counsel suggested that the accused was not admitting what he had done, but only telling his fellow-prisoners what the Law was saying he had done.

The Judge, Baron Channell, began his careful summing up just before 6 p.m., going thoroughly into the nature of "circumstantial" rather than "direct" evidence. He advised the jury, in fact, to consider first what evidence there was apart from the scientific witnesses or the alleged admissions. He pointed out that it was known that Steed had suggested they walk home together, whereas Eldridge claimed that they had separated very soon after starting out, and he contrasted Pooley's evidence of seeing them together with Eldridge's demonstration to the Police of his roundabout way home alone. The Judge was also clearly not impressed with the Defence's understanding of the train conversations.

The jury retired for about 15 minutes at 7.30 p.m. returning with a verdict of "Guilty"; the prisoner had nothing to say, so the Judge put on the black cap and addressed him in stern words about his dreadful deed, advising him to avail himself of the spiritual counsels which would be offered him, for there was no hope of mercy for him this side of the grave. Sentence of death was then passed upon Alfred Eldridge.

A few days later it was announced that Eldridge had confessed to the murder; he said he had received great provocation. On the way home, Steed had accused him of owing "some halfpence", and pushed and hustled him about. Eldridge warned him that if he did that again he would serve him out. Steed pushed him a third time into the road, when Eldridge knocked him down "and being excited by his passion and remembering past grievance, he stamped on him and kicked him, but without any intention of killing him". After that confession he said he felt happier than he had done since boyhood.

With another condemned man he listened to the admonitions of the prison chaplain, and received Holy Communion. On the Monday before the execution date, their photographs were taken, to be given to their wives. Mrs. Eldridge was unable to travel to visit him for health reasons, but his brother went to see him, and accepted the picture for her. On Thursday August 20, Eldridge and his fellow prisoner (a soldier who had killed his baby son under the influence of drink), were taken out to the scaffold in front of Maidstone Gaol at noon, before a large crowd, which included members of the dead man's family. Eldridge said "I don't know how it is, but I never felt so happy in all my life". When the nooses were placed round their necks, and the hoods over their heads, the hangman Calcraft shook their hands, withdrew the bolt from the drop and "the wretched men were launched into eternity". The account of the execution adds that the scaffold was surrounded by black cloth, so that the spectators lost sight of the bodies as they fell; only the tops of their white caps could be seen. Finally, according to the Gazette, "The bodies hung for the usual time, when they were cut down, and the crowd dispersed".

POSTSCRIPT

Naomi Connor, who had a nine-year-old son by her first marriage, later married George Turk, her escort when the body was discovered. A gravestone at Herne records the burial in 1877 of Alexander Hawtrey Connor, aged 23 – a stone placed "by his mother, Naomi Turk".

Albert Steed, who at the age of eleven had gone with the cart to fetch his father home, died in 1939 at the age of 87. At the time of the murder, Richard Steed's household, as seen in the 1861 Census, included his wife Hannah, three young daughters, and Albert. The reports of the case reveal that the elder daughter was married, and as Julia, wife of James Hammond, gave evidence of the extent of her father's injuries. There was, however, another member of the family, not in the Census household, nor mentioned in the newspaper: a son William, old enough to have left home.

William married his cousin, Ann Maria Steed, and later kept the "Pig and Whistle" at Hawthorn Corner, not far from the railway cutting where his father had kept his shanty. He died in 1923 aged 81. He knew the story in great detail, of course, and would take his children on regular walks to the scenes associated with the crime in almost ritual fashion, to impress the facts on their minds.

His son Frank, born in 1897, died comparatively young in 1948, but he too carried on the tradition, and in turn took his children to see the site of the quarrel and told the story of his grandfather's murder.

The first draft of this account, based on the newspaper reports, was already written, with some puzzling ambiguities, when the writer was taken by Frank's son Alan Steed to the traditional landmarks, and heard the legend of the hollow in the ground when Richard Steed was struck down, a hollow which obstinately refused to be levelled up. Today the spot is overgrown, overtaken by the corner of Moat Wood; but the story lives on, in a chain of oral tradition extending over three generations from father to son, and spanning 120 years.

Principal Sources:

Kentish Gazette, 1863: May 5, 12   July 28   August 4, 18, 25

Personal information by Mr. G. A. Steed and Mrs. M. Croucher of Herne Bay, great-grandchildren of Richard Steed.

An artist's impression of Richard Steed by Colleen Bond, his great great grand-daughter.

171

THE 1927 FLOODS

by

David Ashenden

My father, Leonard T. Ashenden, was closely concerned with the floods around Sturry in 1927. At the time he was General Expenditor for the Commissioners of Sewers. This rather grand title meant that, as Surveyor to the Commissioners, he was responsible for the efficient drainage of the Stour valley from Ashford to the estuary at Pegwell Bay. The Commissioners were a body of interested landowners charged with the responsibility of seeing that the river adequately served the marshes and water meadows then much in demand for grazing and fattening cattle each summer.

The Stour was tidal as far as Fordwich and a delicate balance had to be maintained between high and low water so that the smaller streams bisecting the valley were always well filled. They formed the fences and boundaries between the landowners. The main control was the Stonar Cut at Richborough where the flow was regulated by sluice gates. If the river was allowed to discharge itself unrestricted through the Cut during low tide there was the danger of the streams and dykes emptying themselves into the river; water levels would fall to the extent that stock would get mixed up – a most unpopular happening my father tried to avoid at all costs! Too little water run through the Cut and there was the probability of flooding, especially after heavy rain.

The run up to Christmas 1927 brought some pretty rough weather, and with a full moon over the Christmas period, the Spring Tides coincided with an exceptionally wet week. There was an abnormal amount of water draining into the valley from the uplands. On Christmas Day the wind veered to the East and increased to gale force. This was an ominous combination – the same combination that caused the 1906 flooding of the village.

By mid-afternoon the river was seeping over its banks along the Sturry Road. Mr. Prosser, owner of the two mills – the Black Mill and the White Mill – opened his sluices and ran the mill races at full bore, but they couldn't cope with greatly increased flows. What is now Milner Court playing fields was under water. The two branches of the river joined during the night and the Leopard's Head Public House between the two road bridges was flooded.

Boxing morning dawned with the water roaring across the road 2 feet deep. A car became stuck and was very nearly washed into the mill pool while the unfortunate passengers were pushing it out. Mr. Peel, of Sturry Court Farm, provided a farm horse and cart to convey pedestrians through the flood. In those days a number of people regularly walked to Canterbury – even on Boxing Day! Cars attempted the crossing at their peril. My father provided another horse to stand by to pull any vehicle that spluttered to a standstill when water 'got in the works'. The wise motorists did not attempt to cross under their own power but relied on the four-legged 'Punch'.

The water spread all round the White Mill as far as what is now the Milner Memorial Ground and to the builder's yard. Mrs. Newman, the church verger, unlocking the church that morning found hassocks floating about the aisles. Even after the flood had subsided it took several weeks to dry out the church. The two tortoise stoves, each holding 2½ cwt. of coke were kept burning day and night. In the meantime services were held in the Parish Room, sadly demolished in the last war when land mines devastated the village.

As always there was a humorous side to the catastrophe. During Christmas night, Mr. Prosser's hen houses were swept away and his chickens took refuge on the fences and bushes surrounding the mill. My brother, who kept his canoe at Bridge House, could be seen on Boxing Morning paddling after some panic-stricken birds that had taken flight when Mr. Prosser, in his own rowing boat, had collided with their erstwhile perch! Strangely, the two mariners succeeded in accounting for practically all the chickens.

Later in the day, my brother and I went to the lower land of Whatmer Hall Farm adjacent to the marshes to rescue more chickens marooned in bushes and trees. Just about where Bretts machinery stands was a jumble of sheds belonging to Mr. Amos in which lived a variety of pigs, chickens and cats. Of the cats there was no sign; the pigs had removed themselves to higher ground and were huddled in a corner of our land by the railway; the chickens, resting safely on their perches until Mr. Amos opened the flooded sheds, took off and flew with surprising agility to the nearby willows.

Farther along, towards Westbere, Mr. Waters, the well-known 'looker', also kept a few chickens. The 'looker' was employed by the graziers on a free-lance basis to 'look' the stock each day and report if anything was awry. There was, of course, no grazing in the winter.

Mr. Waters' chickens were very much 'free range', picking up their living on the marsh. They roosted mostly in some willows along our boundary. That day, the trees were standing in about two feet of water and, wisely, the birds had not moved from their overnight perches. It was a simple matter, at dusk, to wade out to them and put them into sacks for Mr. Waters to take to his house in the Island Road.

Photograph by courtesy of the late Arthur Bournes

A casualty of the flood in the Fordwich Road, Sturry

173

Those who suffered most on account of the flooding were the residents of Fordwich. The main street was awash, with houses on both sides flooded. On the Sturry side of the river the water reached almost to the Welsh Harp public house. A Flood Relief Fund was opened by the Mayor of Fordwich who was, I think, Mr. Daniel Brice.

Further afield, Canterbury was partially flooded. Pound Lane, North Lane, the Westgate were under water, and I can remember walking over King's Bridge with my father and standing in water almost immediately. The situation was aggravated by the restricted mill-races of the two mills belonging to Messrs. Denne & Son, the one in St. Radigund's, the other at the end of North Lane. In an effort to hold back the water to relieve Canterbury, my father had the mills at Chartham, Chilham and Wye close their sluices and this certainly eased the flooding in Canterbury. But it did not help Sturry and Fordwich sandwiched between the mass of water bearing down from Canterbury and the upsurge from the coast with each high tide.

After the flood came the frost. Burst pipes and ice everywhere! The Westbere Marshes were one vast skating rink. Several of us learned to skate that winter! Wherever I went with my father the scene was the same – thick ice across the valley with just a ribbon of open water winding down the middle. It was said one could skate from Fordwich to Sandwich, but as far as I know, no one put it to the test. It was done, however, in 1906 – by Mr. Prosser and one or two hardy friends.

BROOMFIELD HALL in 1930, restored by JOHN WESTON ARNOLD, showing the croquet lawns. The house was demolished in 1961.

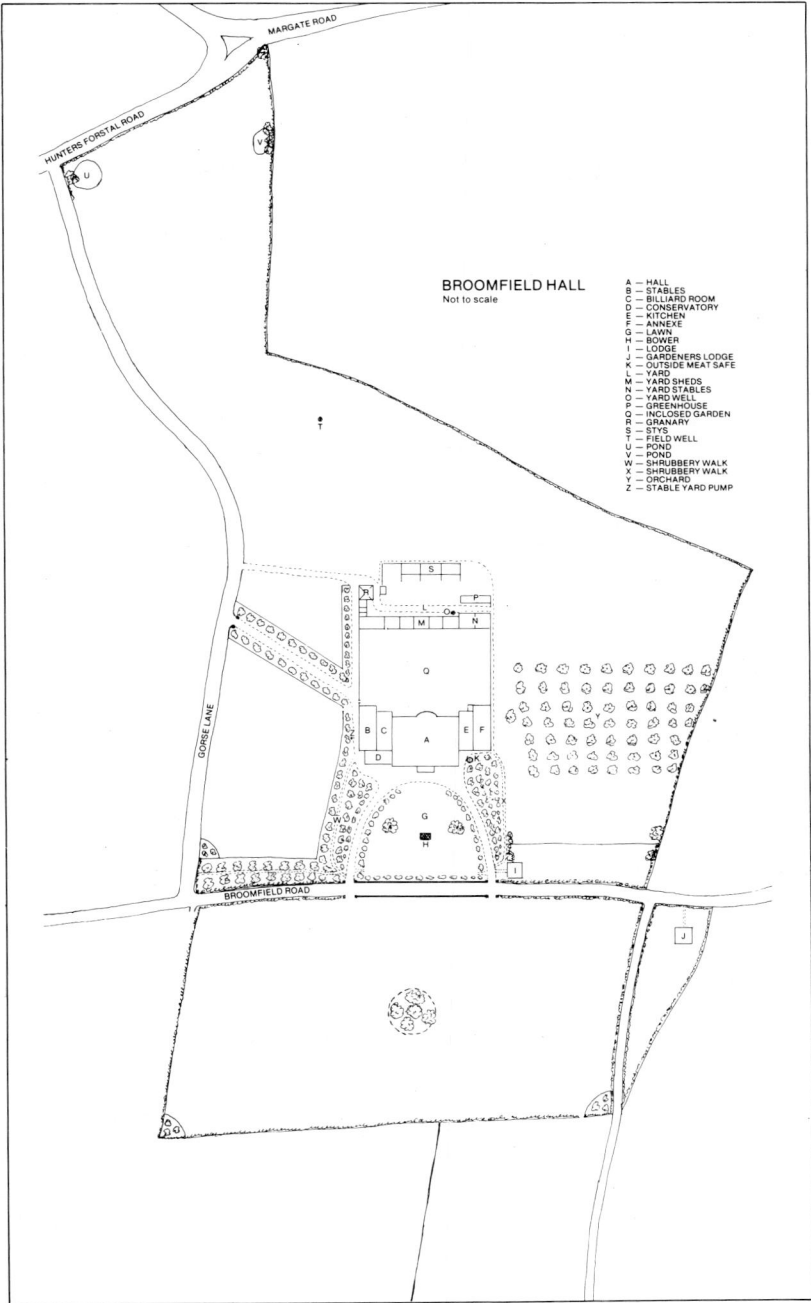

MARGATE ROAD

HUNTERS FORSTAL ROAD

GORSE LANE

BROOMFIELD ROAD

BROOMFIELD HALL
Not to scale

A — HALL
B — STABLES
C — BILLIARD ROOM
D — CONSERVATORY
E — KITCHEN
F — ANNEXE
G — LAWN
H — BOWER
I — LODGE
J — GARDENERS LODGE
K — OUTSIDE MEAT SAFE
L — YARD
M — YARD SHEDS
N — YARD STABLES
O — YARD WELL
P — GREENHOUSE
Q — INCLOSED GARDEN
R — GRANARY
S — STYS
T — FIELD WELL
U — POND
V — POND
W — SHRUBBERY WALK
X — SHRUBBERY WALK
Y — ORCHARD
Z — STABLE YARD PUMP

THE AMOS FAMILY

by

Brian Austin.

Every village has its large family, but in Hoath there were two, the Amoses and the Dales. I was related to the Amoses. Being related to such a large, close family means that recounting stories and events can be achieved with comparative accuracy.

My great grandmother, Daisy Amos, met her husband, William, who was born at Herne Street in 1881 whilst in service at the Old Rectory, Hoath, at the turn of the century. Mr. Amos used to drive around the village with horse and cart delivering flour for his employer, Mr. Ebenezer Fuller of Old Tree Mill, Hoath. Having been married at Kennington Church, Ashford, the birthplace of Mrs. Amos, the couple moved in 1909 to Hole Cottages, Herne, the birthplace of Harry Wells, V.C. Although within the parish of Herne, the ruins of these cottages can still be seen at the bottom of Old Hawe Lane, which runs from the top of Ford Hill. It was at this home where all ten Amos children were born between 1910 and 1932.

During World War I William Amos served with the Buffs in France, and when on leave would have to walk from Herne Bay Station down Old Hawe Lane to his home, the same long walk endured by his two eldest sons in World War II. My Great Aunt, Mrs. Gertrude Marsh (née Amos), recalls how frightened they were as children when the Army horses came galloping down the lane, for they were grazed in the meadow opposite the cottages.

After the Great War, William Amos went into the building business, but a crippling injury caused by falling from the roof of a building brought an end to this venture.

All of the Amos children went to school at Hoath (either the old school, now the village hall, or the new school) and approximately 30 Amos children have been on the register (remembering that Mr. Amos' younger brother, Harry, himself was father of 13 children).

By the Second World War, the Amoses had moved to Dalby Cotts, Hoath, next door to Aunt Aggie's sweet shop. These old cottages were condemned when the family moved in and are long since demolished; in fact all that remains behind the modern bungalows which are built on the site of Dalby Cotts are the fruit trees, planted many years ago by Mr. Amos and still flourishing.

The two eldest boys, William and Reginald, followed in their father's footsteps by serving in the Buffs during the War. William was invalided out of the Army, but Reg went on to serve in such places as North Africa and Burma where he was killed in action in 1945, the Buffs' final campaign of the Second World War.

After the War, although now married and with grandchildren of their own in some cases, the family remained local. Mr. Amos worked for the Rural District Council and retired to 5, Woodview, Hoath, where he died in 1961 aged 80. Mrs. Amos remained in good health and spirits, such that she was able to endure the premature deaths of three of her children.

It was always with great pride that she furnished the photographs of her husband and son with poppies, and it is perhaps ironical that she died on Remembrance Sunday 1979.

FIRWOOD, HERNE COMMON

A Georgian-style house, according to a photograph of about 1880, it may have been the one referred to in 1800 by Hasted (vol. ix, p.85) – 'an elegant new house built on the common, belonging to Mr. Lyddell'. It may be relevant that George Liddell of the parish of St. Mary Magdalene, Bermondsey, was married to Mary Tassell at Herne on 29 October, 1795. There is no evidence of any other contemporary house on Herne Common.

On the 1840 Tithe Map it appears as enclosure 522, part of Herne Common Farm, owned by John Palmer, and described as 'House, Lawn and Garden, 1 acre, 1 rood, 10 perches'.

It is said to have been used as a summer holiday residence by Douglas Jerrold, the Victorian journalist and humorist, the author of 'Mrs. Caudle's Curtain Lectures'. He was a friend of Charles Dickens, and invited him to visit him at Herne, but Dickens turned the idea down (July 1844). Jerrold's connection with Herne and Herne Bay is said to have ended by 1852.

The 1851 Census shows it as occupied by John Palmer, aged 65, his wife and his three sisters, together with two female domestic servants, and a farm servant aged 19. Palmer described himself as a 'Farmer of 88 acres employing one or two men; but for free trade would employ four' – an intriguing political comment!

In the 1930's it was occupied by an equerry of the Prince of Wales (later King Edward VIII); then it was turned into a 'roadhouse' and re-named 'The Silver Slipper'. The house was gutted by fire, and later demolished.

Photograph by courtesy of the Herne Bay Records Society

FIRWOOD COURT, HERNE COMMON

HOATH SCHOOL

by

Joy Webster

Hoath Church of England School opened in 1860 in the building now used as the Village Hall. A plaque on the wall tells us that 'This Tablet was placed here to commemorate the indefatigable exertions of the late Sarah-Ann Collard in raising the funds for the erection of this school house'. I have not been able to discover anything about the early years as the first entries in the School Log Book are for the year 1902 when the Headteacher was Miss Hocken. She and her assistant, Miss Thomson, both retired in April 1905 after thirty years' work in the school. There were two classrooms, in the smaller of which the Infants were 'awkwardly seated at long desks placed on the ledges of a high gallery' (H.M.I. Report 1911). This gallery was removed and dual desks provided in 1912. The main classroom housed Standards I to VI, aged 7 to 13 years, all of whom were taught by the Headteacher until after 1915 when various uncertificated assistants are mentioned. There was also living accommodation for the teachers, with a scullery and living room downstairs and a staircase (now removed) leading up to the bedroom. These rooms were used until the school closed in 1928 – there is reference in the Log Book to the 'unpleasant proximity of the boys' offices' and to the school having two days holiday so that the rooms could be 'whitewashed etc.' ready for a new teacher to move in. Living conditions were obviously not ideal and it is not surprising that there were many occasions when the school closed early on the last day of term 'to enable the teachers to meet the London train'.

There are many complaints about poor attendance due to chicken-pox, measles, mumps, colds and influenza. Ringworm was common and one boy was absent for 3 months with this. In June 1902 other causes of absence are mentioned; ' . . . parents fruit and pea-picking and also the sudden and dangerous illness of our beloved King having cast a gloom over the village. Also, postponement of the Coronation Festivities added to the children's sorrowful appearance'. In 1919 the Headmistress wrote of the 'constant promiscuous!!! half days for quite unnecessary reasons of certain children . . . decisive steps ought to be taken to stop it'. But despite admonitory lectures by the Attendance Officer the problem continued. Mothers took them out on fine days, and the weather had a far more marked effect on attendance than nowadays as both heavy rain and heat waves caused children to stay away. In 1926 there was an outbreak of diphtheria in the village and eight children were in hospital.

Reading the Log Book one gains an impression of a school where much good work was done despite poor conditions and overcrowding. Those Heads who remained for some years obviously became attached to their pupils and accustomed to the conditions – it is those who came on supply or for short periods who provide the most vivid picture of the school. Miss Growns, who was in charge from October to December 1905 wrote: 'The monitress is no use whatever as a teacher, so I have the whole six Standards and the Infants to teach (72 pupils present this week). Unless good help is forthcoming my health will thoroughly break down . . . it requires three good teachers to work up such a backward school. The children are terribly cramped and so short of books they have to look over . . . Lights are required very badly here all the winter months, as several times we have not been able to see to work. Also, it is very cold in the mornings although the cleaner lights the fires as soon as she can see'.

In 1922 Mr. G. A. Turner (H.M.I.) wrote of the 'cramped and crowded conditions. There are two classes in the main room . . . The stove stands out from the wall, there are desks for 54 children, a piano, cupboards, and some boards used for making a platform for concerts and public meetings. Most of the school material is piled in corners for want of cupboard room, and there is very little space for free movement. The walls and ceiling are dirty. On the day of inspection 59 children were being taught in this room'.

There must have been great rejoicing in October 1928 when the new Hoath Council School opened and the children moved into a building with well-lit rooms surrounded by a pleasant playing field. Problems continued, however. In the first year the school had a succession of two head teachers and eight assistants, some of whom stayed only a few days, and there was a shortage of books, pencils and other equipment. During the next few years the school was very crowded with up to 90 pupils aged 5 to 14. The playground and field were often flooded due to inadequate drainage.

In 1935 Sturry Central School opened. The senior pupils from Hoath were transferred to the new school and Hoath School itself took on the form it still retains as an Infant and Junior School of between 40 and 50 pupils.

Children at Hoath Primary School about 1925
The picture includes Ronald Foreman, Charlie Cage, Tommy Holmes, Victoria Cage, Elsie Bounds, Muriel Amos, Kathleen Pretty, Reginald Haffenden, Frederick Wells, Winifred Curtis, Hilda Amos, Nellie Amos, Winifred Amos, Dorothy Hollands and Clifford Miles.

Photograph by courtesy of Mrs. W. Wells

Hop-growing Parishes in 1835 and 1951 with acreages

	1835	1951
Chislet	20	8
Fordwich	17	0
Herne Bay	41	0
Hoath	40	15
Sturry	42	0
Westbere	12	0

Acres of hops being grown in parishes in Kent.

	1835	1951
Acres of Hops	25,740	12,645
Number of Parishes	263	129

A Survey of the Agriculture of Kent

by G. H. Garrad, O.B.E., N.D.A., C.D.A. (Hons.) Wye College.

pub. Royal Agricultural Society of England
County Agricultural Surveys No. 1
16, Bedford Square, London WC1. 1954.

A photograph taken about 1928 of Workman on Ford Farm.
They are (from left to right) Archibald Chapman, Robert Hubbard, Cecil Castle and Robert Cage.

Photograph by courtesy of Miss A. Chapman

Abbot, Abp., 31, 38
Acomb, Pastor, 120
Allen, 5
Allen, S. T., 77
Alsopp, Frances, 82
Amos, Mr., 173
Amos, family, 176
André, Bro., 139
Andrews, James, 117, 118
Apulderfield, Elizabeth, 43, 45, 46
Apulderfield, Mildred, 43, 46, 48
Apulderfield, William, 43, 44, 46, 54
Aragon, Katherine of, 46
Arthur, Prince, 46
Arundel, Abp., 20, 31
Ashenden, L. T., 172
Athanasius, Bro., 139

Badcock, Wm., 78
Baldock, Joseph, 117
Ball, Robert, 93
Baret, John, 78
Barley, James, 75
Barling, Joe, 150
Barnes, D'arcy, 127
Barrow, Mr., 170
Bartlett, Fr., 162
Bates, John, 28
Beadle, Mr., 162
Beard, Richard, 94
Beasley, Edward, 120
Beck, Theophilus, 5, 35
Bede, the Ven., 3
Belyetere, Wm. le, 86
Benedict, Bro. Jos., 140
Bennett, Martha, 121
Benstede, Andrew, 28, 29, 60, 61
Bery, Agnes, 32
Bery, William, 32
Best, Mary, 92
Bigglestone, W., 94
Bird, John, 120
Bissaker, Ann, 118
Bix, Richard, 82
Bix, Susan, 82
Blake, James, 137, 138
Blandford, Rev. Thomas, 120
Bollen, Daniel, 82
Boniface VIII, Pope, 31
Bonner, Bishop, 73, 74
Booth, General, 119
Bowes, Dr. T. A., 7, 162
Bowker, William, 49
Boys, Sara, 63
Boys, Thomas, 63
Brand, Gordon, 155
Brand, Ronald, 154, 155
Brent, John, 7
Brent, Roger, 44
Brent, William, 42, 44
Brice, Charlotte, 119
Brice, Daniel, 174
Brice, George, 119, 120
Brice, Hope, 160
Bridges, Sir Brook Wm., 115
Brooke, Susan, 32
Brooke, Thomas, 32
Brown, Wm., 120
Bruce, J. M., 160

Brus, Margery, 45
Buchanan, Rev. James, 54, 60, 100, 101, 102, 128, 130, 131
Buckhurst, John, 77
Bundock, Jonathan, 118, 119
Bysmare, Elizabeth Agnes, 58
Bysmare, Margaret, 58
Bysmare, William, 58
Bysmer, Bartholomew, 32
Bysmer, Richard, 32
Bysmer, Robert, 32
Bysmere, Alexander, 28
Bysmere, Thomas, 26, 28
Bysmere, William, 28

Calcraft, 170
Camoys, Thomas, Baron, 56
Caton, John, 29
Cawley, Rev. D., 86
Cecil, Sir William, 52
Chakbon, Isabella, 64, 65
Champagnet, Fr. Marchellin, 136
Channell, Baron, 170
Chapman, Copper, 117
Chapman, William, 80
Charles I, 38
Cheneys, 43
Chichele, Abp., 28
Christian, Thomas, 120
Chumald, Bro., 139
Clarke, Joseph, 32
Clarkson, Jonathan, 120
Clere, Wm., 45
Clerk, Richard, 82
Cobb, John, 28
Cobbett, Wm., 96, 97
Cobham, Sir Alan, 153, 154, 156
Codrington, T., 9, 10, 13
Cole, A. E., 119
Collard, E., 94
Collard, Edward, 122
Collard, James, 94
Collard, John, 122
Collard, Sarah-Ann, 178
Connor, Alex H., 171
Connor, Naomi, 167, 171
Constant, Wm., 85
Cottew, F. W., 152, 153, 155
Cranmer, Abp., 38, 72, 73
Criol, Nicholas, 40
Crippen, Wm. F., 119
Cromwell, T. K., 100
Cullen, Elizabeth, 167
Currie, Henry, 137

Darley, John, 28, 56, 58, 59
Daubeney, Rev. Giles, 100, 124
Davidson, Abp., 138
Dawkyn, Sir W., 32, 34
Dean, Abp., 38
Deacon, Wm., 34
Decoopman, Edward, 137, 138
Deedes, Wm., 115, 116
Defoe, Daniel, 5, 98
Denne, Alfred, 136
Denne, Ann, 136
Denne, Elizabeth, 136
Denne, Frances, 136
Denne, George, 122
Denne, John, 136

Denne, Thomas, 136
Dering, Sir Edward, 22
Dering, Sir Edward C., 115, 116
Dering, G. C. A., 125
Dering, George, 122
Dickens, A. G., 117
Dickens, Chas., 177
Digges, James, 43
Digges, Mildred, 43, 48
Don, Kaye, 154
Downing, Prof. G., 137
Drake, Michael, 115
Duncombe, John, 43, 54
Dunkyn, Tymothy, 75
Dunkyn, Wm., 82

Edward II, 4
Edward VI, 51, 73
Edwards, Passmore, 128
Elcock, Christopher, 63
Eldridge, Alfred, 166, 167, 168, 169, 170
Elizabeth, Queen, 74
Engham, Elizabeth, 60
Epsly, Jonas, 117
Evans, Sir John, 7
Evans, Wm., 124

Fairbrass, Fredk. Wm., 120
Fiennes, Celia, 96
Finch, Sidney, 150, 152, 154
Fitter, R., 100
Flint, T. J. W., 120
Foche, Ann, 92
Fogge, Sir John, 42, 44, 46, 49
Fortescue, Sir John, 46
Frampton, T. S., 32
Freeth, Stephen, 85
Fryer, Wm., 115
Fuller, Ebenezer, 94, 176
Fuller, Edward, 94
Fuller, Richard, 108
Fuller, Thomas, 40, 49
Furnace, Mr., 140
Furser, Anne, 82
Fussell, L., 98, 99, 100, 122
Fusser, John, 82
Fyneux, Anne, 43, 48, 49
Fyneux, Elizabeth, 45, 47, 61, 63, 98
Fyneux, Jane, 43
Fyneux, Joan, 48
Fyneux, John, 40, 41, 43, 46, 48, 49, 61
Fyneux, Sir John, 6, 29, 40 et seq., 41, 42, 43, 54, 98, 105
Fyneux, Margaret, 62
Fyneux, Mildred, 43
Fyneux, Richard, 41
Fyneux, Robert, 40
Fyneux, William, 41, 46, 48, 49, 98

Gambrill, T. B., 94
Gammon, Mrs. C. L., 128
Gardiner, Bishop, 73
Gifford, Master, 42
Gipps, G., 69
Glynne, Sir Stephen, 34
Godynestre, Hugh de, 55
Goldfinch, John, 94

Goldstone, Reginald, 43, 46
Goldstone, Thomas II, 34
Goodlad, 78
Goodman, 163
Goodwin, Joseph, 122
Gore, Joseph, 120
Gore, R. J., 120
Gower, Sgt. W. H., 168
Gray, F. G., 126
Gray, Henry, 60
Greenhill, Mr., 77
Greenstead, Sarah, 117, 118
Greenstead, Wm., 118
Grey, Lady Jane, 74
Grinall, Mr., 76
Growns, Miss, 178

Haekins, 137
Hales, John, 42, 46
Halle, Elizabeth, 55, 56, 57
Halle, Peter, 55, 56, 57
Hammant, Wm., 128
Hammond, James, 171
Hammond, Julia, 171
Hammond, Thomas, 63
Harbour, S., 8
Hardres, Dorothy, 62
Harnett, J. B., 141
Harnett, Wm., 119
Harvey, E., 150
Hasted, Edward, 31, 64
Hatch, Joseph, 79
Hatch, Thomas, 79
Hatch, William, 79
Haute, Richard, 44
Haute, Sir Wm., 42, 44, 49
Haward, Thomas, 120
Hearn, Martin, 154
Hearne, Richard, 78
Head, Sir F. Bond, 109, 110, 111
Henry VII, 46, 52, 54
Henry VIII, 38, 52, 72
Hilder, Charles, 122
Hob, Lawrence, 32
Hobday, Thomas, 118
Hocken, Miss, 178
Hogbin, John, 118
Holbein, H., 48
Holland, Chas., 94
Holman, John, 93
Holman, William, 128
Hoode, Richard, 34
Hoskins, W. G., 122
Houson, George, 117
Hubbert, Elizabeth, 48
Hubbert, Henry, 45, 48
Hubbert, James, 48
Hughes, Henry, 119
Hunt, Robert, 21, 34
Huntley, John, 117
Hussey, Arthur, 32
Hutt, John, Snr., 117
Hyghmore, William, 32

Igglesden, Sir Chas., 94, 119
Illingworth, Capt., 154
Ince, Dr. A. G., 7
Ingleton, Lily, 150
Ingram, Rev. Delavel, 137
Ireland, 100
Islip, Abp., 104
Ive, Nicholas, 32

James I, 31, 103
James, Bro. Edward, 140
Jameson, Dr. W., 167, 168, 169
Jarvys, John, 30
Jencke, 75
Jenkins, Dr. Frank, 12, 13
Jeny, Master, 43
Jerrold, Douglas, 177
Johnston(e), D. E., 10
Judge, Alfred, 94
Jutzi, Mr. Alan H., 30

Kempe, John, 117
Kennard, Anne, 81, 82
Kennard, Augustine, 81, 82
Kennard, Elizabeth, 82
Kennard, George, 81, 82
Kennard, Hammond, 81,
Kennard, Johanna, 81
Kennard, John, 81, 82
Kennard, Mary, 82
Kennard, Richard, 81, 82
Kennard, Sampson, 81, 82
Kennett, Robert, 32
Kerner, Richard, 86
King, William, 118, 119
Kingsford, Daniel, 93
Kingsland, David, 94
Knell, Barnabas, 21, 22
Knight, Samuel, 80
Knoller, Thomas, 32
Knowler, George, 34
Knowler, Robert, 108

Laflin, T., 144
Lanfranc, 69
Langton, John de, 19
Larkin, Richard, 119, 167, 168
Latimer, Hugh, 74
Laud, Abp., 21, 38
Lawrence, Freda Brand, 152, 154
Lawrence, family, 93, 94, 122
Lawrence, Rev. H. J., 155
Lawrence, W., 120
Leland, John, 38, 40, 45, 52, 97, 98,
  99, 102
Lenthal, family, 60
Leo, Bro., 140
Liddell, George, 177
Lindredge, Thomas, 104
Liveing, Dr. Edward, 137
Loverick, Anthony, 60
Loverick, Constancia, 60
Lowes, Alice, 34
Lowes, Richard, 34
Luther, Martin, 72
Lychfield, John, 75
Lynsted, Bartholomew, 43, 48

McMullen, Edward J., 138, 140
McNair, Lieut. E. A., 147
Mais, S. P. B., 100
Manwood, Peter, 75
Marsh, Mrs. G., 176
Marshall, R. N., 149
Martin, Brian, 160
Martin, J. E., 127
Mary Tudor, 74
Matthew, Thomas, 38
Maxted, Edward, 121

May, George, 118
Maycot, Agnes, 64, 67
Maycot, Anthony, 64, 67
Mayers, Mr., 75
Mears, George, 80
Milles, Richard, 92
Milles, Samuel, 92
Minter, William, 94
Moat, Josiah, 119
Mooney, Richard, 137
Morley, Thomas, 62
Morphy, Cpl., 150
Morse, J. J., 137
Morton, Cardinal & Archbishop,
  34, 38, 39, 44, 45 46, 51, 52, 88
Moys, John, 110
Moyse, 78
Musk, Rev. Mark, 121

Nash, R., 94
Naylor, C. B., 34
Neeve, James, 118
Nethersole, John, 42, 44, 46
New (Niewe) (Nyewe), Thomas,
  20, 26, 31
Newman, Mrs., 172
Newman, Daniel, 92
Newman, Danyell, 92
Newman, Decimus, 92
Newman, Elizabeth, 92
Newman, Dr. Francis, 92
Newport, Harry, 133
Newton, John, 118
Northumberland, Duke of, 74

O'Connell, John, 138
O'Rourke, Jarlath, 139
Ovenden, Henry, 120

Packer, Jonathan, 94, 118
Palmer, F. W. J., 124
Palmer, John, 122, 177
Parker, Abp., 38
Parkes, Henry, 75
Parkinson, Capt., 154
Parks, Rev. T. J., 142
Parnell, James, 118, 120
Paston, Elizabeth, 45, 47, 62
Paston, Sir John, 45, 61
Pavy, Dr., 169
Pearce, Samuel, 127
Peckham, Abp., 16
Peel, Mr., 172
Pembrook, Gilbert, 122
Pembrook, J. K., 125
Pencestre, S. de, 17
Petts, Wm., 167
Phelip (Philip), Christina, 27, 28,
  58, 59
Phelip (Philip), Matthew, 26, 28,
  45, 54, 58, 59
Phelip (Philip), William, 26, 44,
Philip of Spain, 74
Philipot, Thomas, 40, 54
Philp, Brian, 9, 10, 13, 14
Pitcher, Mary, 121
Pitcher, Thomas, 121
Pooley, Isaac, 166, 168, 170
Port, Mrs. James, 127
Porter, Elizabeth, 117
Powell, Wm., 130
Poynings, Sir Edward, 44, 46

Prescott-Westcar, C. W., 125
Prosser, Mr., 172, 173, 174
Prude, Thomas, 61

Reeve, Jos, 78
Reid, Whitehead, 153
Reynolds, Thomas, 109
Richard III, 44
Ridley, Anne, 72
Ridley, Christopher, 72
Ridley, Nicholas, 38, 49, 72, 73, 74, 117
Roberts, E. A., 133
Roberts, J., 133
Roberts, J. H. Snr., 132
Robinson, Beatrice, 120
Robinson, Elizabeth, 81, 82
Robinson, Thomas, 117
Rogers, Rob. B., 119
Rogers, Sarah, 119
Rogers, Sister, 119
Rolfe, 150
Roper, Christopher, 44
Roper, Elizabeth, 48
Roper, Jane, 43, 44, 48
Roper, John, 42
Roper, Margaret, 44
Roper, William, 44, 46
Rose, Francis, 144
Rossetti, Dante G., 101, 108
Ruskin, John, 100, 101, 102
Ruskin, Wm., 102
Russell, John, 117
Rust, Mary, 1596, 63
Ryder, George, 75

St. Leger, René de, 151, 156
Salisbury, The Marquess of, 51
Saunders, Mrs., 168
Sayer, George, 119
Scott, Sir John, 42
Sea, John, 62, 63
Sea, Martha, 62
Sea, Sara, 62
Seager, May, 149, 150, 151, 154
Seager, Muriel, 151
Seager, William, 155
Sedley, Sir John, 108
Sedley, Sir Wm., 108, 109
Seers, Henry, 74
Segrave, Sir Henry, 154
Sellyng, William, 42, 43, 46
Setterfield, Mr., 160
Seymour, Charles, 122

Seynclere, Sir John, 56
Seynt, Nycholas, 75
Shakespeare, Capt., 122
Sherwood, 109
Shipman, James, 26
Shrubsole, Sarah, 92
Simpson, James, 132
Singleton, Widow, 117
Slater, Frances, 136, 137
Slater, Mary, 136, 137
Smith, John, 62
Smith, Thomas, 62
Soane, Sir John, 88
Somner, William, 40, 46
Sondes, Earl, 125, 155, 156
Sondes, Anthony, 46, 48
Sondes, Elizabeth, 48
Sondes, Joan, 46, 48
Spanton, Mrs. Frank, 165
Spencer, Richard, 32
Spratt, Thomas, 110, 117, 118
Spratt, Wm., 118
Springate, R., 94
Stack, Air Chief Marshal J., 152, 157
Stack, Capt. T. N., 152, 153
Stainbank, Robert, 80
Staines, Elizabeth, 119
Stamp, Prof. L. Dudley, 154
Steed, Alan, 171
Steed, Albert, 171
Steed, Ann Maria, 171
Steed, Frank, 171
Steed, Hannah, 171
Steed, Richard, 166, 167, 168
Steed, William, 171
Stephens, Mr. & Mrs. B., 72
Stephens, Mrs. R. B., 160
Stewart, Ethel, 137
Stewart, Florence, 137
Strangford, family, 44, 46, 49
Street, George, 102
Stupple, John, 117
Swinford, Mrs., 161
Swinford, John, 115, 122

Tappenden, Thomas, 118
Tassell, Mary, 177
Taylor, Dr., 169
Taylor, Jehu, 115
Taylor, Rowland, 120
Taylor, Thomas, 94
Telford, Thomas, 6
Terry, John, 54

Terry, Richard, 54
Teynham, Lord, 46
Thomson, Miss, 178
Thorp, Harry, 74
Tinfrey, John, 75
Torney, Edward, 122
Trow, Alfred, 115
Turk, George, 167, 171
Turle, George, 118
Turner, G. A., 179
Turner, John Bunce, 120
Twyman, Henry, 71, 90
Tyll, family, 42, 46
Tyndall, Richard, 49
Tyngewick, N. de, 19

Urban, Bro., 139

Varham, Sarah, 34
Varham, Vincent, 34
Viney, Josiah, 130

Wacher, J. J., 125
Wacher, Thomas, 122
Wacher, Wm., 125
Waleys, Dame Margaret, 56
Waleys, Wm., Kt., 56
Walker, Supt., 168
Ward, Thomas, 140
Ward, Mr. Valentine, 120
Warham, Abp., 28
Warner, James, 132
Waters, George, 173
Watmer, William, 103
Watkins, Dr. and Mrs., 95
Watson, Wm., 115
Weatherly, Anne, 68
Webb, Thomas, 110
Webster, Peter, 82
Welby, John, 108
Wells, Sgt. Harry, 146, 176
Whatmore, Geoffrey, 103
Whitworth, Wm., 82
Winchelsey, Abp., 16, 19, 24, 31
Wise, Ted, 150
Wood, John, 86
Woodruff, C. E., 24, 31
Wooton, family, 93, 146
Wooton, Thomas, 127
Wyatt, Sir Thomas, 74
Worrell, H. B., 120
Wyborn, Mr., 163
Wyndham, R., 100

Young, Thomas, 75

EDITORIAL POST SCRIPT

Another volume is proposed in this occasional series treating the area bounded by the sea, the river Stour, the Forest of Blean and the Wantsum Channel as a broad whole. In making this corner of England the subject of further study it is hoped to have contributions that reflect a deeper and broader view of the Stour Lathe, and take a longer perspective of its history. A number of articles have had to be held over from this book owing to pressure of space.

HERNE BAY STATION AND APPROACHES SEEN DURING THE PREPARATION FOR ELECTRIFICATION

On 15 June 1959 electric train service commenced on the railway between Gillingham and Ramsgate via Herne Bay (the old London Chatham and Dover route). Work on the electrification of the line began some years before and this photograph shows the 'up' end of Herne Bay station and its approaches as it was in July 1958. The 'third rail' was by then already in position and white concrete channel sections to carry the feeder cables can be seen in the foreground and stacked against the goods shed (extreme left). After electrification the goods shed was let to private business and its crane and approach rails removed. The signal box, the station master's house (right centre) and the water column were demolished. Soon after this view was taken, the two upper quadrant starting signals at the ends of the up platforms were replaced by colour light signals. In the right foreground are the points controlling access to the coal wharf. This has been converted to a BRS road-freight park and its rail tracks lifted. Also in the photograph is seen a Class C 0-6-0 freight locomotive shunting the midday Margate – Faversham goods. This service has long since been discontinued and the locomotive withdrawn and broken up.

Photograph by P. Ransome-Wallis